IMAGES
of America
LITTLE SWITZERLAND

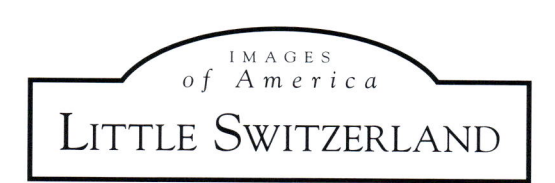

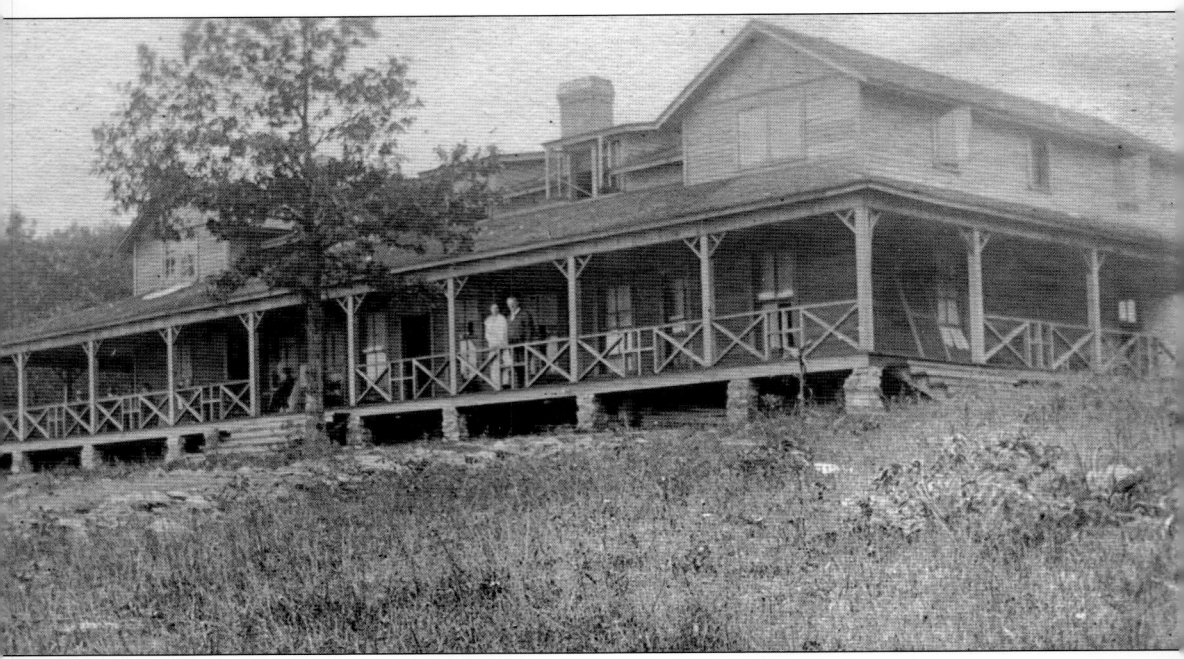

Operated by Ida Clarkson Jones, the Switzerland Inn has been the focal point of the Switzerland Company development since it opened in the summer of 1911. Originally a two-story clapboard structure, the building was renovated and enhanced through the years to serve as a haven for clientele from throughout the world. Age and increasing demands for lodging spelled the end for this building in 1970, when it was torn down, and a portion of today's Switzerland Inn was constructed on its site. (Courtesy of Cama and Robert Merritt.)

ON THE COVER: A beautiful day is the perfect excuse for a picnic, and the McKinney and Hand families are enjoying a meal together. Pictured from left to right are (standing) Maude McKinney and Viola Hollifield; (kneeling) Gerta Waycaster, Ida McKinney, Thelma McKinney, Jane Buchanan McKinney, Mildred McKinney, and Harriet Hand. (Courtesy of Davis and Jann Godwin.)

IMAGES of America
LITTLE SWITZERLAND

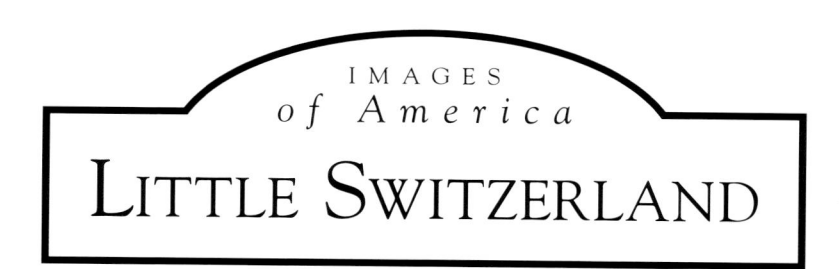

Chris Hollifield and David Biddix

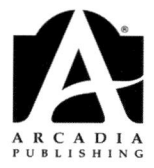

ARCADIA PUBLISHING

Copyright © 2010 by Chris Hollifield and David Biddix
ISBN 978-0-7385-8615-1

Published by Arcadia Publishing
Charleston, South Carolina

Printed in the United States of America

Library of Congress Control Number: 2010922024

For all general information contact Arcadia Publishing at:
Telephone 843-853-2070
Fax 843-853-0044
E-mail sales@arcadiapublishing.com
For customer service and orders:
Toll-Free 1-888-313-2665

Visit us on the Internet at www.arcadiapublishing.com

Contents

Acknowledgments		6
Foreword		7
A Contributor's Note		9
Introduction		10
1.	Up the Spoon Camp Road: Heritage of a Hardy People	11
2.	"This Is the Place:" The Switzerland Company Establishes A Colony	27
3.	The Scenic: The Blue Ridge Parkway Brings Challenge and Change	41
4.	Nature's Playgrounds: The Camps and Wildacres	53
5.	Seasons on the Mountain: Faith, Family, Friends, and Fellowship	71
6.	Living off the Land: Mother Nature's Bounty	101
7.	Beauty Spot of the Blue Ridge: Little Switzerland Today	119
Bibliography		127

ACKNOWLEDGMENTS

A special acknowledgment goes to the hard work and expertise of Greg S. Burnette, who assisted with the collection of interviews and materials for the book. Without his help, the quality of this work would be diminished.

We also acknowledge the research, photography, and proofing by Marsha Biddix. Thank you for your hard work!

A special thank you also goes to the Centennial Committee of Little Switzerland for their assistance in identifying potential sources for materials.

The authors would like to thank the following individuals and organizations for their contributions to Little Switzerland: Daniel Barron, Dr. Stan Black, Frank Brown, Phillip and Jean Buchanan, Ruby Buchanan, Todd Bush, Bill and Judy Carson, Chestnut Grove Baptist Church, Robert and Cama Clarkson, Sarah Clarkson, Verdie Mae Cox, Kelly Gibson, Hugh and Carolyn Glenn, Lloyd and Nelle Glenn, Alex Glover, Davis and Jann Godwin, Minnie Hoilman, Frank Hollifield, Hazel Webb Hollifield, Susan Hollifield, Tommy and Lillian Hollifield, Maude Hughes, Coles Jackson, Gary Jensen, Clarkson Jones, Ann Kernahan, Judith Knight, Judy Collis Koon, Betty Mace, Cole Martin, Pat Mitchell, Bernice McKinney, Bill McKinney, Guss McKinney, John McKinney, the U.S. National Park Service's North Carolina Collection at the Pack Library in Asheville, the North Carolina Collection at UNC–Chapel Hill, North Carolina State Archives, Jean Nydegger, Markine Ostling, Ruth Parsley, William S. Powell, Mike Queen, Alan Schabilion, the Southern Historical Collection at UNC–Chapel Hill, Eugene Self, Nancy Snipes, Carrie Washburn, James Self, Anne Mitchell Whisnant, Wildacres Resort, and Bob Young.

Foreword

My first awareness of Little Switzerland was its scent. It was 1945, and I was eight years old, driving with my parents for my second summer at As-You-Like-It, the girls' camp at Little Switzerland. When we reached the top of the mountain on Highway 226-A, I became aware of new aromas sifting through the open car windows. The scent of galax and humus under the rhododendron slicks was interesting and so different from the odors I was accustomed to in the summer heat of my native South Carolina. Today, I still remember this early occurrence and my reaction to it. The fragrances recalled memories of the camp, and I could barely contain my excitement to get back there again. Marvelously for me, in 2010, this experience of returning to Little Switzerland has changed very little since my youth, except that I now approach our home from the direction of the Blue Ridge Parkway, in too much of a hurry to drive the older and slower scenic route that I traveled as a girl.

Even before we purchased property here, my summers and other visits to Little Switzerland dominated all planning for my yearly agenda. I recognized early that this was a place that stimulated as well as quieted me. I tried to convey these feelings about Little Switzerland to our children; so each summer, as we turned up the mountain on Highway 226-A, I began my annual speech and urged them to practice gentleness of tone and behavior during their summer together. We laugh about those early days now, but we all agree about the message: that when we approach Little Switzerland, the stresses of our daily lives in the flatlands must be left at the foot of the mountain, leaving ourselves free to absorb anew all that this special life has to offer us.

This intense connection of mine to our colony and its surroundings can be easily explained on one level alone six generations of my family have been summer residents here, from 1912 to 2010. More specifically, my father and I, our three children, and our eight grandchildren have all grown up in Little Switzerland from our earliest childhood. Our lives have been full of tales of Little Switzerland's past, its founding in 1910 and its early development, the coming of the automobile, electricity, and telephone, the building of the Blue Ridge Parkway, the paving of roads, and other modern developments of the late 20th century.

For the first 54 years of Little Switzerland's existence, my family's history was entwined with the girls' camp called As-You-Like-It, operating from 1914 to 1945 and owned and operated by my great-aunt, Marie Gaillard Dwight of Charleston, South Carolina, with the help of her sister, my grandmother Louisa DuBose Dwight Cathcart of Columbia, South Carolina. The camp operated from 1945 to 1965 as Glenlaurel under the ownership of Jeanette Boone and Helen McMahon of Sweetbriar, Virginia. My family lived at the camp rather than in the summer colony, and I stayed there also, first as a camper and then as a counselor.

As-You-Like-It, purported to be the first girls' camp in the western North Carolina mountains, was located 2 miles of easy walking southwest from Little Switzerland, under the Bearwallow overpass and down the girls' camp road, or between milepost 336 and 337 off of the Blue Ridge Parkway. It was an important element in the growth of Little Switzerland, for during its existence, it had approximately 100 or more persons each summer to feed and nurture at a time when Little Switzerland was still quite undeveloped. The camp and the visitors it generated made an economic impact in the area, as well as a social one; sometimes guests from the summer colony were invited to attend the camp plays and musicals, square dances and Sunday dinners. When the camp ceased to operate about 1958, it became the prey of vandals who tore down the chestnut cabins for the wood, took up most of the rock walls and steps for the stones, and set fire to the larger buildings after stealing most of their furnishings. Today the property is a jungle of weeds and thorns, and only the internal map in my head guides me around. The loss of the camp took away our family base in Little Switzerland until, in 1971, my husband and I purchased our Little Switzerland home on the Bearwallow Road. Today both of our daughters have homes here, and we are once again deeply entrenched in this magical place.

Obviously and thankfully, I am not the only person to have these strong feelings about being on our mountain. The growth of Little Switzerland over the past 100 years is a testament to this same emotional connection and to the strength and tenacity of the colony's charms: those who came could not stay away but remained to be mesmerized by surprises everywhere. From the tiniest lichens to the beauty of the distant forested vistas, from the quieting fogs to the absolute splendidness of sun-filled days, Little Switzerland is a tapestry of glorious nature spread out openly for all to see.

Before the summer development began, there were local mountain residents who lived in the area, mostly on the northwest side of Chestnut Ridge, scattered in the valleys and coves, hollows and dips in the mountain to keep them out of the wind and extreme weather. The summer community was on the southeast side of Chestnut Ridge, hugging the highest areas for the most dramatic mountain views. These two peoples lived some distances apart, but they became closely connected, each needing the other and what he had to share. The new development, as well as Camp As-You-Like-It, benefited immeasurably from the vast knowledge, advice, and expertise of these generous people, among whom were fine craftsmen, builders, stonemasons, woodsmen and hunters. These native residents also benefited from this joint connection. For just as their ancestors long ago saw the beauty of this mountain land and wrestled it from the Cherokees, so in 1910 another wave of pioneer settlers came, this time to create Little Switzerland, not with guns but with money. Thus the lives of the local residents improved with the infusion of cash from this mutually satisfying partnership.

The important relationship between the newcomer and the native must be honored in our 2010 celebration of the 100th anniversary of the founding of Little Switzerland. For though the name "Little Switzerland" originally referred only to the summer settlement developed within the original 1,100 acres, today, 100 years later, the name encompasses much more. It includes all peoples living around both sides of Chestnut Ridge and its environs: summer residents, full-time retired persons, and local residents, some of whom are descendents of the original pioneer settlers. This year we are celebrating not only the 100-year anniversary of the founding of a summer village but also its transformation into the enlarged community of people who share together this beautiful mountain space.

—Coles Cathcart Jackson
Spring 2010

A Contributor's Note

Two old sayings come to mind when I think of Little Switzerland: "You can never go home again," and, "You may take the boy out of the mountain, but you can't take the mountain out of the boy." After being away for 25 years, I have indeed come home again to my beloved Little Switzerland.

Little Switzerland shares with its namesake majestic mountain peaks, cool summers, and a healthy environment. No wonder the first settlers fell in love with its mystique and beauty.

Many wonderful memories of growing up on Rich Knob Farms and on our place on McKinney Mine Road come to mind. We were poor as far as this world's values are concerned, but we were wealthy living in a wholesome environment of gorgeous nature with a strong ethical and spiritual component. We labored hard putting up hay, cutting wood, mowing, and surviving the rough winters. Honesty and a strong work ethic were instilled in me, qualities I am thankful to possess. I also enjoyed our recreation times of playing football in the yard behind Chestnut Grove Baptist Church, occasional horseback riding, fishing, and exploring the forests and mountains. After a hard day's work we would go to the Switzerland Store and buy pork and beans and Vienna sausages. We also enjoyed going to the store beside the Chestnut Grove Church that was run by Lewis and Josephine Young.

In returning to the mountains, I also relish the spiritual edge that makes our region unique. My deep religious convictions and call to ministry are rooted in this rich culture. Fiery gospel preaching, melodious singing, and firm Biblical teaching laid the foundation of my spirituality. Fond memories of the ministry of Rev. Homer Murdock Jr. at Chestnut Grove Church in the early 1980s flood my soul.

The rich traditions of the Burnette, McKinney, Hollifield, Glenn, Self, Queen, Collis, Boyd, McGee, Ballew, Washburn, and Mace families also make Little Switzerland special. Being a Burnette, I am especially proud of our Scottish heritage. I remember so many, many stories that my dad, Claude, and my uncles, Lonnie and Harley (Bunk), used to tell. One such story is about little George Wilson. One day aunt Mattie McKinney came out on the porch and yelled "Juss [her husband Jessie], don't you cheat Little George." Uncle Jess shouted back, "Cheat little George the dickens—he's running away with everything on the place!" And there scurried Little George down the road from the smokehouse with a ham under each arm!

Traits of ruggedness, stubbornness, honesty, integrity, and humor are evident in all the families of our mountains who descend from English, Scottish, Scotch-Irish, and German heritage.

Relations between the natives and summer residents were also important. With the help of the mountain people, the Little Switzerland colony was a success. Personally, I am especially thankful to summer residents Joseph H. Walker, Lawrence Clements, and Leland R. Bryan for their help and encouragement in my educational and career pursuits.

My late aunt, Carrie Buchanan Burnette, was a local historian who wrote of Little Switzerland many years ago and was also our family historian. She instilled in me a passion for our mountain heritage and a desire to preserve the stories of the past. I have thoroughly enjoyed helping David and Chris with the interviews and compilation of this book. The pictures and historical content infuse in me great love and pride for this unique and mystical place—Little Switzerland.

Happy 100 years!

—Greg S. Burnette
Spring 2010

Introduction

Chestnut Ridge has stood for eons at the edge of the Blue Ridge, its long, flat summit marking the edges of the Toe and Catawba River valleys, the Toe making its way to the Mississippi while the Catawba flows to the Atlantic. In a land claimed as a hunting ground by both the Catawbas and Cherokees, the hardy English, German, Scottish, and Scotch-Irish pioneers of early America moved into the region following the Revolutionary War. Carving a life in this new wilderness was a struggle. The mountainous terrain made transportation difficult, so small communities sprang up where roads (such as they were) allowed. One such place was the community of Phenoy, whose post office was opened in 1896 by a young Reid Queen at his father's house near present-day Lake Laurel. He also ran a store near Black Mountain Baptist Church for a few years before heading to Marion and a career in real estate.

Queen brought Heriot Clarkson to the mountain in 1909, showing him vistas from atop Grassy Mountain. This inspired Clarkson to return to Charlotte and, with other investors, to form the Switzerland Company, buying property on the mountain to establish a resort. Access to the property was limited to horse trails and toe paths. Clarkson knew that for their investment to succeed a good road was needed, and the company constructed the Etchoe Pass Road from Gillespie Gap (and the nearby Mount Mitchell train station) to the Switzerland Inn. Clarkson joined the Good Roads Movement and began lobbying for a statewide system of modern highways to connect county seats. One of the roads he worked for was North Carolina 19 (now North Carolina 226A), which was to go from Marion to Bakersville. He campaigned to have the route follow a ridge to Little Switzerland, where it would join the Etchoe Pass Road, continuing on to its destination. His success in establishing the highway improved access to the resort, and it began to flourish.

A powerful member of the Democratic Party, Clarkson was campaign manager for North Carolina governor Cameron Morrison, and he was involved with major policy decisions made in North Carolina around the beginning of the 20th century. He also served as an associate justice of the North Carolina Supreme Court. He was very much a man of his times.

With Clarkson and the road, major changes came to Little Switzerland. The old way of life for natives was radically altered, while summer residents were introduced to a way of life vastly different from their own. The two cultures would come together and form a symbiotic relationship that would be beneficial to both, with economic opportunities opening up for locals and essential needs being provided for the summer residents. Friendships formed and a social structure that promoted interaction between the two groups developed. This promoted growth and opportunities for both. This is their story.

One

Up The Spoon Camp Road
Heritage of a Hardy People

The Proclamation of 1763 set up an artificial barrier barring pioneer settlers from ascending the Blue Ridge Escarpment to seek their fortunes. Following the Revolutionary War, soldiers for the fledgling United States and other settlers began pushing through that barrier into new territory. They built trails up and across the Blue Ridge into the rich valleys and river bottoms. As the population increased and choice land became harder to find, settlers began looking to the higher mountains for room. They followed these trails, like the Spoon Camp Road, which led from the Grassy Creek community to Little Switzerland, back up to the heights of the escarpment, settling on the rich but steep terrain.

Life here proved to be much different than in the lowlands. The mountains presented a natural barrier to easy transportation and trade. Weather at the higher elevations was another challenge, its extremes shortening the growing season and requiring extra preparation for the winter months. These factors combined to force the settlers to be largely self-sufficient, growing their food and making their clothes and tools from the resources of the land. The Buchanans, Burnettes, Collises Hollifields, McKinneys, and other families took on this challenge and settled what was to become Little Switzerland.

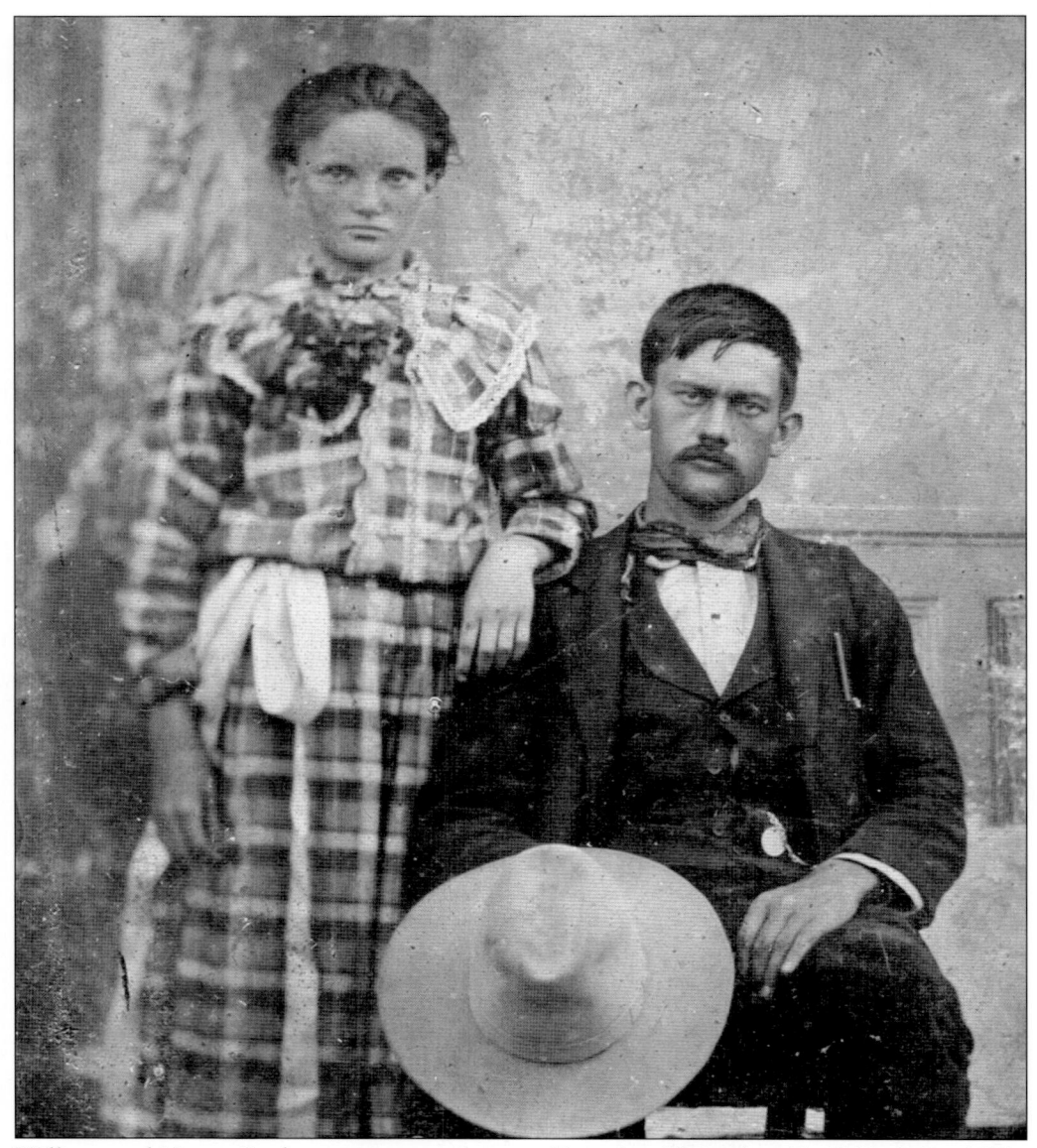

William and Nancy Buchanan pose on their wedding day, November 11, 1860. A Civil War veteran, William taught school before enlisting. He joined the Confederates and was wounded in Virginia. From the battlefield, he wrote letters to his bride, which have survived. Afterwards, he returned to teaching through 1897. Nancy married William when she was 18, and the couple settled in the area, rearing nine children. (Courtesy of John McKinney.)

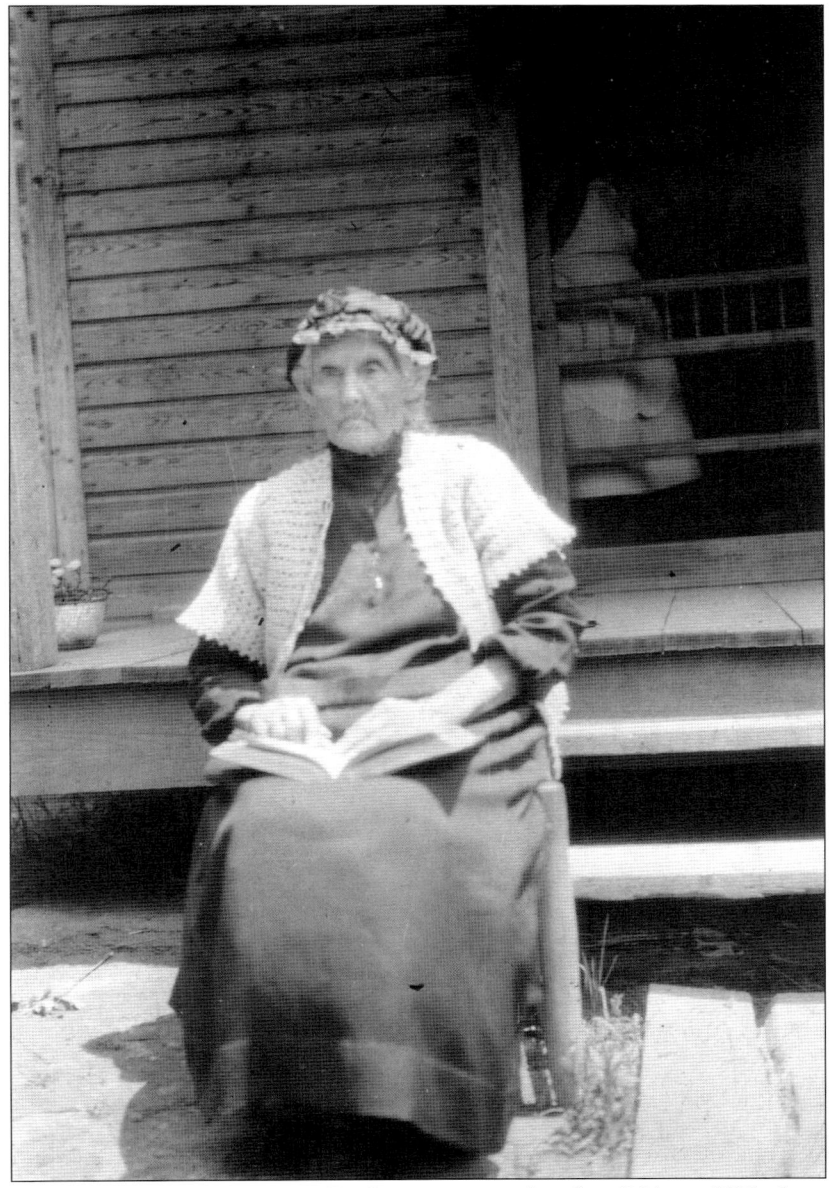

Ninety-three-year-old Nancy DeWeese Buchanan sits reading her Bible in 1935, the year of her death. She was born in Missouri on February 2, 1842, returning to North Carolina with her mother Rachel DeWeese and two sisters at age five. She married William Buchanan, a schoolteacher, on November 11, 1860, and settled on land set aside for them in Little Switzerland. Nancy managed the household while William was away in the Civil War for four years. The couple continued to add acreage to their farm. Nancy became the matriarch of the community, the "mother of the mountain," as she was involved in the lives of both native and summer residents. Nancy sold the majority of the land that the Switzerland Company acquired for the summer colony in 1910, with Judge Heriot Clarkson granting her a life estate so that she could remain in her home. When she passed away, Clarkson sponsored a monument for her grave site that is in the Buchanan Cemetery, located near the present-day Switzerland Inn. (Courtesy of Betty Mace.)

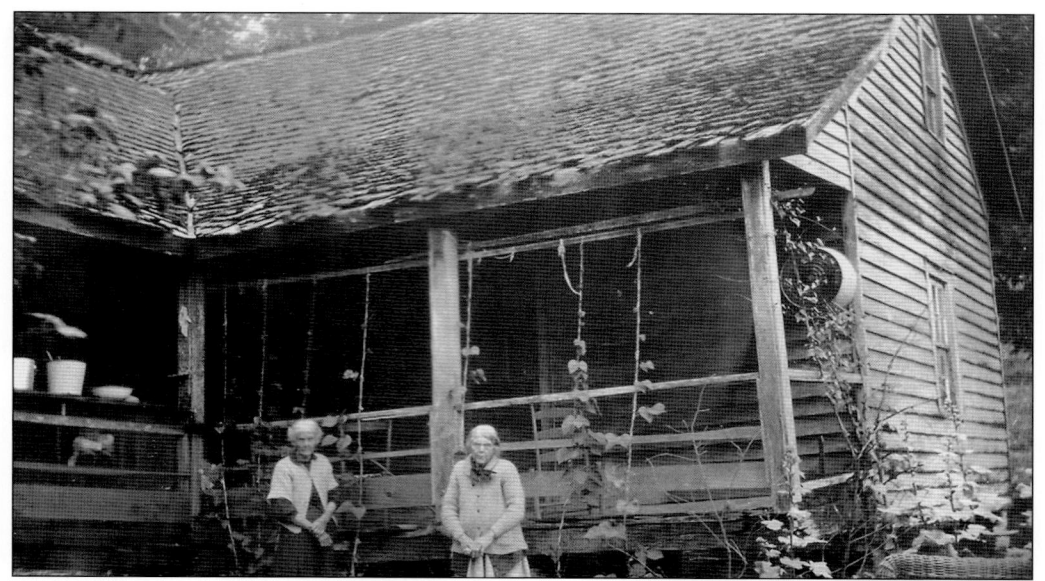

Nancy Buchanan visits with her sister Mary Biddix at Nancy's home on the Spoon Camp Road. William Buchanan built this home in the late 1800s on land later sold to the Switzerland Company. Nancy was allowed to live here until her death in 1935. The remnants of the house stand today just off Grassy Creek Falls Road near the Blue Ridge Parkway. (Courtesy of John McKinney.)

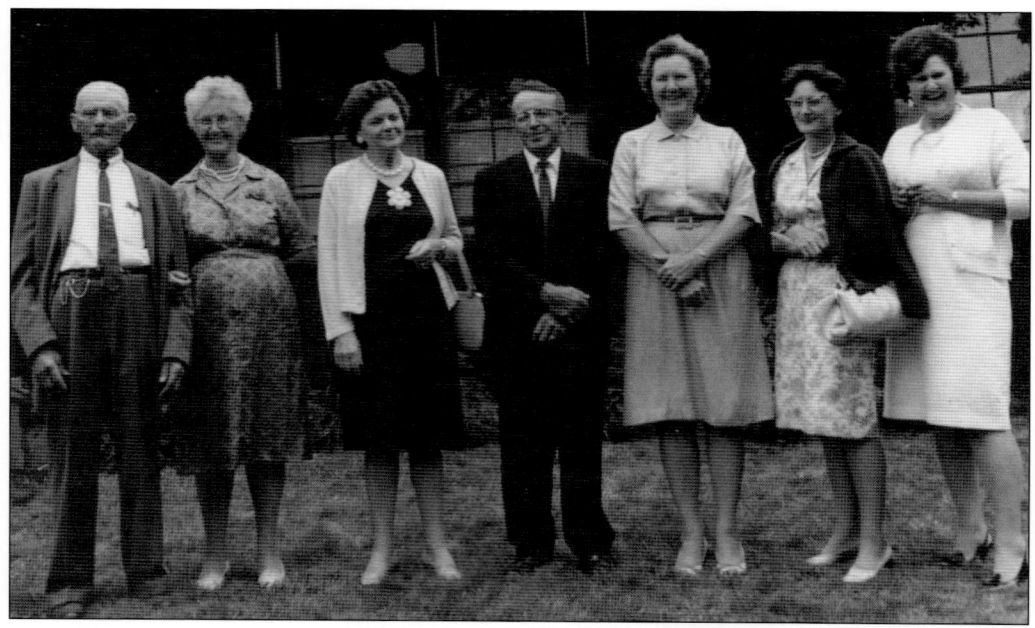

Robert Winfield Buchanan was a carpenter and farmer who built a home near the Little Switzerland Tunnel. It was taken when the Blue Ridge Parkway came. His daughter Carrie Washburn, as of this writing, is one of the oldest current residents at age 96. Pictured here from left to right are Win Buchanan, Effie Hollifield, Erie Carter, Charlie Z. Buchanan, Carrie Washburn, Wilma Eaves, and Gladys Piper. (Courtesy of Carrie Washburn.)

Uncle Molt Schism, pictured with wife Melissa, was a noted carpenter whose talents also included making caskets. Melissa was the daughter of Mother Nancy Buchanan and was well known for her quilting and for her skills with laundry, being known as the best wielder of the flat iron on the mountain. (Courtesy of Ruby Buchanan.)

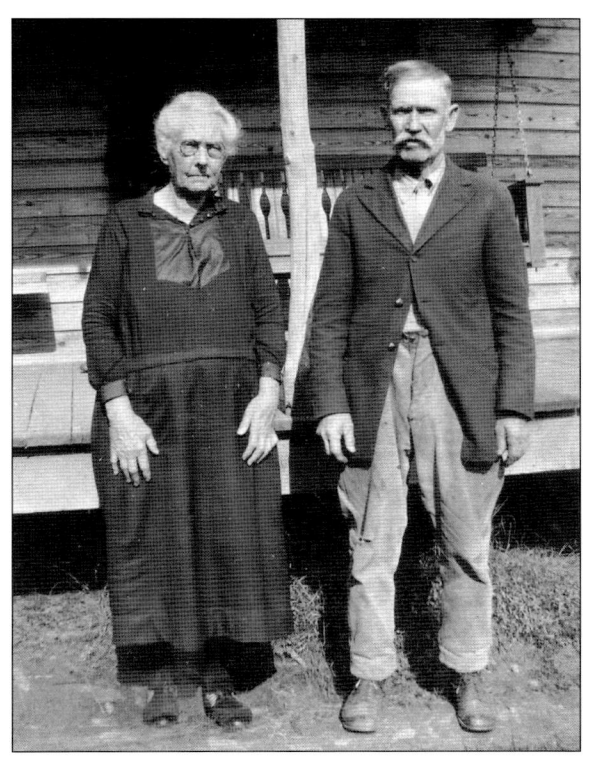

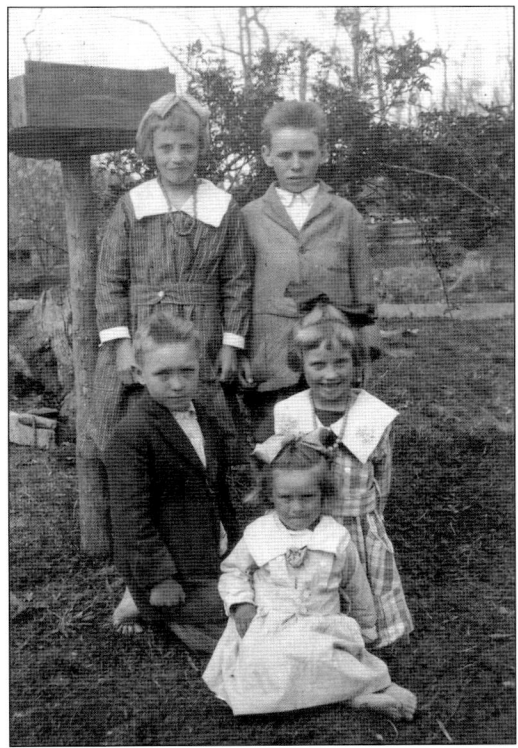

The Smith grandchildren of Molt and Melissa Schism pose for a photograph. At top are Maude and Frank; in the middle are Bert and Verdie Mae; and at the bottom is Josephine. Frank ran the Switzerland Store; Bert fought in World War II; Verdie Mae is famous for her flowers and for her canning; Josephine and husband Louis Young ran a store. Maude passed away prematurely in 1936. (Courtesy of Bill and Judy Carson.)

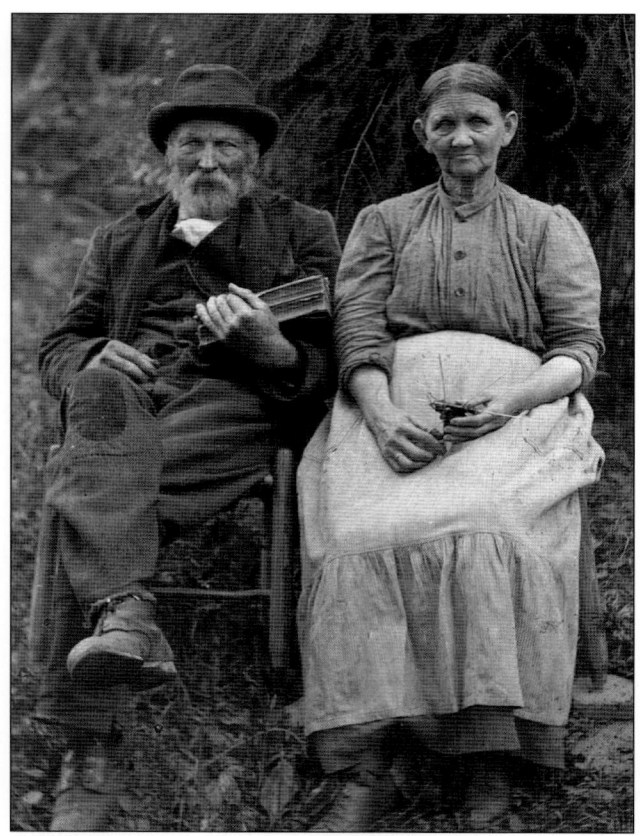

Cyrus and Caroline Burnette were the progenitors of the Burnette family of Little Switzerland. Cyrus, a Civil War veteran in the Union Army, was a farmer who helped others learn to read and write, even the children of former slaves. Caroline, daughter of Charles McKinney Jr. and Elizabeth Washburn, was a granddaughter of "Cove" Charles McKinney, who had four concurrent wives and 42 children. (Courtesy of John McKinney.)

Emily Burnette, daughter of Cyrus and Caroline McKinney Burnette, is pictured below with James Poore and sons Elliott (left) and Theo Hollifield in the 1890s. Born and raised in Armstrong, she was very prominent among the summer residents, working for the W. A. Avant family from Charlotte. Her sons worked in a logging camp. Theo was killed in an accident in 1908. (Courtesy of Greg S. Burnette.)

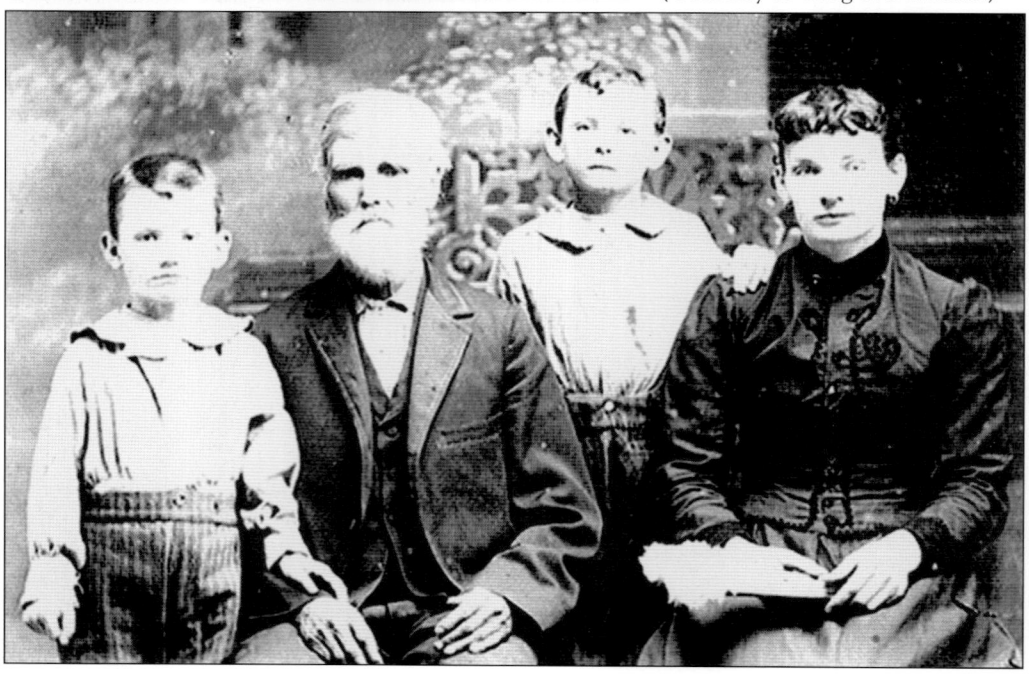

Elliott Hollifield and his mother, Emily Burnette, pose for a photographer. Elliott worked as a farmer and in logging camps, popular occupations for men around 1900. He was married to Maude Buchanan, granddaughter of Mother Nancy Buchanan, and they had 11 children. His daughter, Viola Hollifield Cashwell, was a noted artist who painted the baptistry scene for Chestnut Grove Church. (Courtesy of Greg S. Burnette.)

The Burnette family poses during a reunion in the 1940s on McKinney Mine Road. These are mainly the descendants of Cyrus and Caroline Burnette. Such family gatherings were common in the spring and summer among the locals, who enjoyed fellowship, good food, and horseshoes. (Courtesy of Greg S. Burnette.)

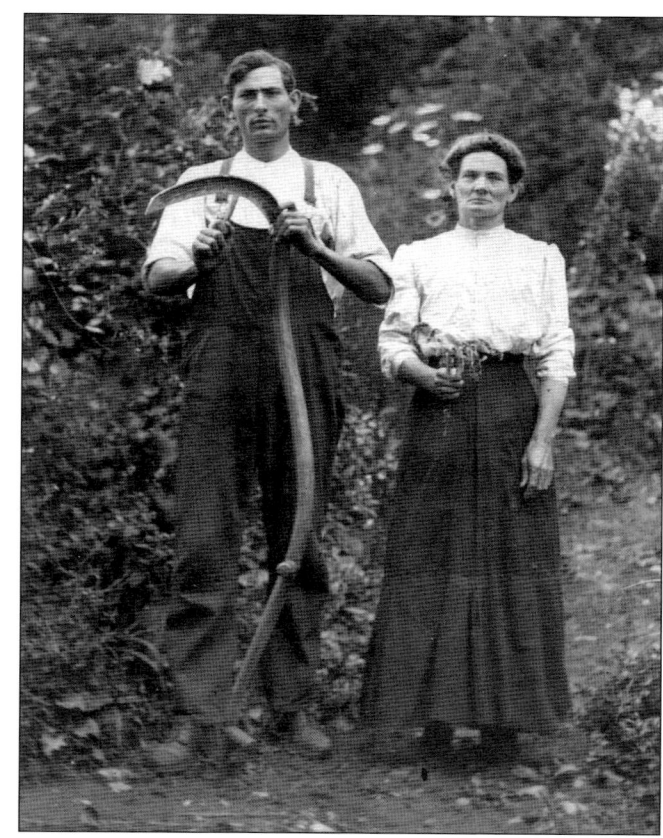

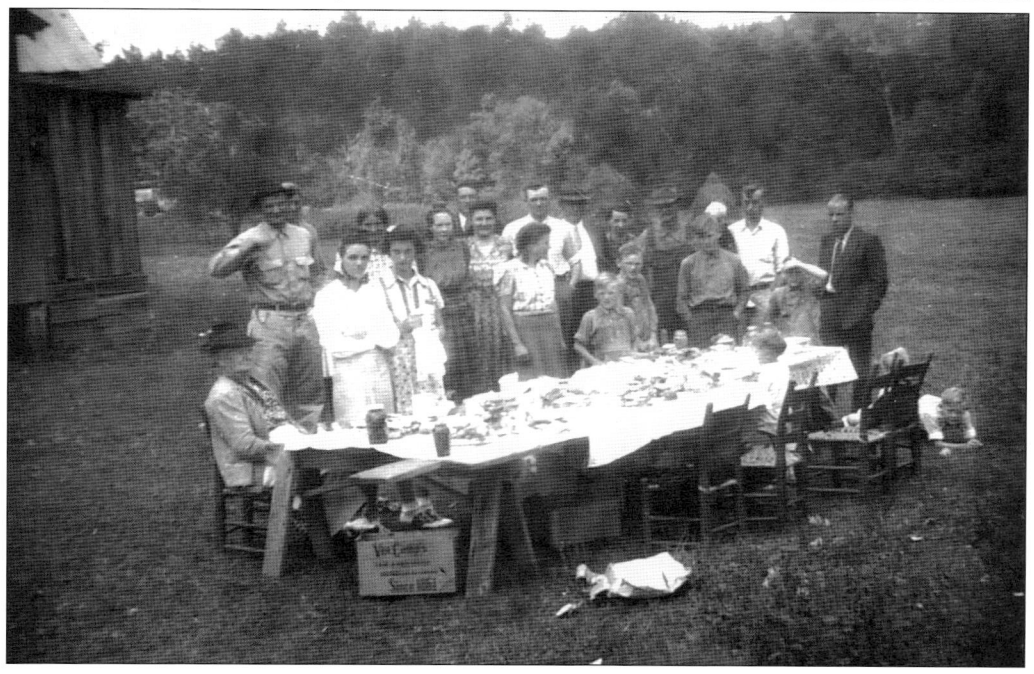

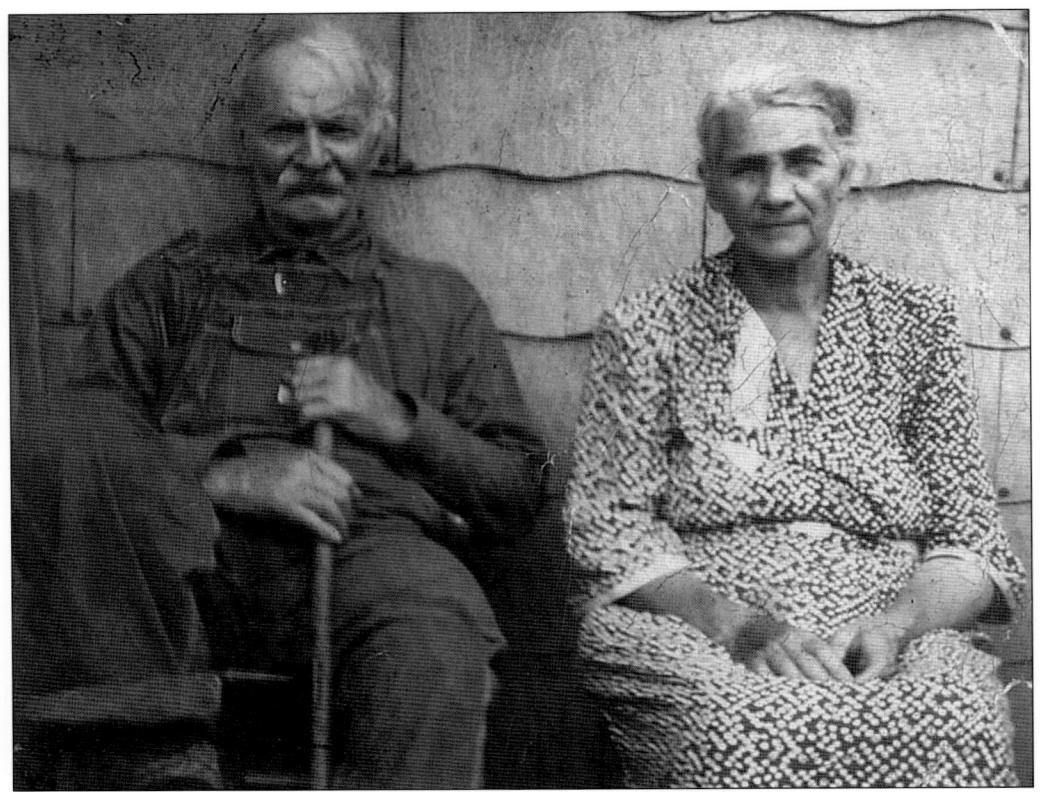

Waites and Maggie Burnette relax at the home of their son Plato. Waites was a farmer who also mined, logged, and carried mail from the Mount Mitchell train station to the Phenoy post office, the precursor to Little Switzerland. He also served as a county commissioner in Mitchell County. Maggie was the daughter of Bill and Beedie Pitman Waycaster. (Courtesy of Greg S. Burnette.)

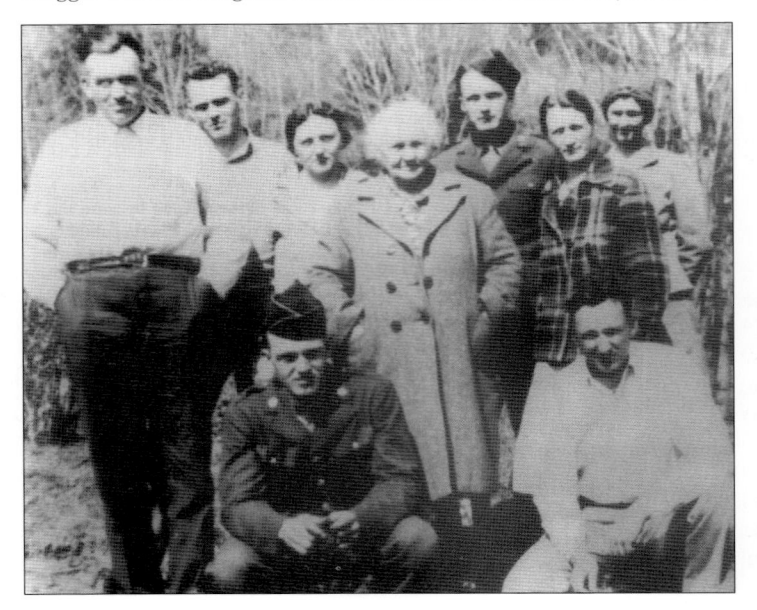

The Boyd family originally settled near Black Mountain Baptist Church and also lived in the Armstrong community of McDowell County, where they were involved in timber cutting. They were known for their musical abilities and staged hoedowns on Saturday afternoons. Pictured here from left to right are (squatting) Fred and Everett Boyd; (standing) Carl, Jack, Clara, Hettie, Jim, Ruby, and Elizabeth Boyd. (Courtesy of Hazel Hollifield.)

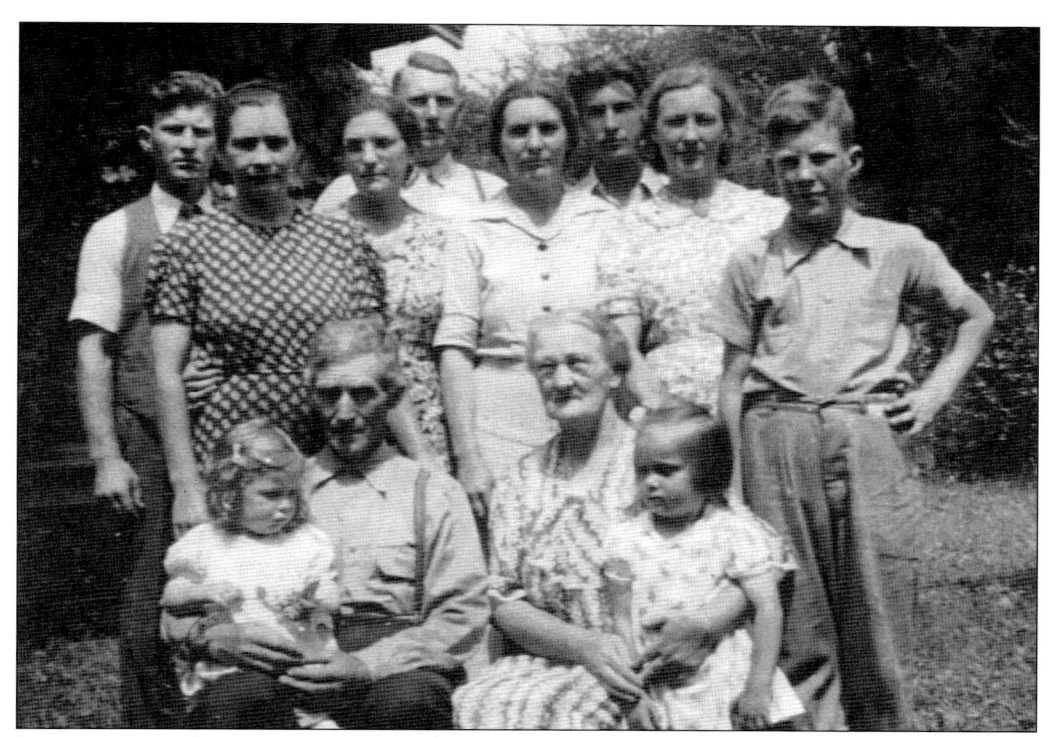

Pictured from left to right are (first row) Maude Self Hughes, D. D. Collis, Jessie Glenn Collis, and Mildred McKinney; (second row) Grace McKinney, Ada Collis, Louise Collis Self, Ivory Collis Hopper, and J. D. Collis; (third row) Glenn Collis, Ralph Collis, and Jim Collis. D. D. was knowledgeable about early mining activity and active in political affairs. A staunch Democrat in a Republican-dominated district, he operated the Glenn voting poll. (Courtesy of Maude Hughes.)

Walter Collis, son of Stephen and Millie Collis, served in the U.S. Navy in the Spanish-American War. Here, he poses for his military portrait. Collis traveled widely, working as a shepherd in Arizona and mining gold in Colorado. He was an avid book reader, loaning from his collection generously. He returned to Little Switzerland and lived with his parents until their deaths. (Courtesy of Hugh Glenn.)

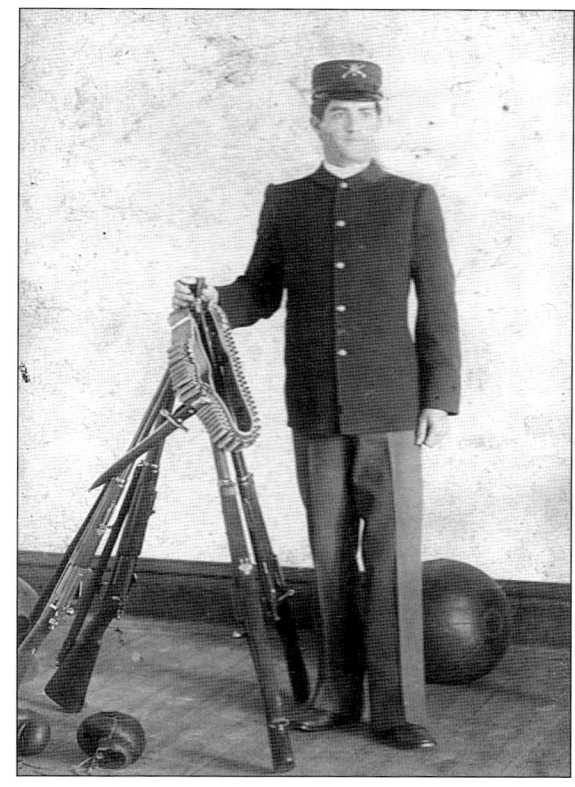

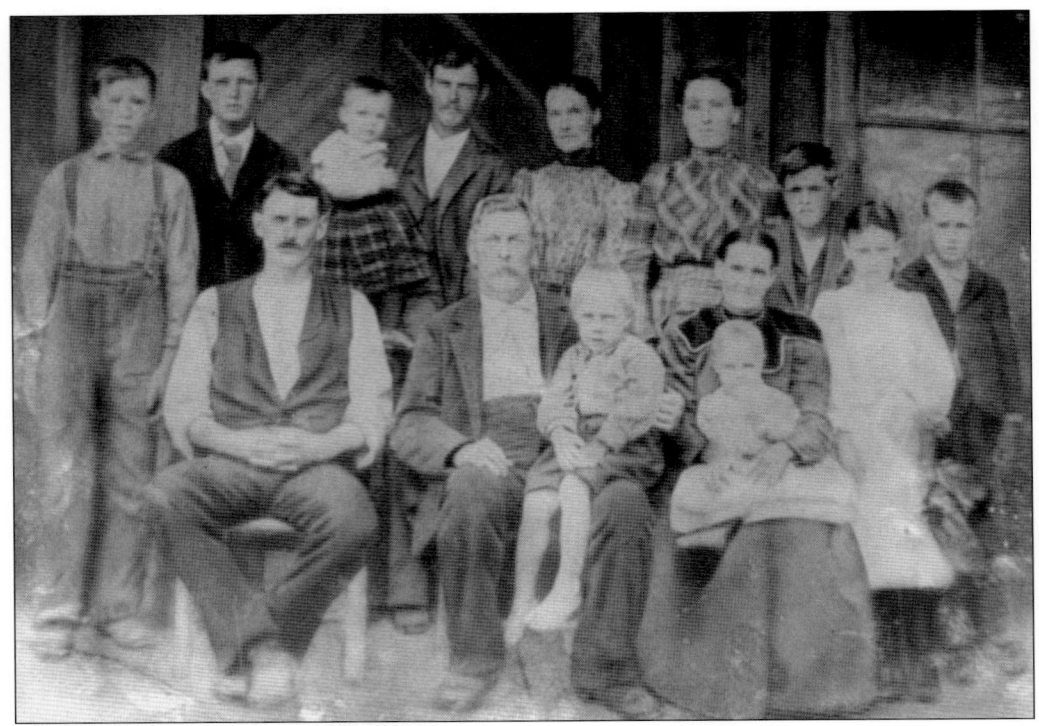

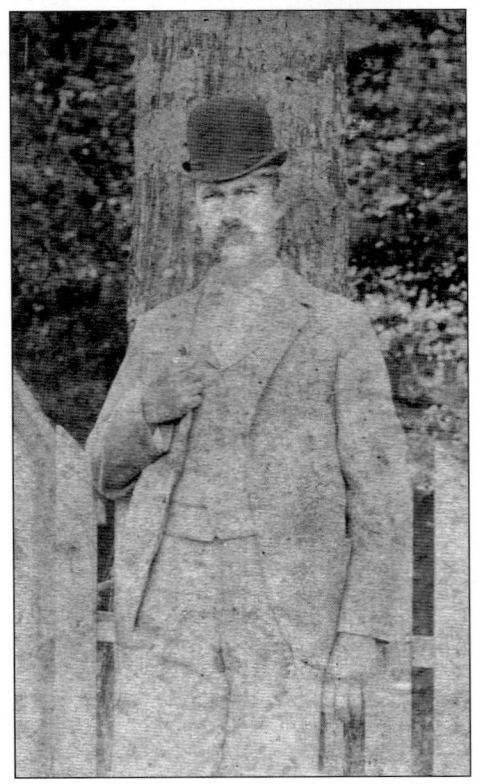

The David M. Glenn family settled in the Chestnut Mountain section in the 1860s. Glenn ran a store, gristmill, and sawmill and owned the Glenn Mines, and the voting precinct was named for him. Pictured from left to right are (seated) Will, David M., Plato, Cordelia McKinney Glenn, Mable Glenn Ballew, and Lessie Glenn Dale; (standing) Jim, Wash, Chesley Buchanan, Carl Buchanan, Alice, Jesse Collis, C. B., and Fred. (Courtesy of Lloyd Glenn.)

Phillip Glenn was a noted carpenter who worked on several projects in the community. He is most known for constructing the original Church of the Resurrection, which was located on the route of the Blue Ridge Parkway, and the Colonel Hill house at Lake Laurel. He operated a commissary that sold goods to road crews constructing the Etchoe Pass Road to Little Switzerland in 1911. (Courtesy of Nancy Glenn Snipes.)

Isaac Hollifield was well known to summer residents as the man who took them from the foot of Mount Mitchell to camp. Married to Millie Shuford, he was born in 1860 and died in 1947. His philosophy on life compared people to leaves, who "drap off one by one. And when your time comes, we'll miss you fer a spell. And then, we'll fergit." (Courtesy of Frank Hollifield.)

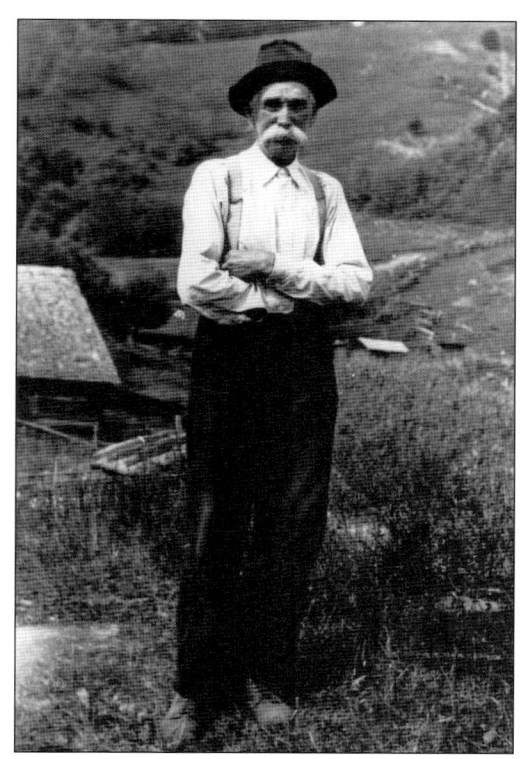

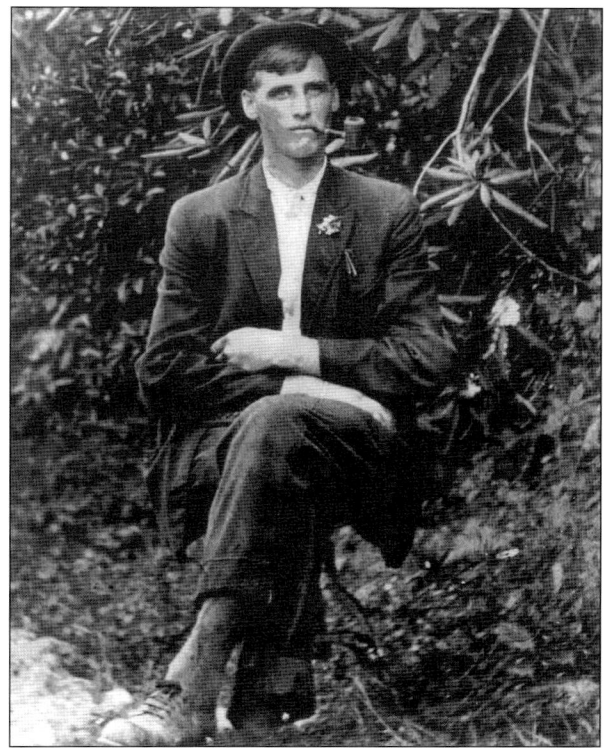

Manley Hollifield, son of Isaac Hollifield, owned a portion of the lands the Switzerland Company purchased to create Little Switzerland. He was also caretaker and right-hand man of Ida Clarkson Jones, owner of the Switzerland Inn. Manley's house, built prior to 1925, still stands on the road to Grassy Creek Falls. (Courtesy of Frank Hollifield.)

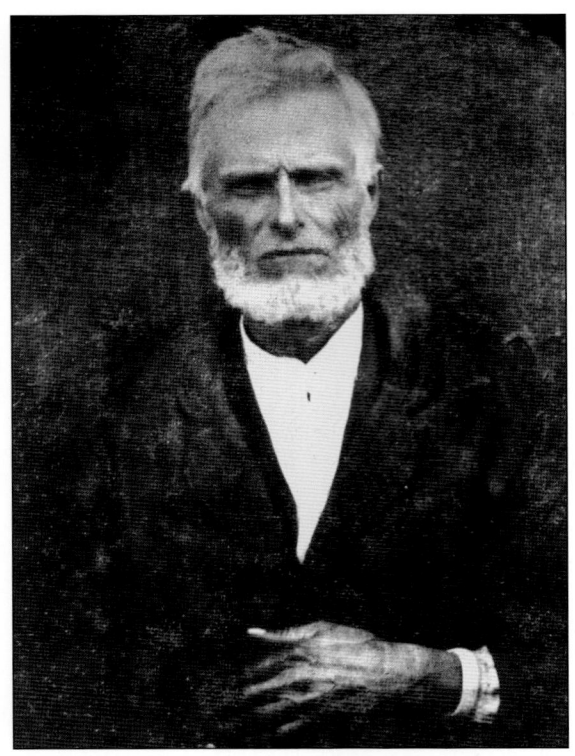

Gray Daniel Hollifield, father of Isaac, was one of the earliest settlers of the region. Born in 1805, he fathered 15 children between two wives. He, along with brother Esom, was one of the first Hollifields to settle in McDowell County. Two prominent Hollifield families in Little Switzerland descended from him. (Courtesy of John McKinney.)

Flurrie (Flora) McKinney Washburn Hollifield works her spinning wheel while Janie Hollifield and Flurrie's son Wade look on. Born in 1824, the daughter of "Cove" Charlie McKinney, Flurrie lived to be nearly 100. Spinning was an important part of family life to the hardy pioneer settlers, as they had to provide for their own subsistence. Using wool and flax, it provided much-needed materials for clothing. (Courtesy of Carrie Washburn.)

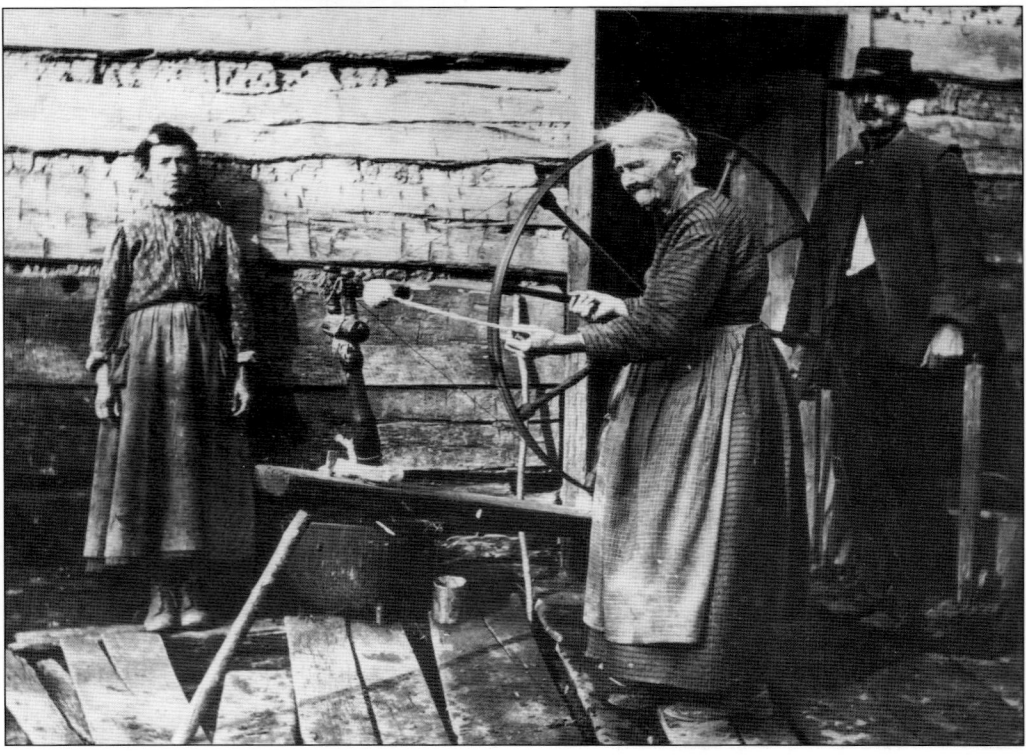

Robert and Susie McKinney (rear) owned and operated a gristmill in the Lake Laurel section in the early 1900s. He was another grandson of "Cove" Charles McKinney. They are pictured with their sons Tom (left) and Lester (right) and daughter Nora. Tom worked in a mica mine in Yancey County. Lester later went on to serve as caretaker of Camp As-You-Like-It for many years. (Courtesy of Ruby Buchanan.)

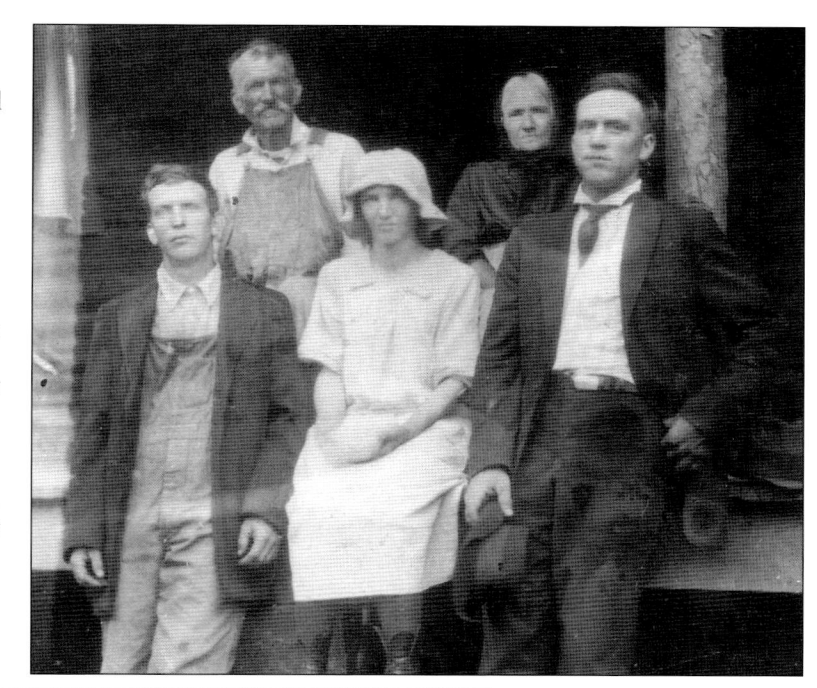

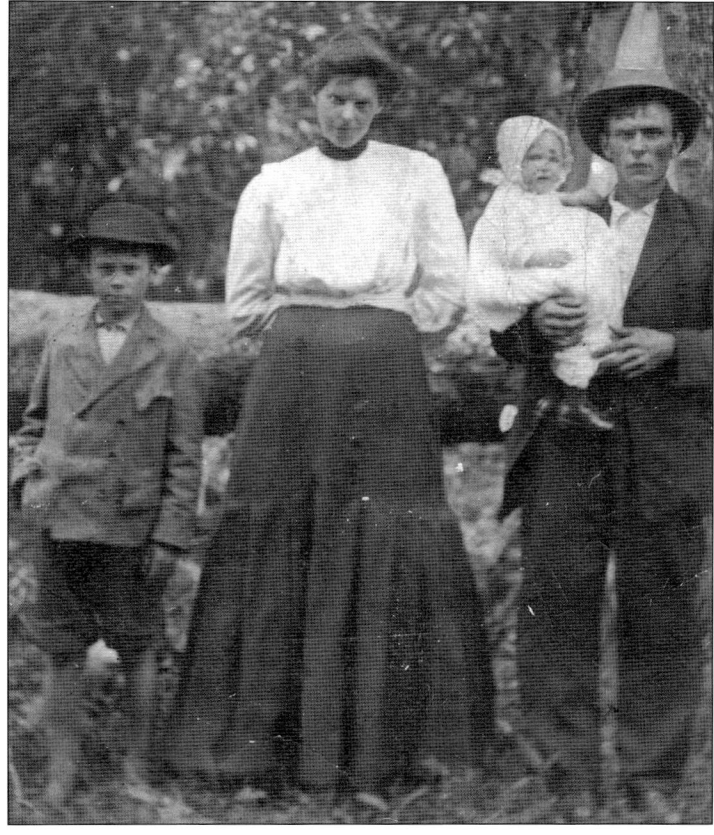

Jane McKinney, pictured here with husband Fons, son Lawrence and daughter Ida, was a daughter of Mother Nancy Buchanan. She was popular with summer residents and visited with many of them regularly. Fons was a skilled rock mason and craftsman who constructed many of the summer resident cottages. Ida later became a schoolteacher in Little Switzerland and Spruce Pine. (Courtesy of Ruby Buchanan.)

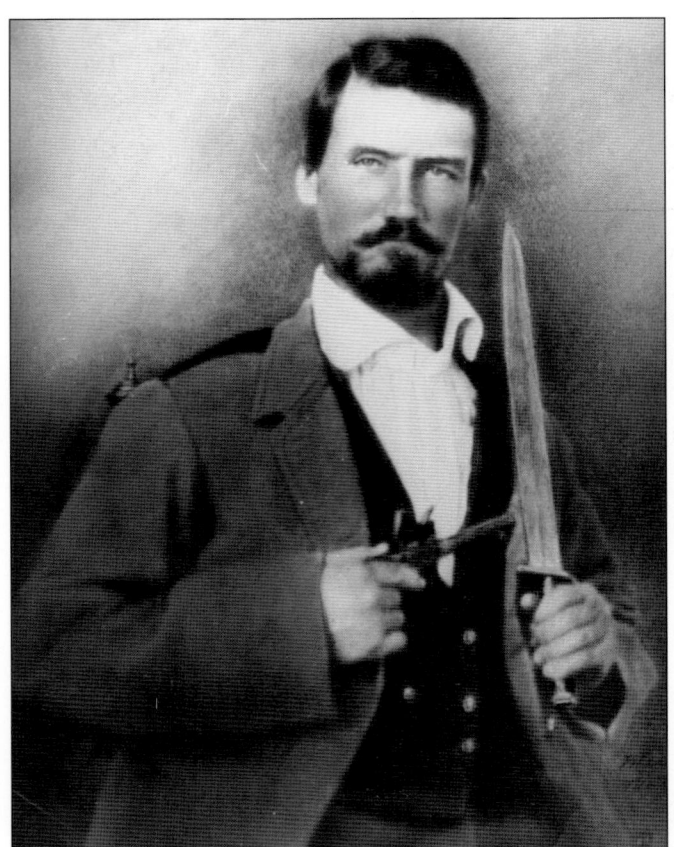

Merritt McKinney was one of the early settlers of Little Switzerland. A veteran of both the Mexican War of 1846 and the Civil War, he raised two families with Susanna Washburn (Grassy Creek) and Mary Hollifield (Little Switzerland). He was afflicted with wanderlust, with legends having him disappearing for months, only to return home. (Courtesy of John McKinney.)

Merritt "Boot" McKinney is pictured with wife Dora and Big Bob on their farm in the Lake Laurel area. Boot and Dora lived in a cabin that dated from Revolutionary War times, and they leased their farm to Charles Stevens Dwight of Charleston, South Carolina, who operated Camp Alpine, a boys' camp, for three years on the property. The cabin still stands on the property. (Courtesy of Bill McKinney.)

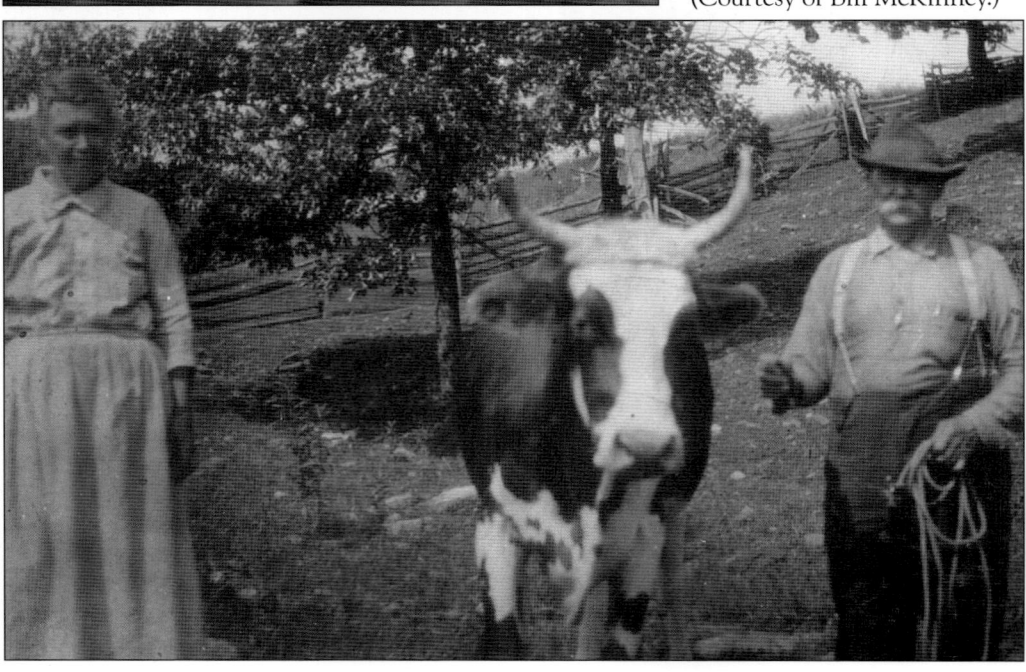

The family of Rufus and Maggie McKinney visits grandmother Susie McKinney. Pictured from left to right are (first row) Susie, Floyd, Merrimon, Clifton, and Landon McKinney; (second row) Nora, Lilly Mae, and Maggie Hollifield McKinney. Merrimon, Clifton, and Landon were well-known stonemasons in the community, working for both locals and summer residents. Their work is still evident in several locations. (Courtesy of Betty Mace.)

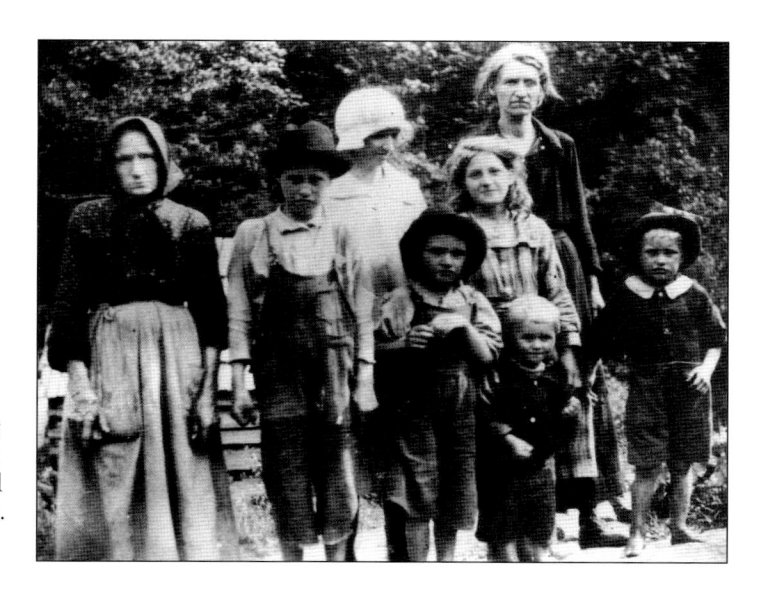

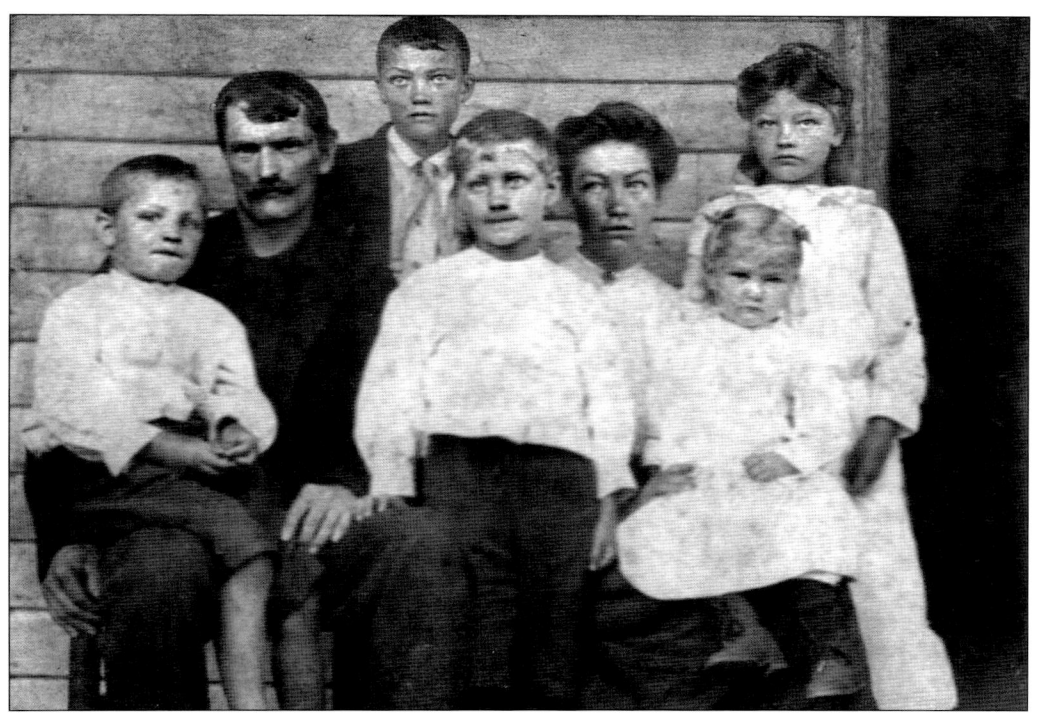

The Alfred and Liller Self family pose on their porch. The Selfs lived in the Lake Laurel section and were carpenters by trade. Fred and Vergie were active members of the Chestnut Grove Church. Seen here from left to right are Fred Self, Alfred Self, Plato Self, Coy Self, Liller McKinney Self (daughter of Mexican and Civil War hero Merritt McKinney), Vergie Self, and Mamie Self. (Courtesy of Maude Hughes.)

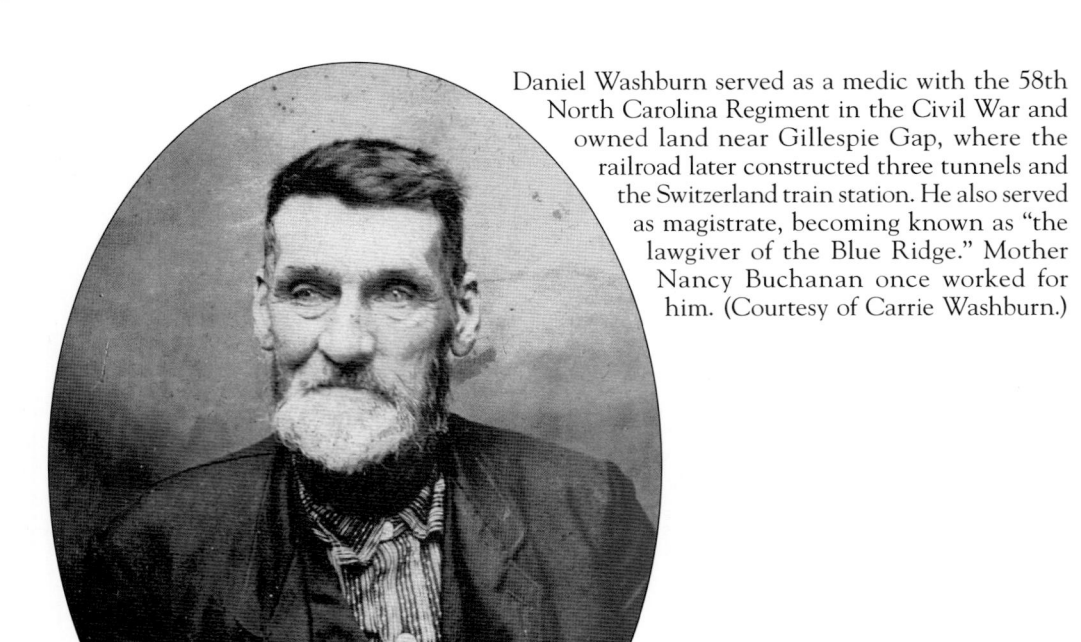

Daniel Washburn served as a medic with the 58th North Carolina Regiment in the Civil War and owned land near Gillespie Gap, where the railroad later constructed three tunnels and the Switzerland train station. He also served as magistrate, becoming known as "the lawgiver of the Blue Ridge." Mother Nancy Buchanan once worked for him. (Courtesy of Carrie Washburn.)

The Mace family came to Little Switzerland from McDowell County. Ed and Etta Mace, pictured here in the 1930s, were among the first Mace families in the area. Ed worked for the Nello Teer Company and was involved in the construction of the Blue Ridge Parkway near Crabtree Meadows. Etta tended house, raising a large family with Ed. (Courtesy of Hugh Glenn.)

Two

"This Is the Place"
The Switzerland Company Establishes a Colony

Heriot Clarkson, a lawyer with the firm of Clarkson and Duls of Charlotte, had a vision. He was seeking a mountaintop paradise where a respite from the summer's heat, combined with scenery and a simpler way of life, would rejuvenate spirits and foster a community. Contacting Reid Queen and Floyd Gardner, real estate agents in Marion, he expressed his desires for property that would meet his dream. Queen, a native of Phenoy, a small community in southern Mitchell County, had an idea of some land that might fill the bill. In 1909, Clarkson, Queen, and Gardner boarded a train to Spruce Pine then set off to view the property on mules up the Spoon Camp Road.

They rode to the top of Grassy Mountain, a clearing with a 360-degree view. In the west arose Mount Mitchell and the Black Mountains; to the south, Linville Mountain, the South Mountains, Turkey Cove and the Catawba River valley; in the east were views of Table Rock, Hawksbill, and Grandfather Mountains; and in the north was Roan Mountain. Clarkson paused, drinking in the display around him. He turned to Queen and Gardner and said "This is the place."

He returned to Charlotte and organized the Switzerland Company, which purchased 1,100 acres of mountaintop property on Grassy Mountain and Chestnut Ridge. The company was named at the suggestion of Anna Twelvetrees, who upon hearing a description of the property declared it to be like the Jura Mountains in Switzerland. In 1910, the company began development of Little Switzerland, creating 1-acre lots, developing supporting infrastructure, and attracting buyers; Ida Clarkson Jones built the original Switzerland Inn, and Clarkson's plans for a utopian community were well underway.

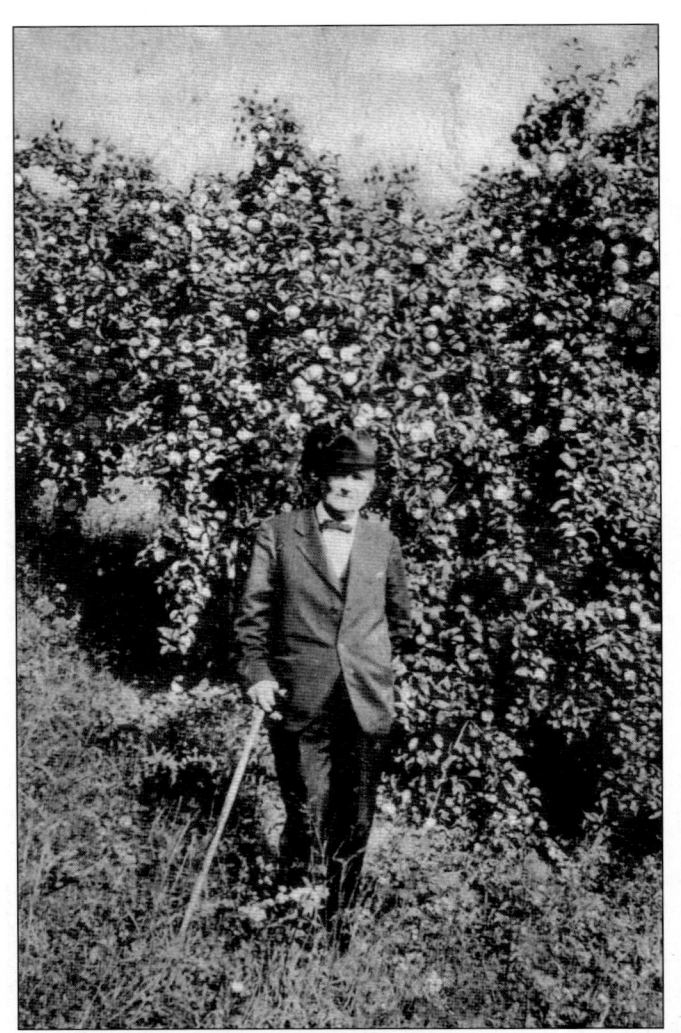

Judge Heriot Clarkson poses in his apple orchard, which was located below current North Carolina Highway 226A across from the Switzerland Inn. Clarkson enjoyed the fresh fruits and vegetables that were in abundance in Little Switzerland in the summers. He also enjoyed mailing a postcard with a family photograph on it each year to friends. This was the 1937 card. (Courtesy of Ruby Buchanan.)

Below, Judge Heriot Clarkson's family gathers for a photograph on his birthday, August 21, 1941, in Little Switzerland. Seen here from left to right are (first row) Mary Pollard, Peggy Clarkson, Francis Clarkson Jr., Helen Clarkson, John Pollard III, Albert Pollard, and Heriot Clarkson II; (second row) Edwin Clarkson, Mrs. Edwin Clarkson, Mrs. Francis Clarkson, Francis Clarkson, Mary Clarkson, Judge Clarkson, Mrs. John Pollard Jr., Cama Clarkson, Mrs. Thomas Clarkson, and Rev. Thomas Clarkson. (Courtesy of Ruby Buchanan.)

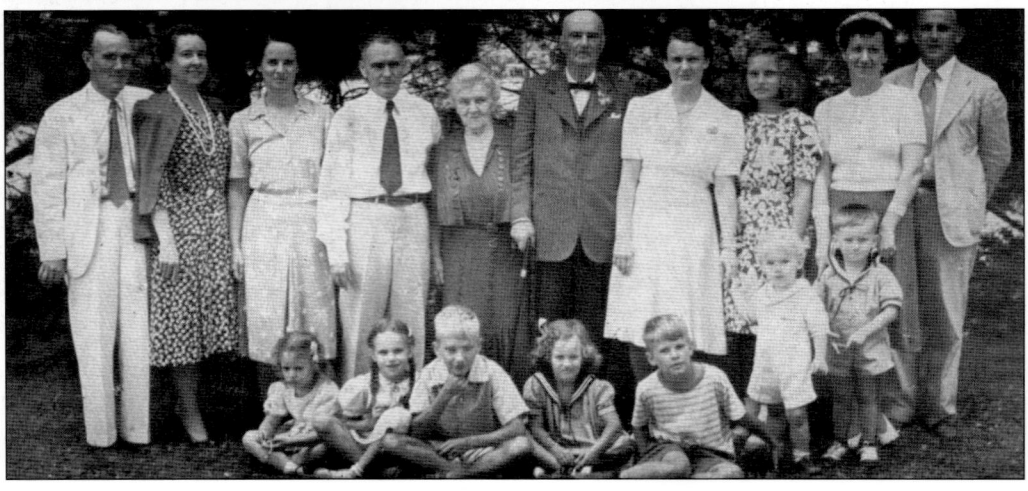

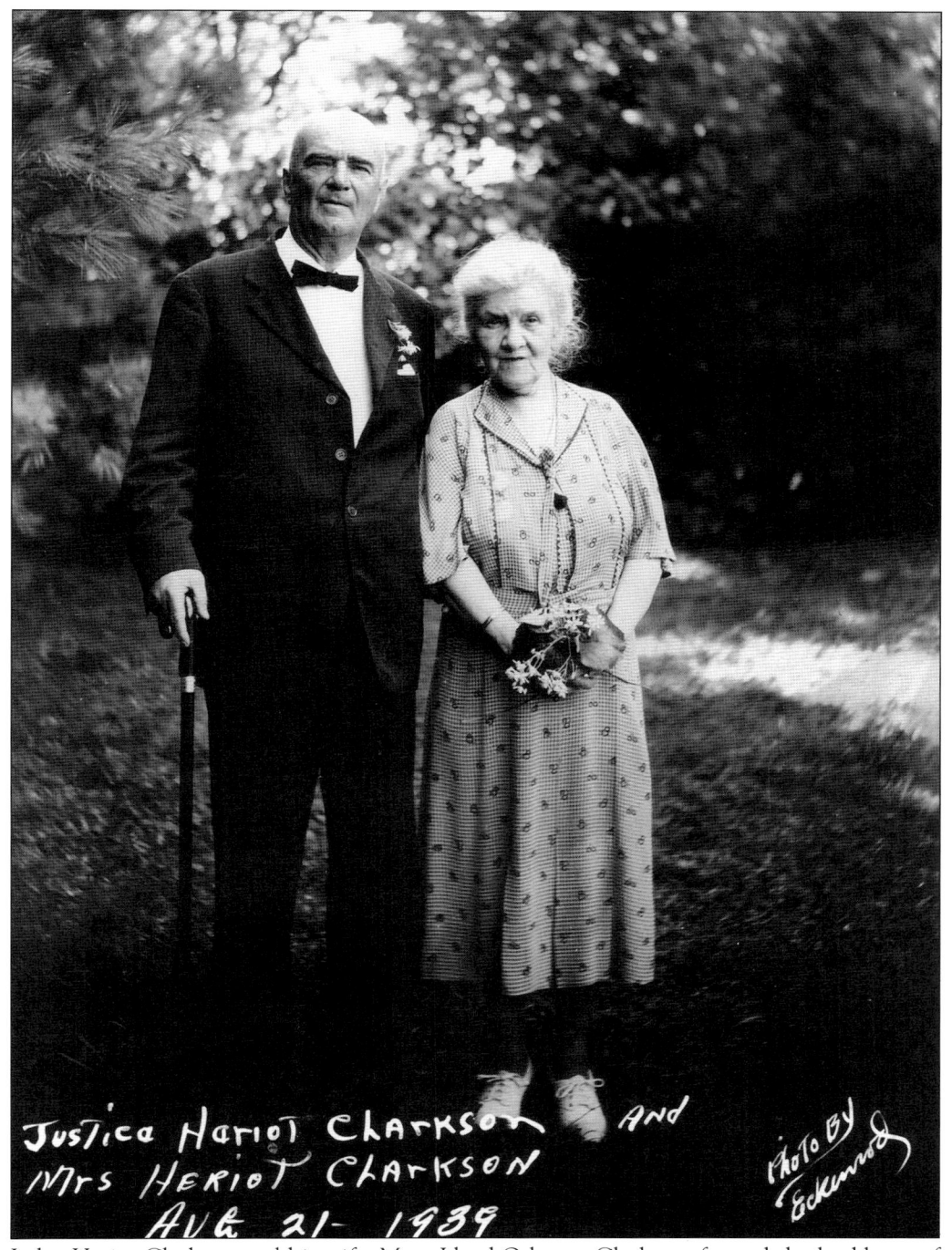

Judge Heriot Clarkson and his wife, Mary Lloyd Osborne Clarkson, formed the backbone of the Little Switzerland community. They helped organize the Church of the Resurrection, with Mary holding rummage sales to raise funds for the church. She was also active with Geneva Hall, coordinating activities held there for the community. This photograph of the couple was taken on Judge Clarkson's 75th birthday. (Courtesy of Sarah Clarkson.)

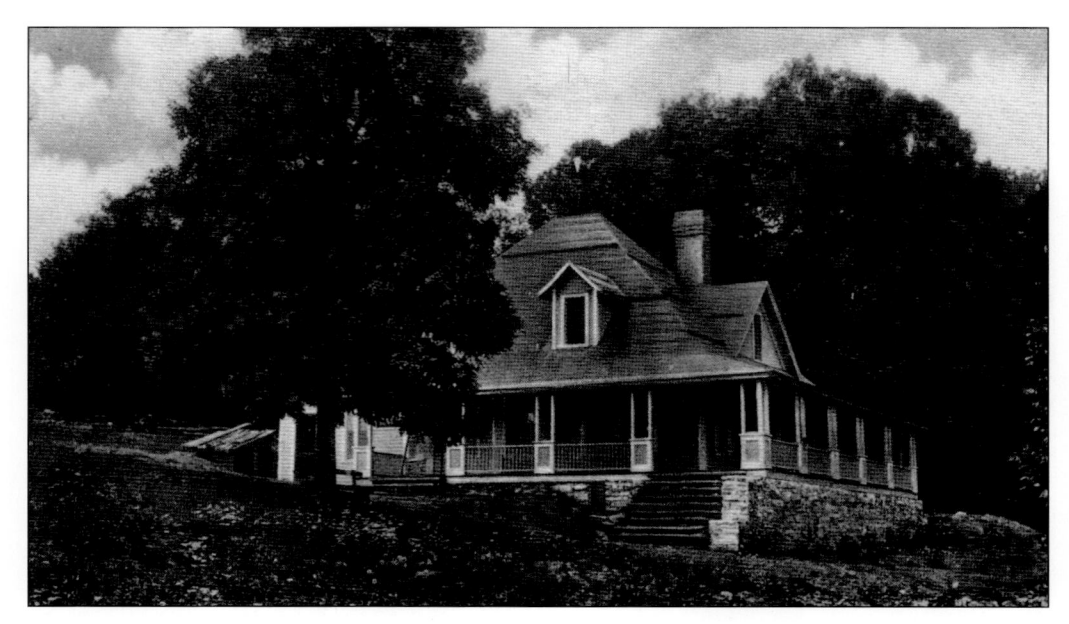

Judge Heriot Clarkson's home, built in 1911, was one of Little Switzerland's first houses. The current Switzerland Inn swimming pool is located where it stood. It was constructed of materials brought by oxen from Marion. Clarkson entertained prominent North Carolina citizens and locals, often in the same day. His annual birthday party attracted the community to celebrate on the grounds. Below, the Clarkson family poses for a portrait on the steps in 1926. From left to right are Elizabeth Clarkson, Eddie Clarkson, Tommy Clarkson, Mary Clarkson, Judge Heriot Clarkson, Peggy Clarkson, Francis Clarkson, Cama Clarkson, and Sarah Clarkson. (Above courtesy of Robert and Cama Merritt; below courtesy of Sarah Clarkson.)

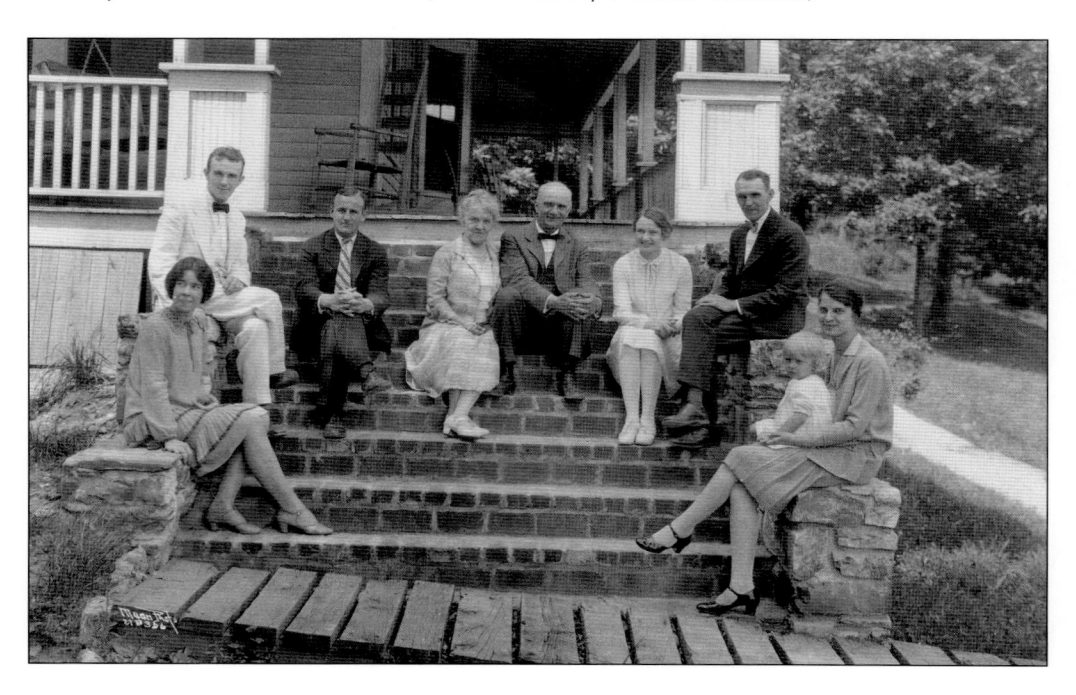

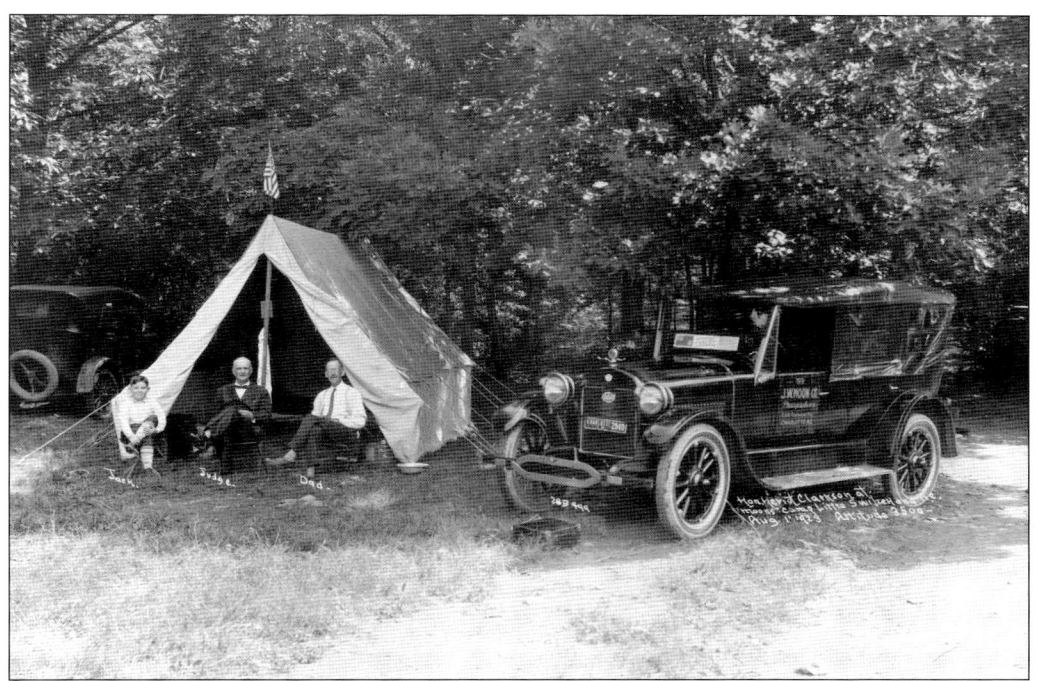

Judge Clarkson had a flair for promotion when it came to Little Switzerland. He spared no expense to attract potential buyers. He produced high-quality printed brochures touting the beauty of the region and featuring photography by the J. W. Moon Company of Charlotte. In the upper photograph, Clarkson visits with Moon and his son Jack at their camp in Little Switzerland during one of their photograph sessions in 1923. Below is the front cover of one of the first Little Switzerland brochures, a hardbound book touting the amenities available to buyers. (Both courtesy of Sarah Clarkson.)

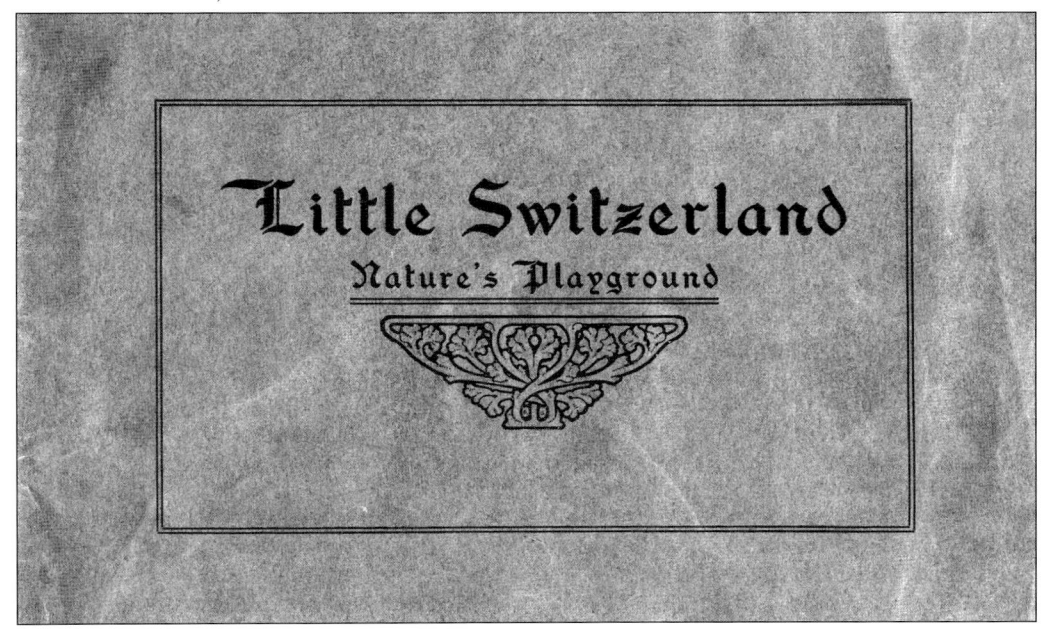

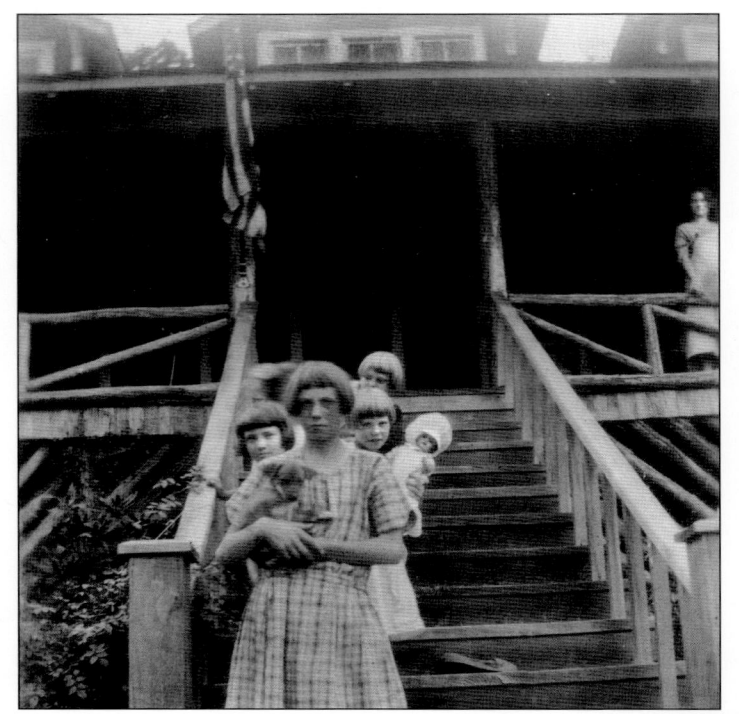

The Switzerland Inn was a focal point of the community after it opened, as both guests of the inn and locals gathered on the front porch to visit. At left, four young women stand on the steps for a photograph. Seen here from front to back are Ida McKinney, an unidentified child, Missouri McKinney (with doll), Edith McKinney, and an unidentified woman at the upper right. Below is a group of workers at the inn. Fons McKinney sits at the upper left of the image. (Left courtesy of Ruby Buchanan; below courtesy of Pat Mitchell.)

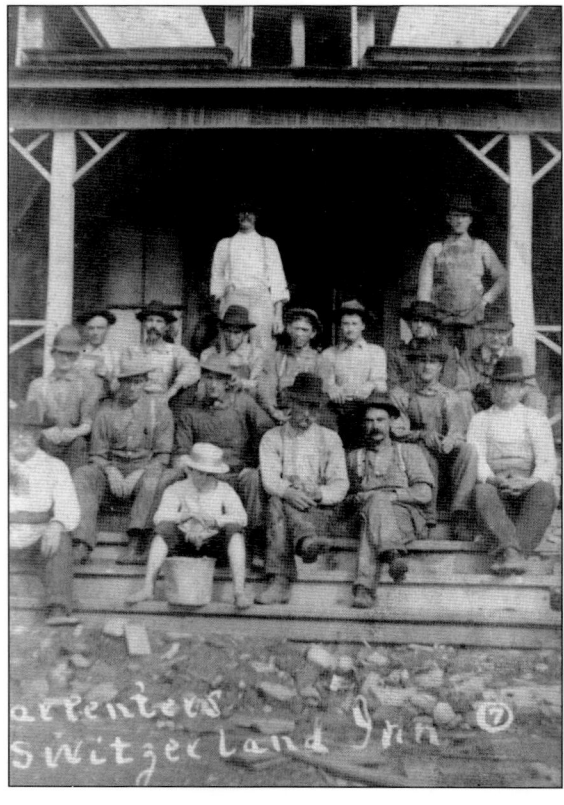

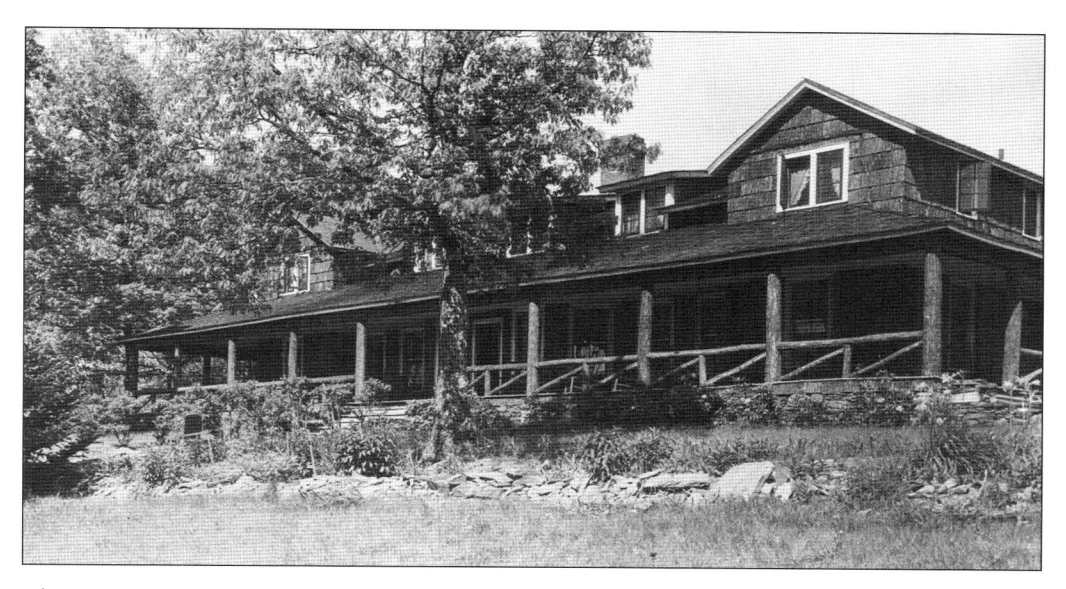

The original Switzerland Inn was operated by Ida Clarkson Jones, Judge Heriot Clarkson's sister. It opened in 1911, a spacious two-story building featuring 25 rooms that was covered with chestnut bark, and was located just below the current inn. Guests paid $7.50 per person per week, which included meals. The restaurant featured a varied menu, often using fruits and vegetables raised by locals. Elegant dining, featuring attentive service by George (pictured below), a waiter at the inn, was a highlight of the stay. Noted visitors to the inn included Biblical scholar and archaeologist William Albright, who authenticated the Dead Sea scrolls, and noted painter Frank Stanley Herring. Later on, Jones added cottages, some of which are still in existence. (Above courtesy of the North Carolina Collection, UNC–Chapel Hill; below courtesy of Clarkson Jones.)

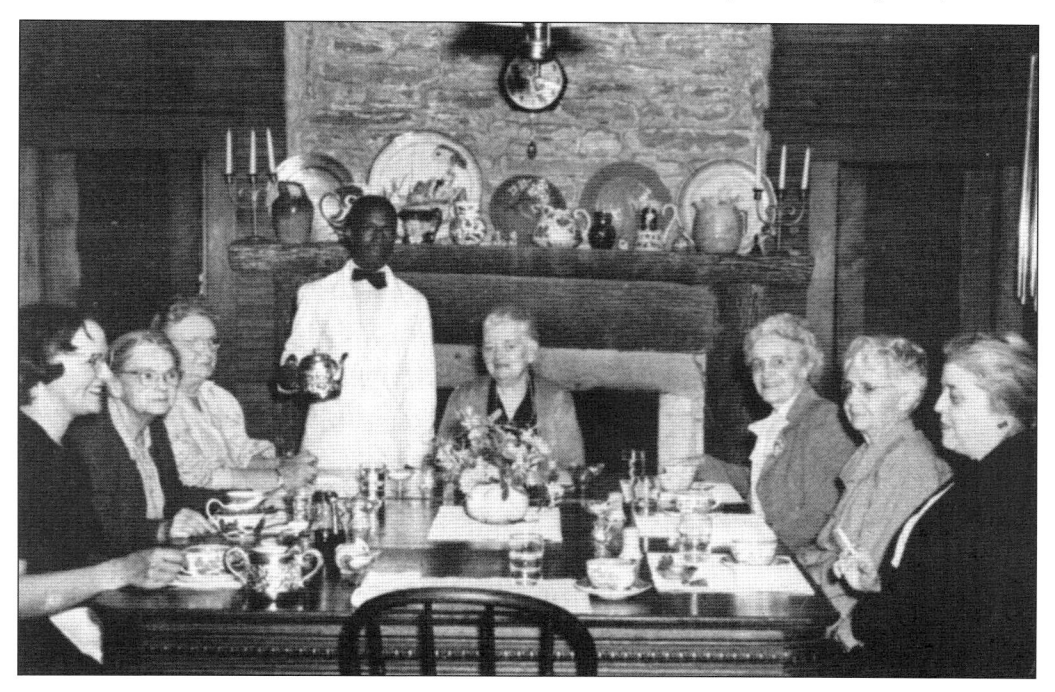

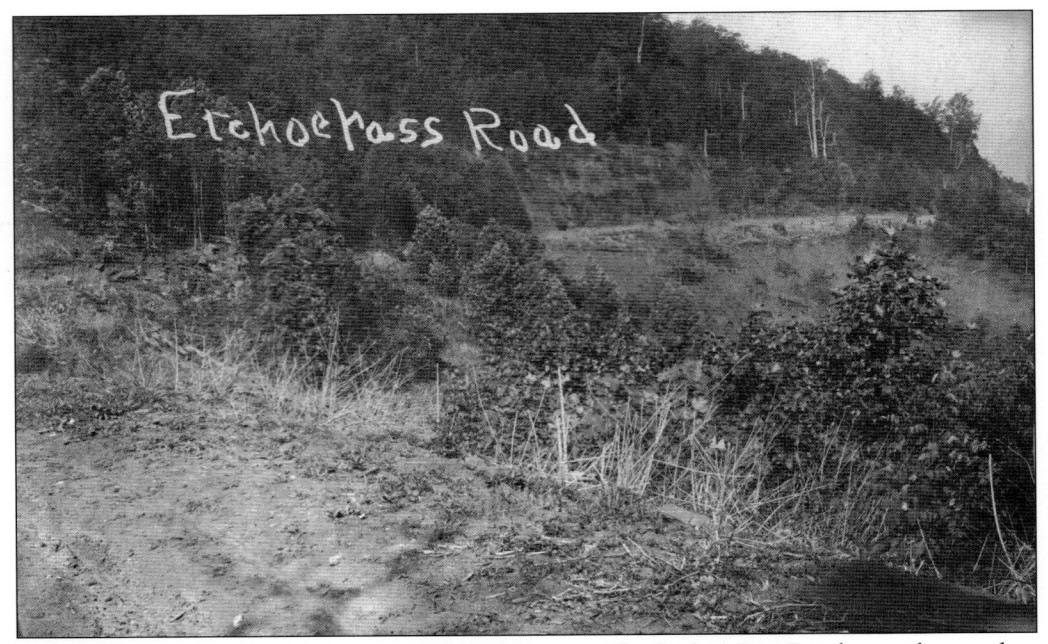

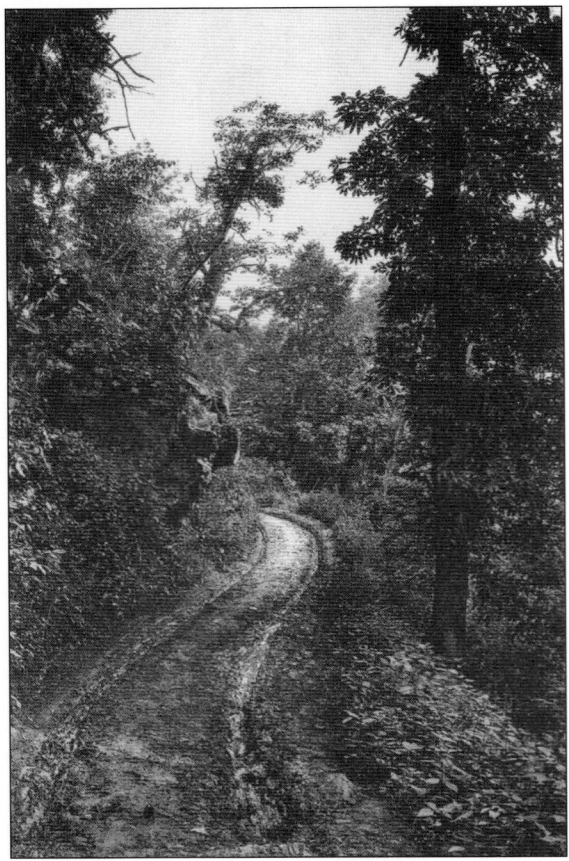

The Etchoe Pass Road wound around the Blue Ridge escarpment from the Switzerland railroad station to the entrance of the resort. The road, commissioned by the Switzerland Company and built under the supervision of David Tappan, was named to honor Gen. Francis Marion (from whom the Clarkson family descended) and his battle with the Cherokee Indians. It is the current North Carolina Highway 226A. (Courtesy of Robert and Cama Merritt.)

The Bearwallow Gap Road was typical of the difficulties faced by travelers and visitors to the Little Switzerland region. This winding route around Grassy Mountain started as a trail that connected the Glenn settlement with Little Switzerland. Several cottages were built along it, and later the Switzerland Store was constructed at the intersection of the road and the Marion Highway (now North Carolina 226A). (Courtesy of Davis and Jann Godwin.)

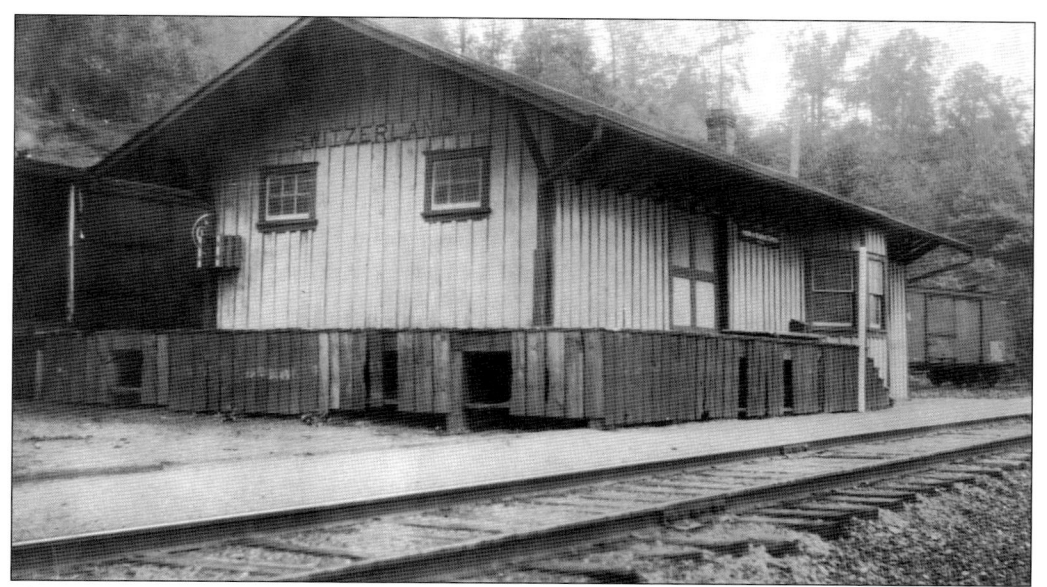

The Switzerland station on the Clinchfield Railroad was where many early summer residents started their Little Switzerland adventure. Trains from the Carolina, Clinchfield, and Ohio deposited passengers for the journey up the Etchoe Pass Road to Lynn Gap, the entrance to Little Switzerland. Judge Clarkson persuaded railroad officials to move its Mount Mitchell (also known as Switzerland) station 2 miles closer to the road to make the journey easier. It was manned during the summer months, and local residents Isaac Hollifield, Fred and Charlie Glenn, Charlie Dale, Fred Buchanan, and Clay, Clyde, and Bud Hollifield all drove the hacks, charging 60¢ for adults, 30¢ for children, and 60¢ per trunk to ride to the resort. (Both courtesy of Davis and Jann Godwin.)

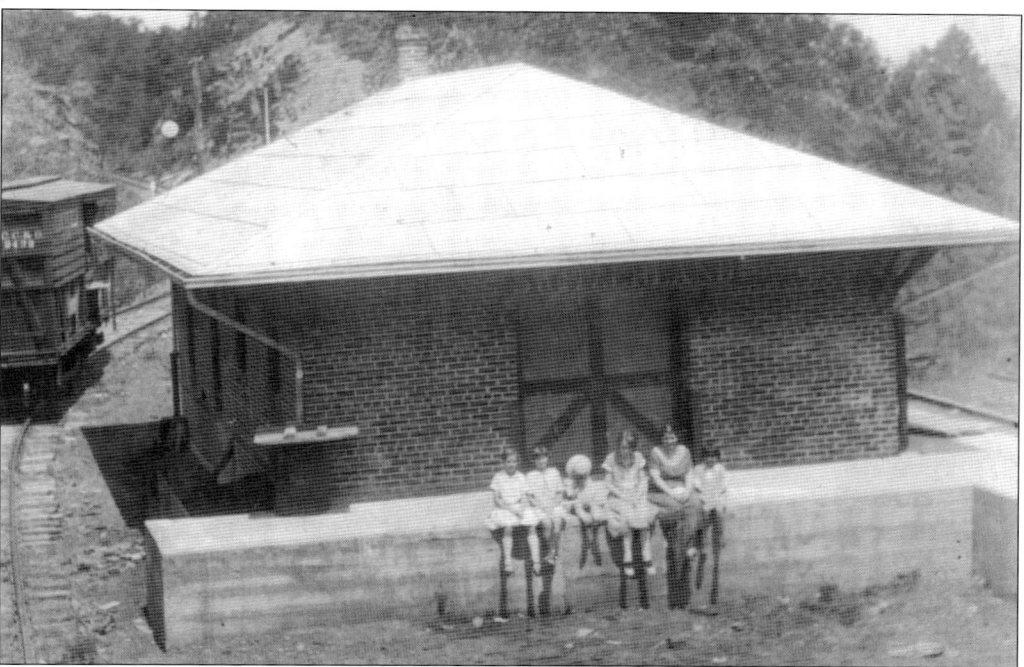

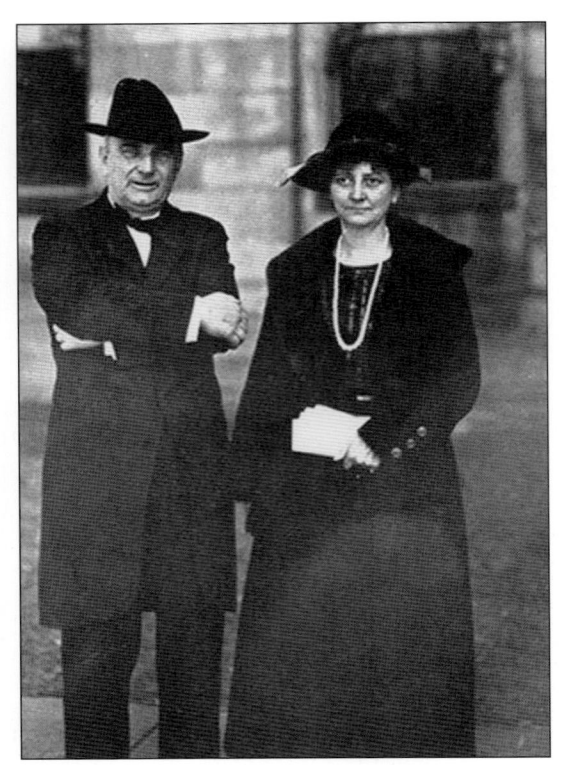

Harriett Morehead Berry, known as the Mother of Good Roads in North Carolina, owned Laurel Ledge Cottage. Pictured with Judge Clarkson, Berry worked through the North Carolina Good Roads Association to persuade the legislature to pass a $50-million bond bringing about North Carolina's modern highway system. She fought political maneuverings requiring counties to contribute half the cost of roads, which would have restricted them to larger cities. Berry spent summers away from her position as acting director of the North Carolina Geological Survey at the cottage. Pictured from left to right at Laurel Ledge below are Harriet Berry, Carrie Washburn, Mary Berry Barnes, Mary Strudwick Berry, John Berry, and Rascal. A 12-mile segment of Interstate 40 near Berry's hometown of Hillsborough is named in her honor. (Above courtesy of the North Carolina State Archives; below courtesy of Dr. Stan Black.)

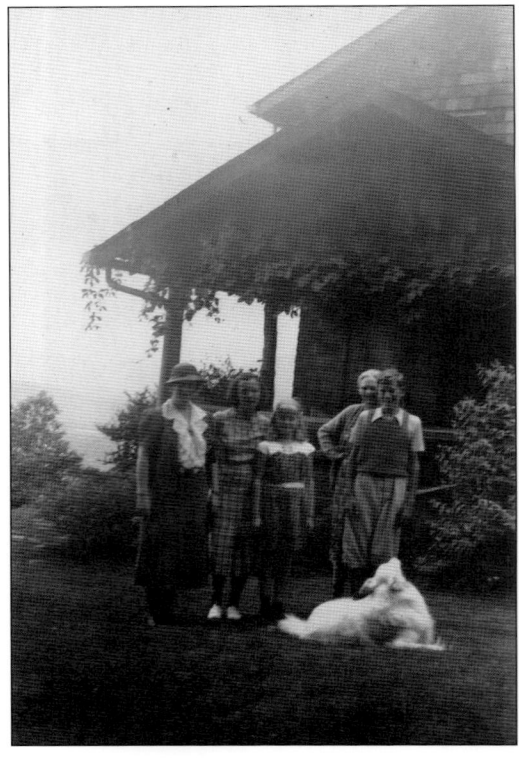

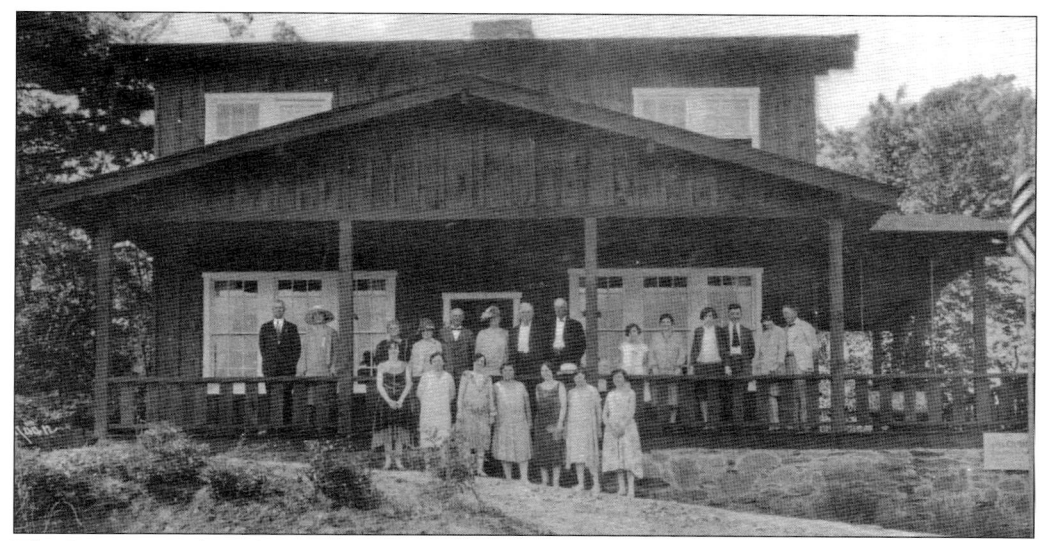

The Business and Professional Women's Club of Raleigh owned the Swiss Chalet, a clubhouse at Noah's Gap, from the 1920s to the 1940s. Mrs. Dess Gurganus, Eugenia Herring, and Mrs. Adali Osborne managed the property. Members of the club vacationed at the house. It was sold to the Gile family of Iowa, who opened it to the public. The property is known locally as "Gile's Pinnacle." (Courtesy of Davis and Jann Godwin.)

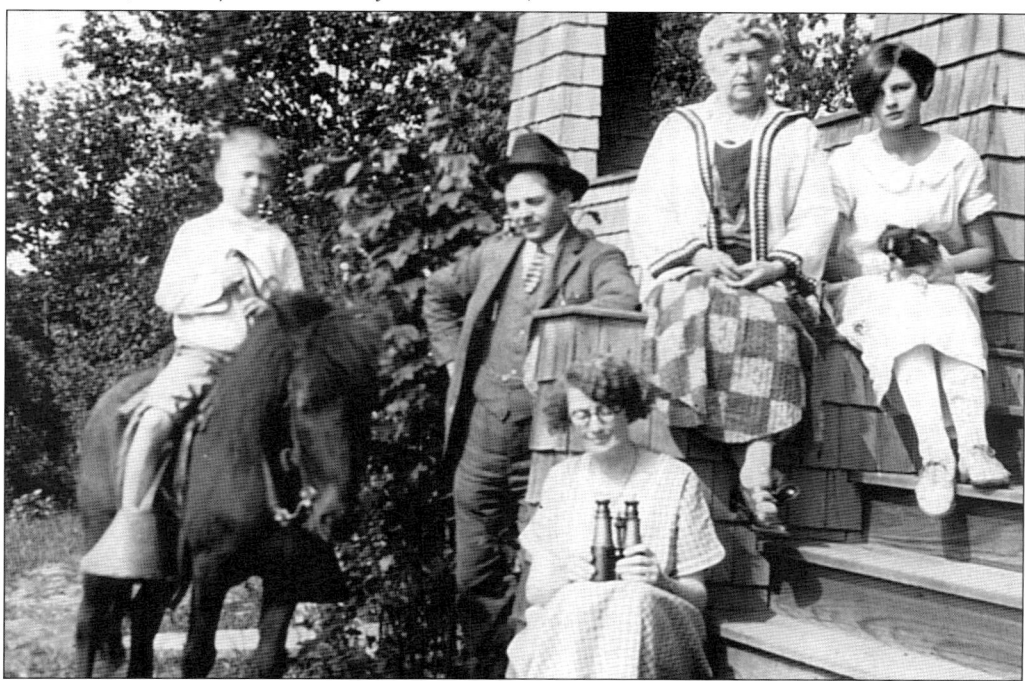

The family of Harry E. and Ida Hand of Orlando, Florida, came to Little Switzerland each summer for rest and relaxation. Hand was sheriff of Florida's Orange County in the 1930s, and as such, he helped the FBI attempt to capture Kate "Ma" Barker, taking part in the gun battle that took her life on January 16, 1935. Pictured from left to right are Buddy Hand, Harry Hand, Ida Hand, Clara Hand Nivens, and Harriett Hand. (Courtesy of Davis and Jann Godwin.)

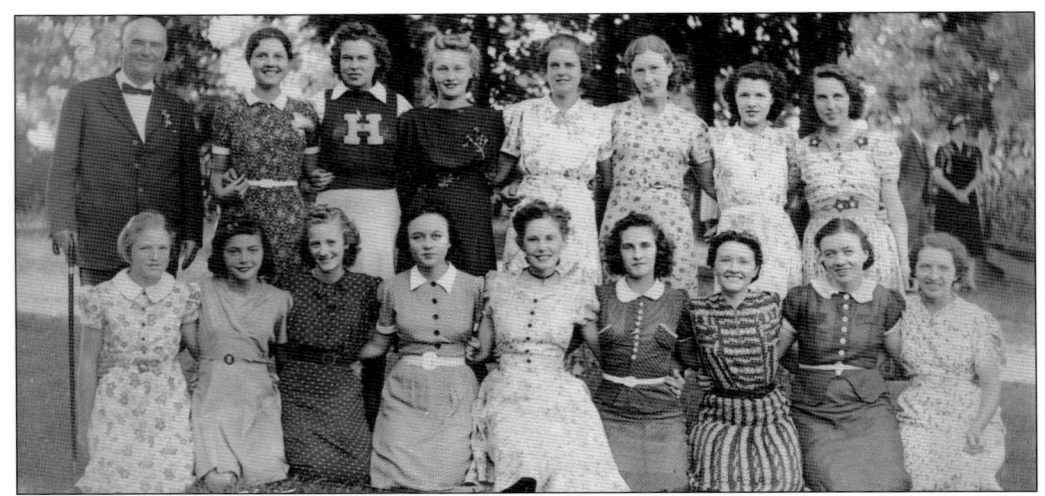

Judge Clarkson had a birthday party each August, and the community was invited. Here, he poses with 16 young women, "the Beauties of Little Switzerland," as part of the celebration in 1939. From left to right, they are (first row) Beulah Hollifield, Margaret McKinney, Helen McKinney, Muriel McKinney, Missouri McKinney Whitener, Josephine Smith, Virginia Gouge, Bernice McKinney, and Nellie Waycaster; (second row) Heriot Clarkson, Elice Hakes, Florence Burnette, Ruby McKinney, Reita McKinney, Ivory Collis, Fay Bradshaw Waycaster, and Verdie Mae Smith. (Courtesy of Ruby Buchanan.)

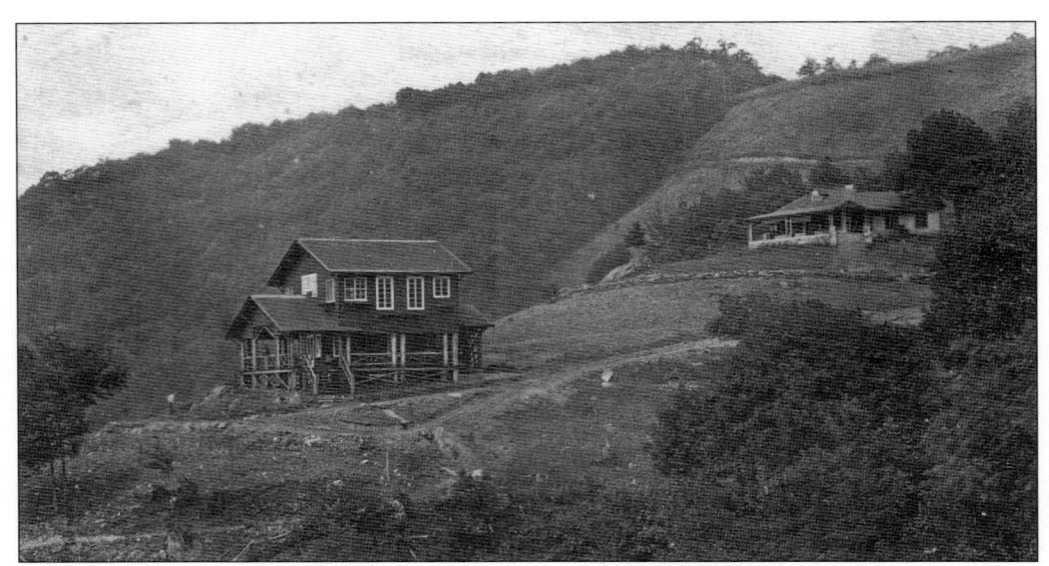

Echo Cottage, above right, was the residence of Judge Charles H. Duls, Judge Clarkson's law partner and an investor in the Switzerland Company. The cottage was popular with boarders, and the name was a derivative of Etchoe Pass. Louisa Duls, who wrote *The Story of Little Switzerland*, lived there. The cottage still stands today on Bearwallow Road. The lower residence is the Sommerville Cottage. (Courtesy of Davis and Jann Godwin.)

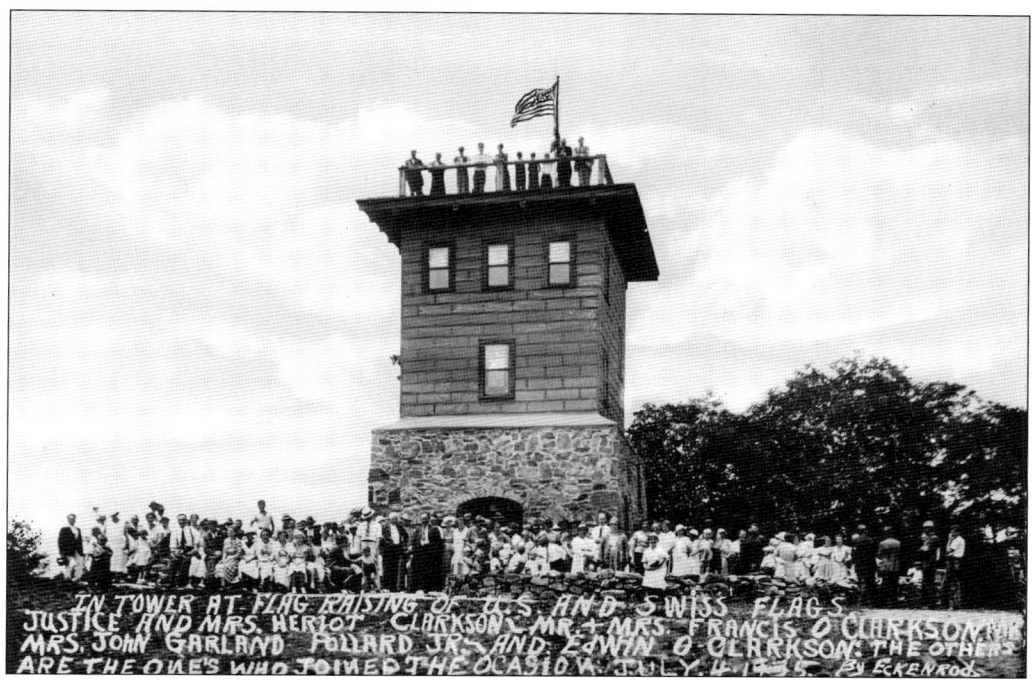

The Clarkson family built Kilmichael Tower as a gathering place for the community and as a tourist attraction. Constructed out of native stone laid by Fate McKinney and other family members, who were aided by oxen Pete and Repete, it featured panoramic views of the mountains. The tower held plaques honoring Judge Clarkson and the men and women from Little Switzerland who served in World War II. It fell into disrepair after the closing of the Wohlford Road, and the wooden upper section collapsed. The plaques were removed and placed on a stone structure next to the Church of the Resurrection. The base was restored in the 1980s as a cottage. The tower was named after the Clarkson family's ancestral holdings in Scotland. (Above courtesy of Frank Hollifield; below courtesy of Jann and Davis Godwin.)

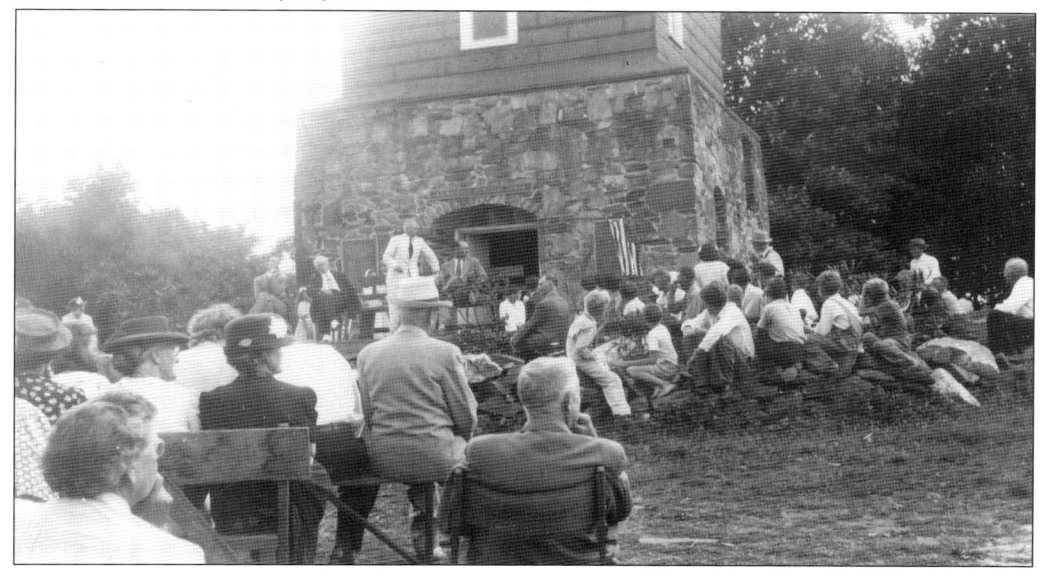

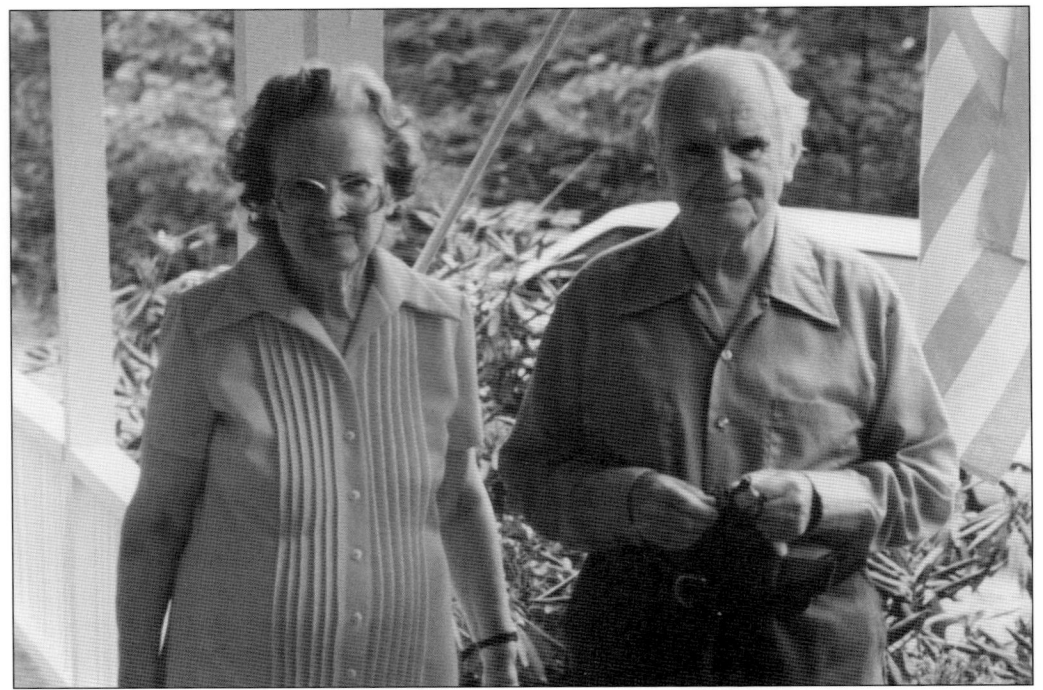

Cama and Francis Clarkson are seen here at their home on Laurel Lane. Francis took over operations of the Switzerland Company following his father's appointment to the North Carolina Supreme Court in 1923. He presided over the colony's expansion, including improvements to the infrastructure and the introduction of electricity. He was a superior court judge and was active in civic affairs in Charlotte, serving on several boards. (Courtesy of Sarah Clarkson.)

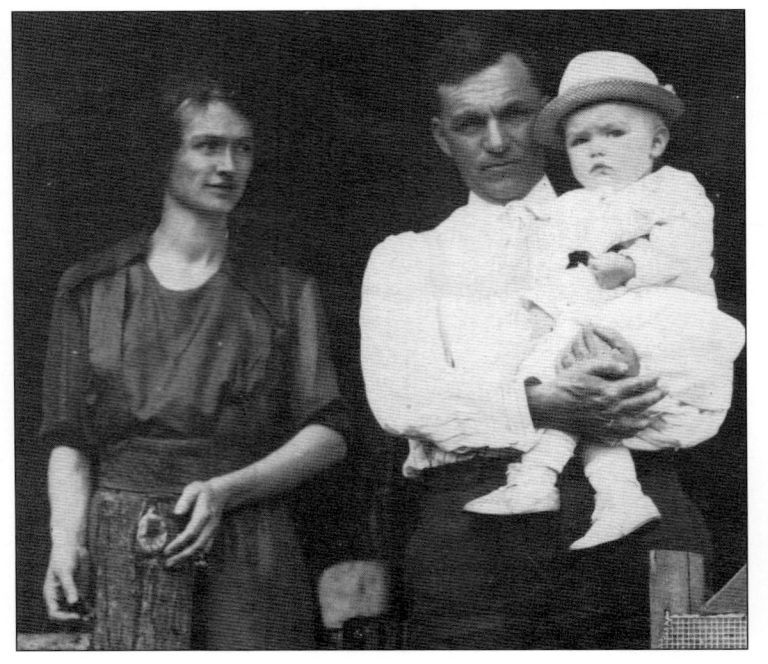

Reid Queen Sr. and Queenie McKinney Queen were important local connections for the Switzerland Company. Queen served as real estate agent, negotiating and buying 1,100 acres to start the colony. Queenie worked at the post office, serving as interim postmistress following E. B. Osborne's death. They are pictured with son Reid Jr. Many feel that without them, there would not have been a Little Switzerland. (Courtesy of Cole Martin.)

Three

The Scenic
The Blue Ridge Parkway Brings Challenge and Change

In 1935, the Switzerland Company learned of plans to route the newly established Blue Ridge Parkway through Gillespie Gap and Little Switzerland on the way to Asheville. Judge Heriot Clarkson and other company investors had campaigned for the Blue Ridge Parkway to go through North Carolina rather than Tennessee. They, along with others, saw the potential for tourism to be enhanced with the road.

R. Getty Browning, a State Highway Commission representative, presented a proposal for 88 acres in Little Switzerland. The Switzerland Company declined the offer, stating that it was too low and offering to settle for $22,000 for the property. The dispute went to court, with the Switzerland Company winning not only $25,000 for the land but also an entrance to the Blue Ridge Parkway, the only commercial entrance granted on the entire highway. The road opened to Little Switzerland on October 30, 1939, and it immediately became a major economic lifeline to the community. Travelers visited the Switzerland Inn and local stores, and the Wohlford Road wound up Grassy Mountain from the Blue Ridge Parkway to Kilmichael Tower. The Switzerland Company seized on the opportunities the Blue Ridge Parkway presented to attract visitors, erecting signs at the intersection enticing tourists to visit the tower and other local attractions. This infuriated parkway officials and, after several bouts with the company over the signs, they closed the Wohlford Road to traffic, essentially closing Kilmichael Tower.

The parkway also brought development such as Crabtree Meadows, a nearby campground, picnic area, and store that offered motorists a place to stop on their journey. As the Blue Ridge Parkway's fortunes go, so does Little Switzerland's economic prospects. Closure of the road can result in lower tourism revenues and can affect jobs. Its importance as an economic lifeline in the area cannot be overstated.

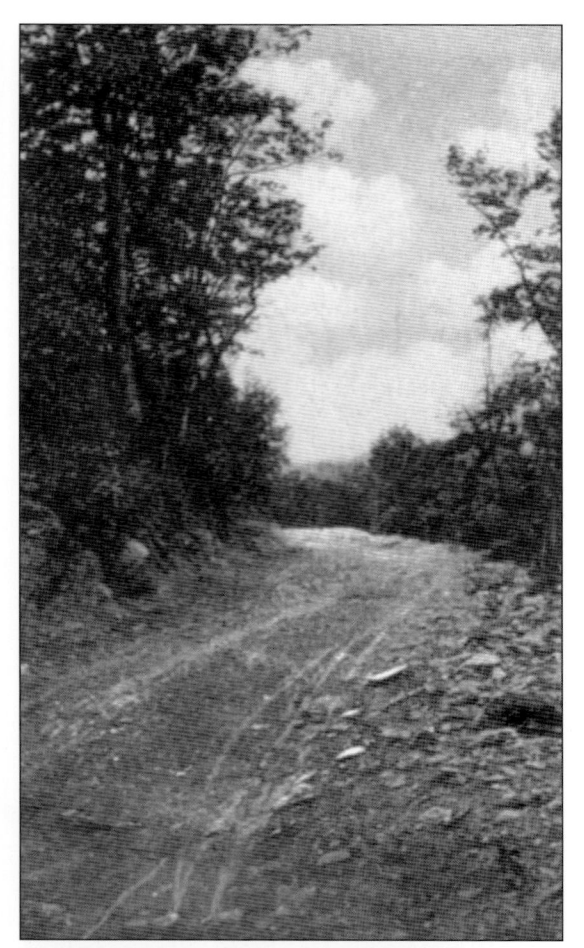

The Crest of the Blue Ridge Highway was a road proposed by State Geologist Joseph Hyde Pratt to run from Virginia to Georgia in 1909. A portion of it, pictured here, was constructed near Altapass, and the Switzerland Company was approached to include the Etchoe Pass Road in the highway, which the company declined. The Blue Ridge Parkway follows the highway from mileposts 317.6 to 318.7. (Courtesy of Sarah Clarkson.)

Construction of the Blue Ridge Parkway through Little Switzerland commenced July 18, 1937, and was completed October 30, 1939. Modern construction techniques, virtually unknown in the mountains at that time, were used to build the Blue Ridge Parkway. Local workers were employed during construction. This is a segment approximately 2 miles from Little Switzerland at milepost 332. (Courtesy of the U.S. National Park Service.)

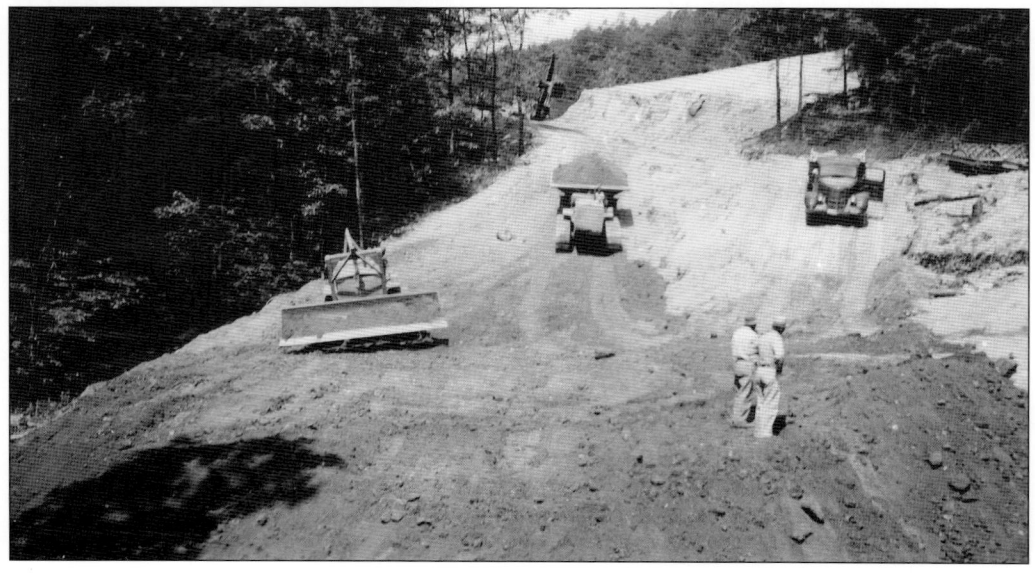

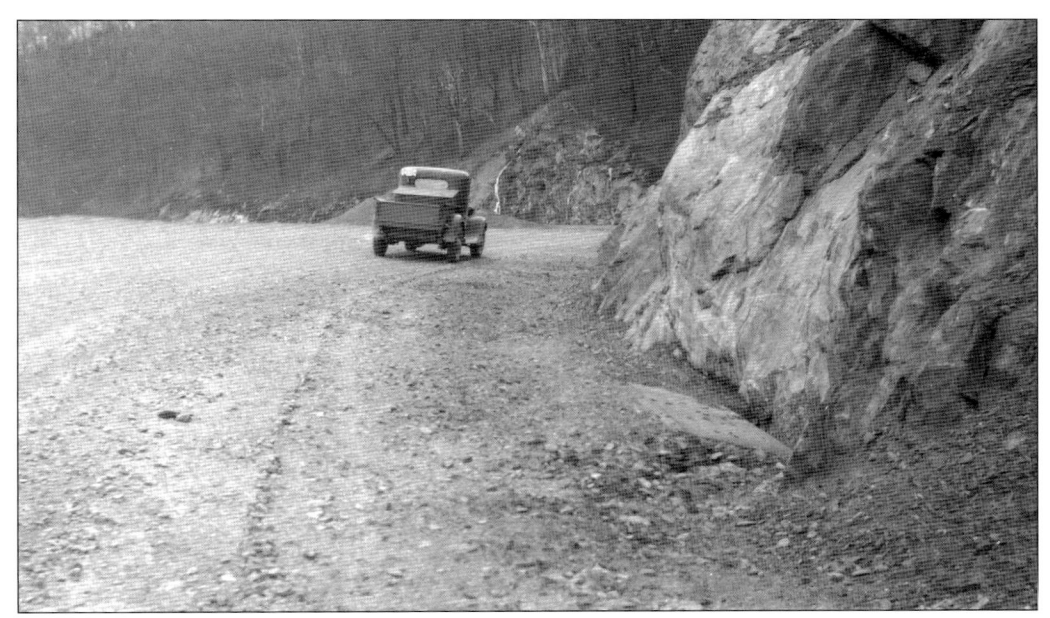

When the Blue Ridge Parkway opened through Little Switzerland on October 30, 1939, visitors were treated to a semi-completed version of the highway. Missing was the smooth pavement of today's road. In its place was a rustic gravel-covered surface with few amenities. The incompleteness did not deter visits, as this truck makes its way near Little Switzerland. Paving of the road did not occur until 1947. (Courtesy of the U.S. National Park Service.)

Stonemasons lay rock at the Buck Creek Gap intersection with North Carolina Highway 80. Italian stonemasons crafted beautiful bridges and culverts on the Blue Ridge Parkway from native stone. This secondary highway connection to Little Switzerland encourages traffic on the Blue Ridge Parkway through the community. Local businesses prefer that Park Service officials use Buck Creek as a detour when the Blue Ridge Parkway is closed. (Courtesy of the U.S. National Park Service.)

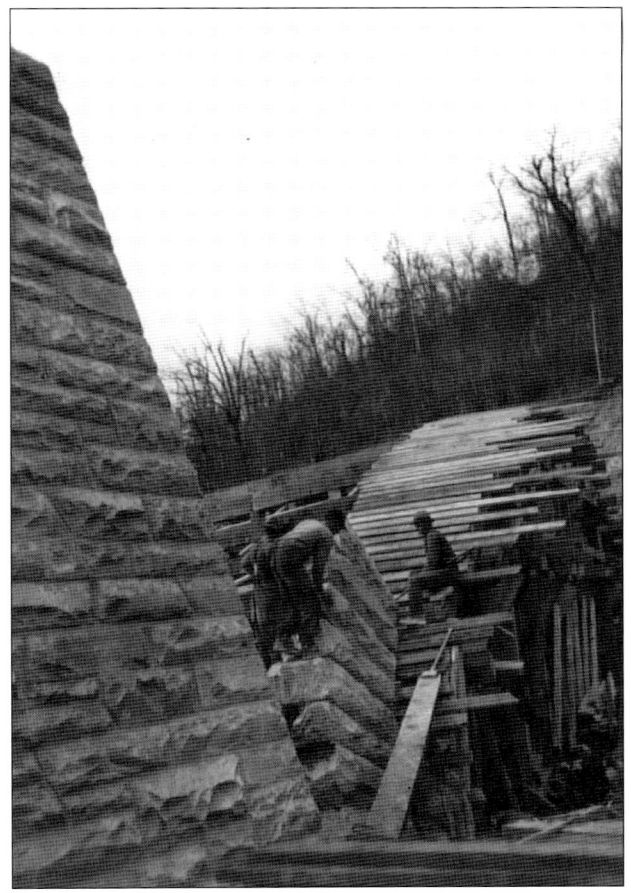

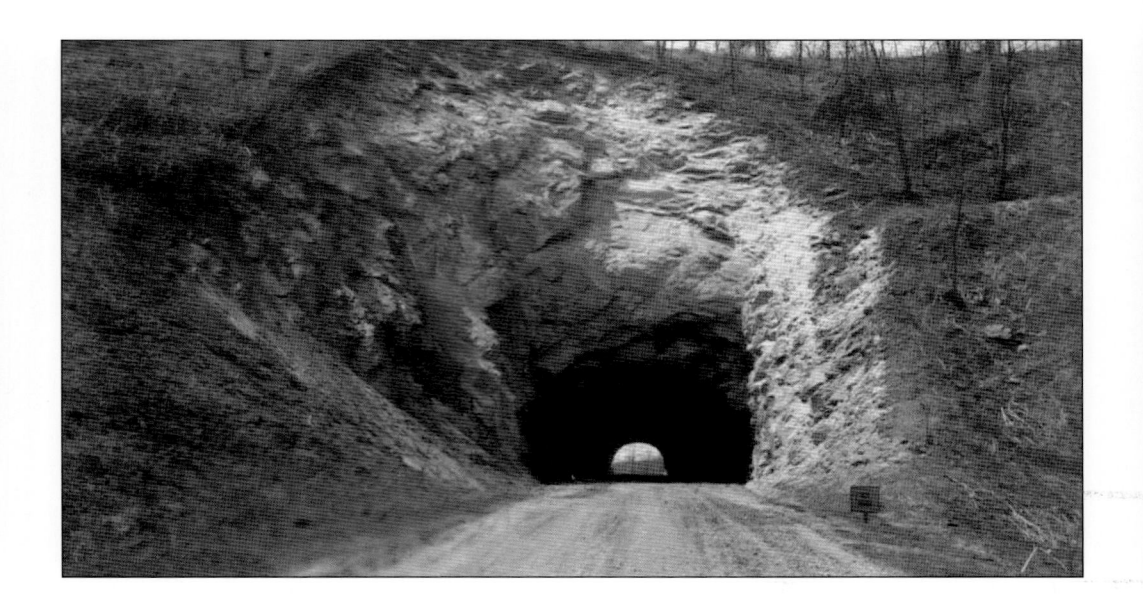

The Switzerland Tunnel, a prominent feature on the Blue Ridge Parkway, is the second longest tunnel on the road. Some 575 feet long, with a height of 19 feet, 8 inches, the tunnel was constructed between 1937 and 1939. The right-of-way near the tunnel contained the homes of the Win Buchanan family and W. R. and Erie Carter, along with the first Geneva Hall and the Church of the Resurrection. The Buchanan house was torn down, while Geneva Hall, the church, and the Carter home were relocated. The facing for the southbound entrance to the tunnel is made of rock quarried from Grandfather Mountain. On the winter solstice, the sun rises and sets directly through the tunnel. (Both courtesy of the U.S. National Park Service.)

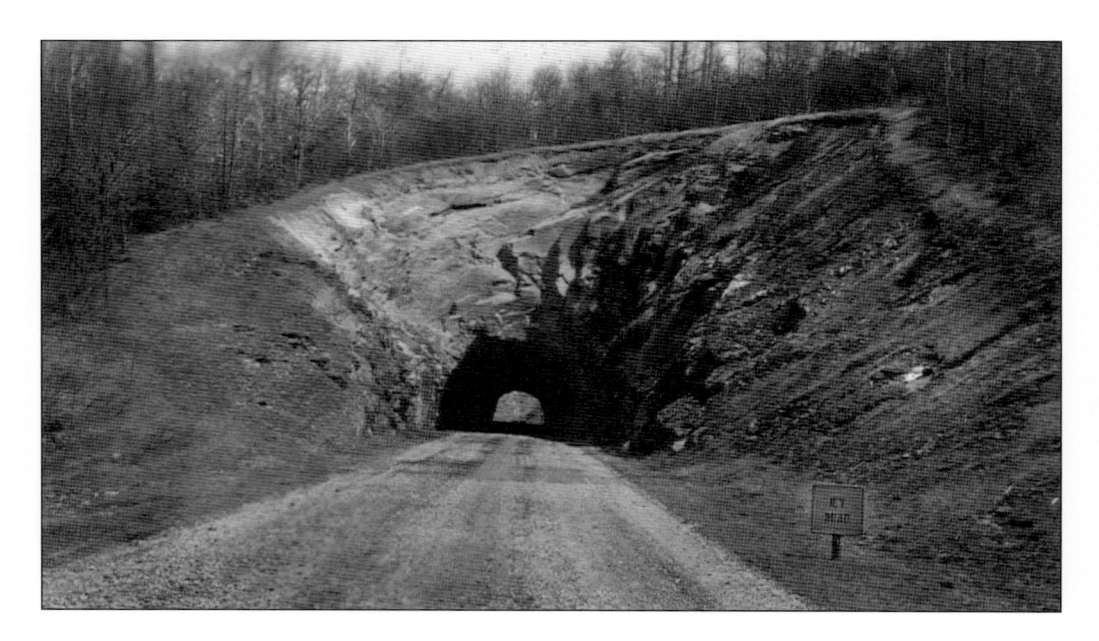

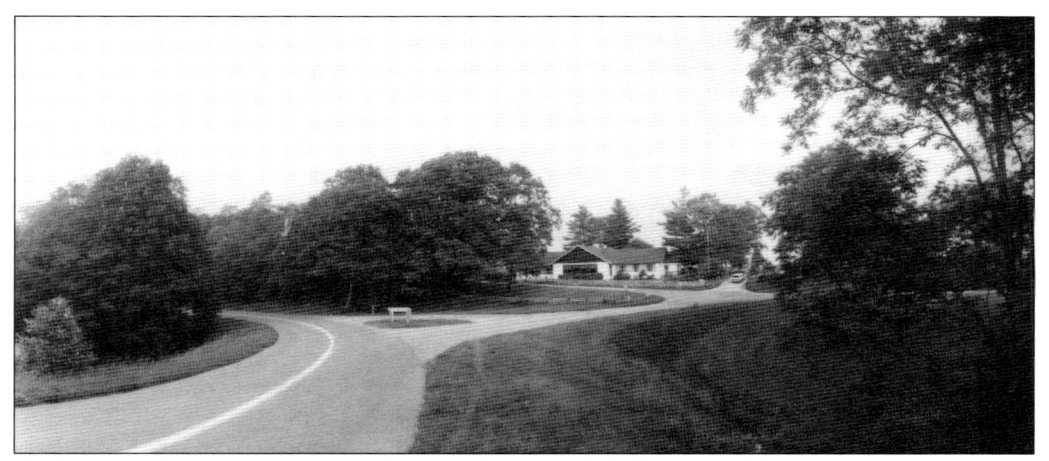

As part of the Switzerland Company's $25,000 settlement with the State of North Carolina of a lawsuit over right-of-way for the Blue Ridge Parkway in 1939, the Switzerland Inn was granted an access directly to the scenic highway, the only such commercial connection on the road. Company advertising later boasted about the exclusive access for the inn. (Courtesy of the U.S. National Park Service.)

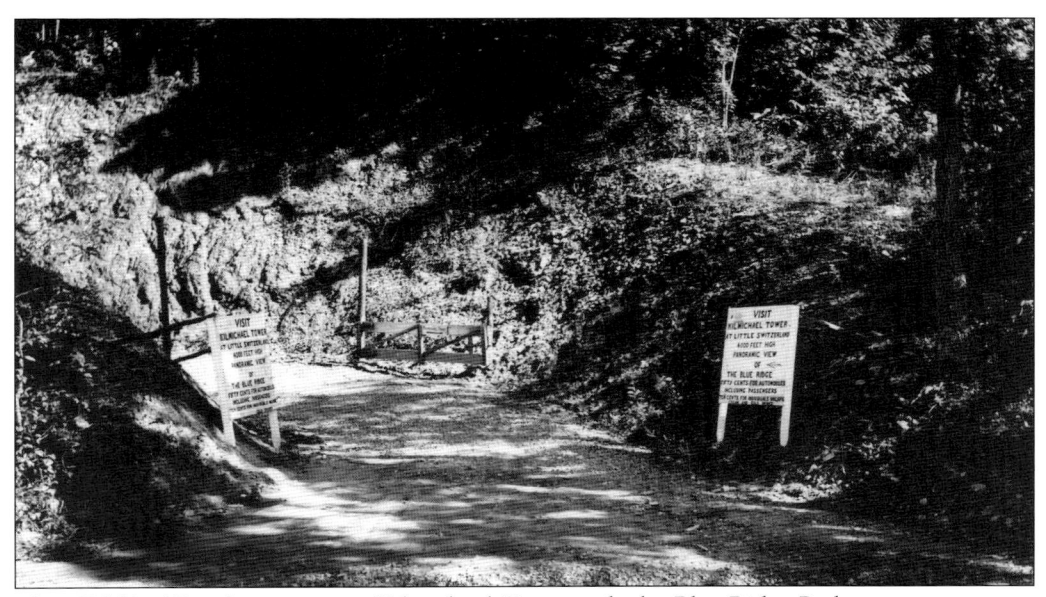

The Wohlford Road, connecting Kilmichael Tower with the Blue Ridge Parkway, was a source of controversy, as the Switzerland Company placed signs promoting it and other attractions on the parkway's right-of-way. They were removed several times before the Park Service closed the road after a long legal battle. Remnants of the road are still in existence and are visible between mileposts 334 and 335. (Courtesy of the U.S. National Park Service.)

45

PROGRAM

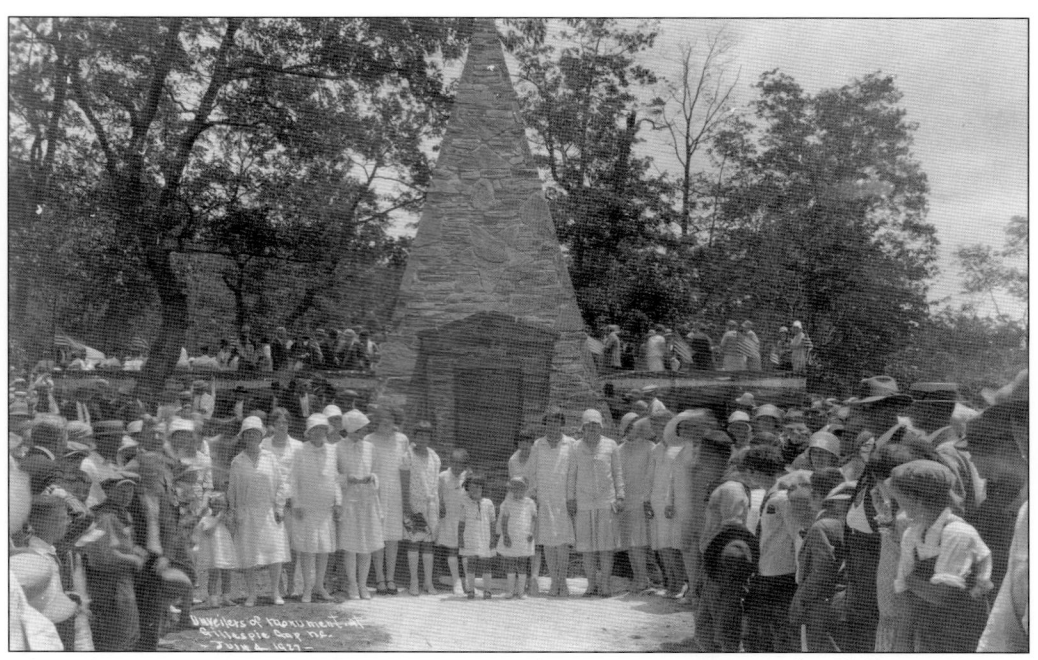

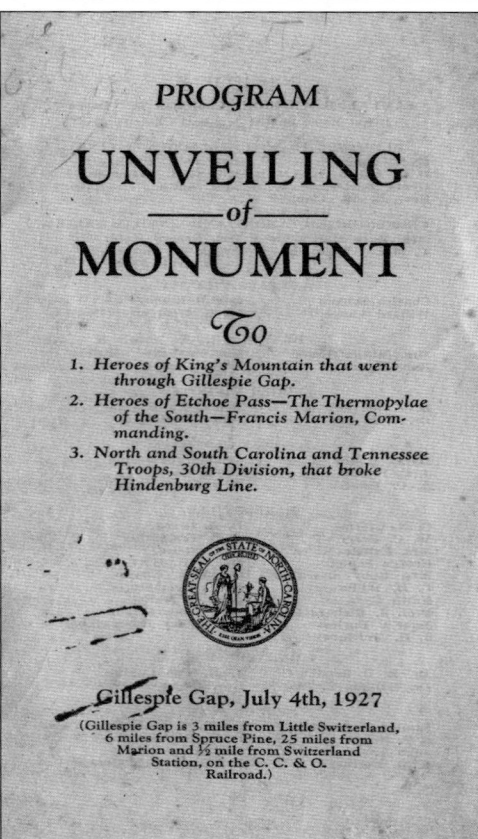

UNVEILING
——of——
MONUMENT

To

1. Heroes of King's Mountain that went through Gillespie Gap.
2. Heroes of Etchoe Pass—The Thermopylae of the South—Francis Marion, Commanding.
3. North and South Carolina and Tennessee Troops, 30th Division, that broke Hindenburg Line.

Gillespie Gap, July 4th, 1927.
(Gillespie Gap is 3 miles from Little Switzerland, 6 miles from Spruce Pine, 25 miles from Marion and ½ mile from Switzerland Station, on the C. C. & O. Railroad.)

A monument was erected at Gillespie Gap to honor the Overmountain Men who marched through the gap on the way to Kings Mountain; to Francis Marion and his battle with the Cherokees; and to the 30th Division, who broke the Hindenburg line in World War I. Judge Heriot Clarkson served on the North Carolina Historical Commission that constructed the marker. A ceremony to dedicate it was held at 11 a.m., July 4, 1927, and featured then-governor Angus McLean, former governor Cameron Morrison, former Secretary of the Navy Josephus Daniels, and other dignitaries. Anna Jackson Preston, great-granddaughter of Stonewall Jackson, assisted in the ceremony. A copy of the program for the day is pictured at left. (Both courtesy of Sarah Clarkson.)

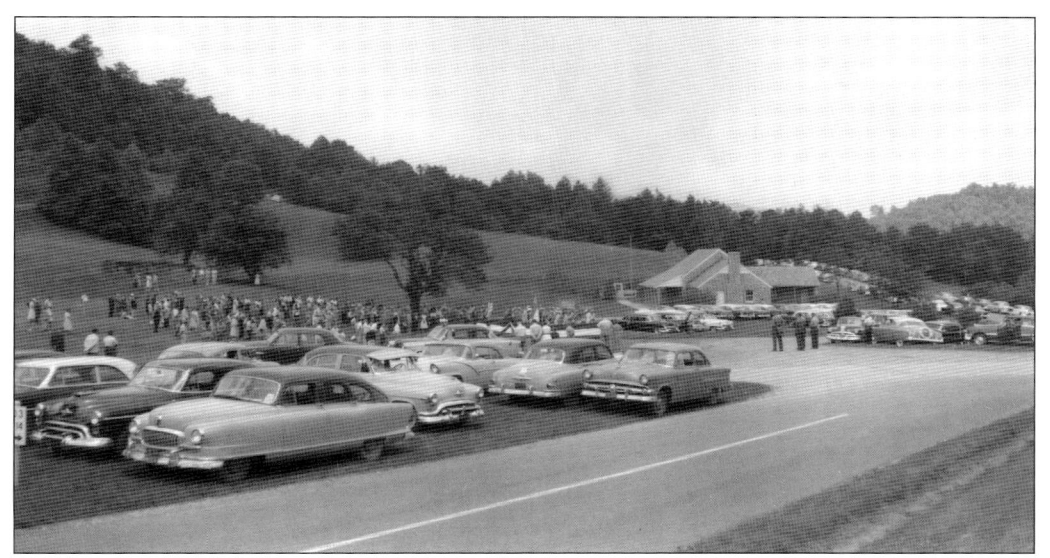

The dedication by Gov. Luther Hodges of the Museum of North Carolina Minerals on June 17, 1955, opened for visitors a view into the economic heart of the region: the Spruce Pine Mining District. Also located on the grounds is the historic marker to the Overmountain Men dedicated on July 4, 1927, which was relocated during the museum's construction. (Courtesy of the U.S. National Park Service.)

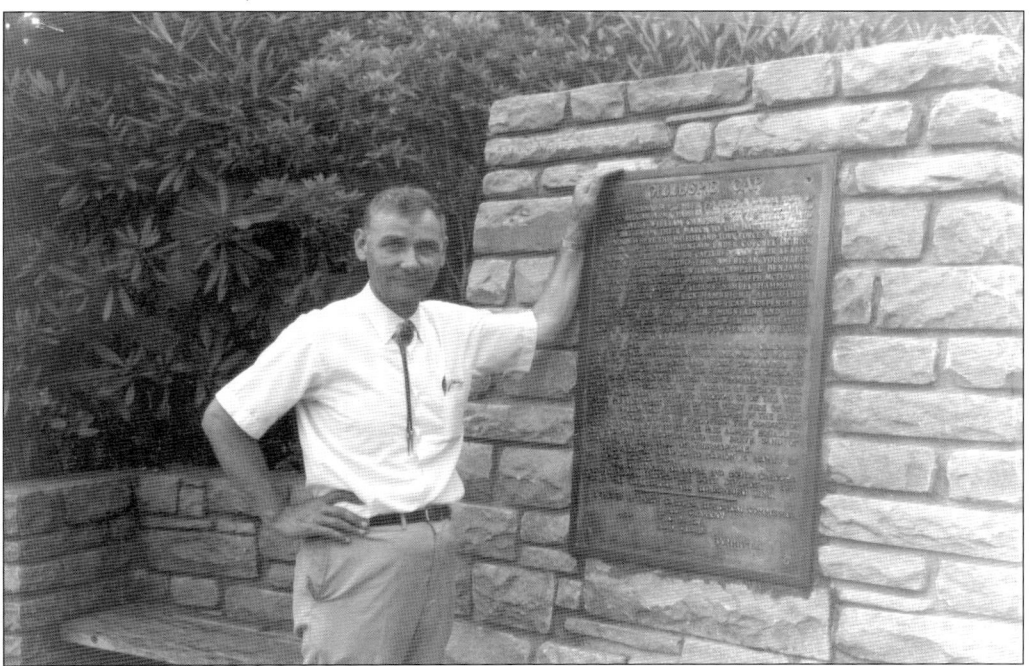

Dr. Harley Jolley, professor emeritus of history at Mars Hill College, stands next to the plaque honoring the Overmountain Men. He is the preeminent historian of the Blue Ridge Parkway and has authored numerous books on it and the region. Jolley is well known for interpretive programs along the parkway, and his enthusiasm for his subject is legendary. (Courtesy of the U.S. National Park Service.)

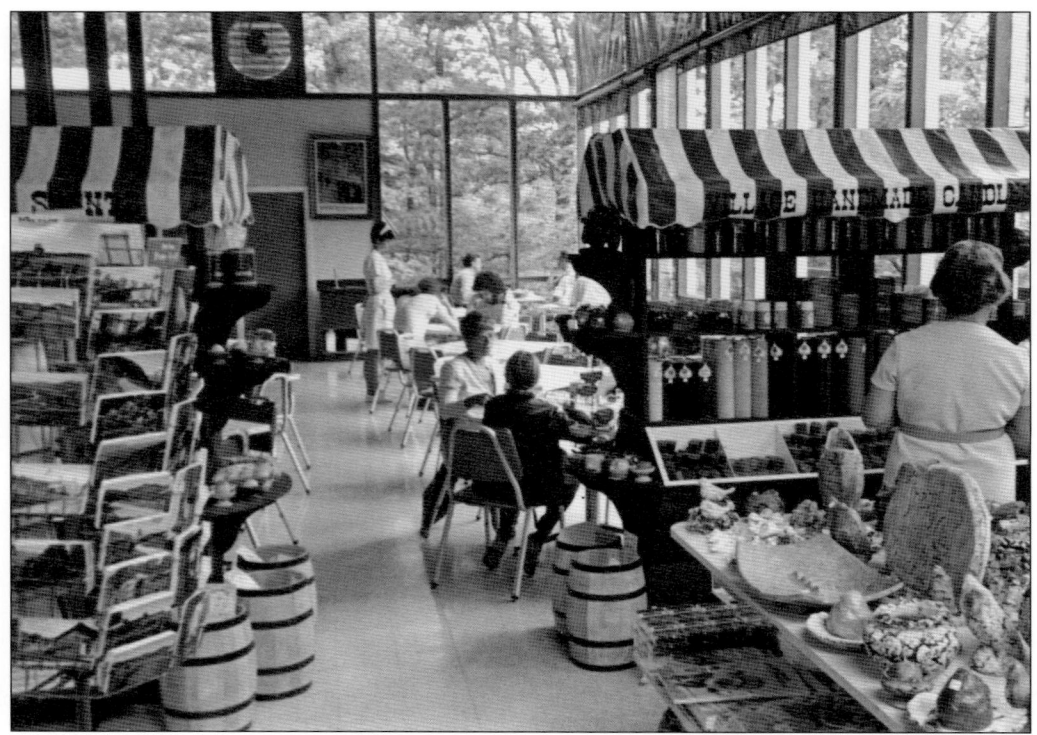

The Blue Ridge Parkway has brought more than traffic to the region. Wayside areas were developed as interpretive sites for local features. One such site near Little Switzerland is Crabtree Meadows. Located at Milepost 339, the original development featured a picnic area, campground, gas station, and hiking trail to Crabtree Falls. Featured above is the coffee and gift shop at Crabtree Meadows, whose building is constructed from rock quarried at Grandfather Mountain. Below is the amphitheater where Park Service rangers host programs on local flora, fauna, and cultural history during the summer months. (Both courtesy of the U.S. National Park Service.)

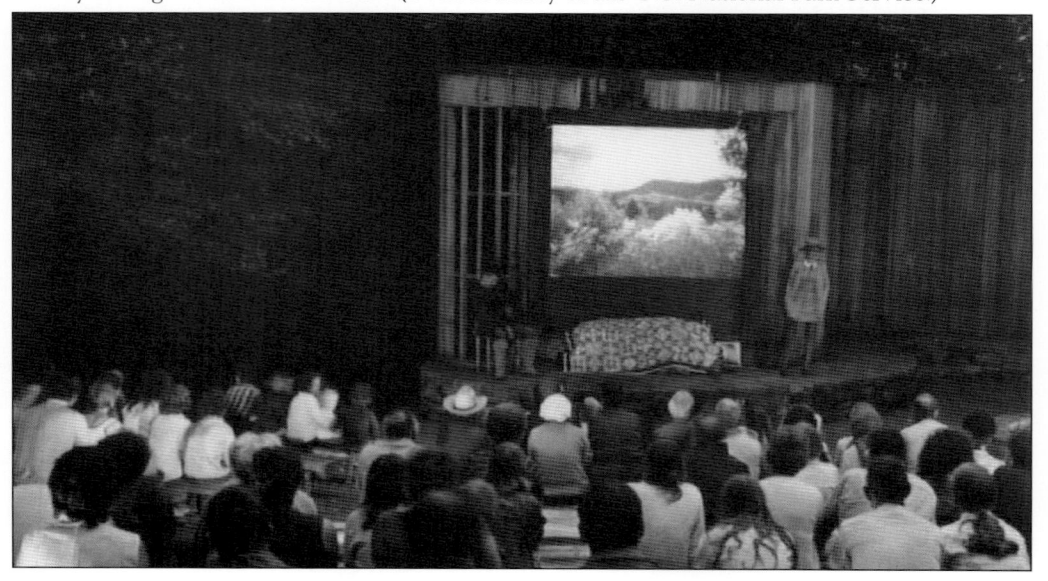

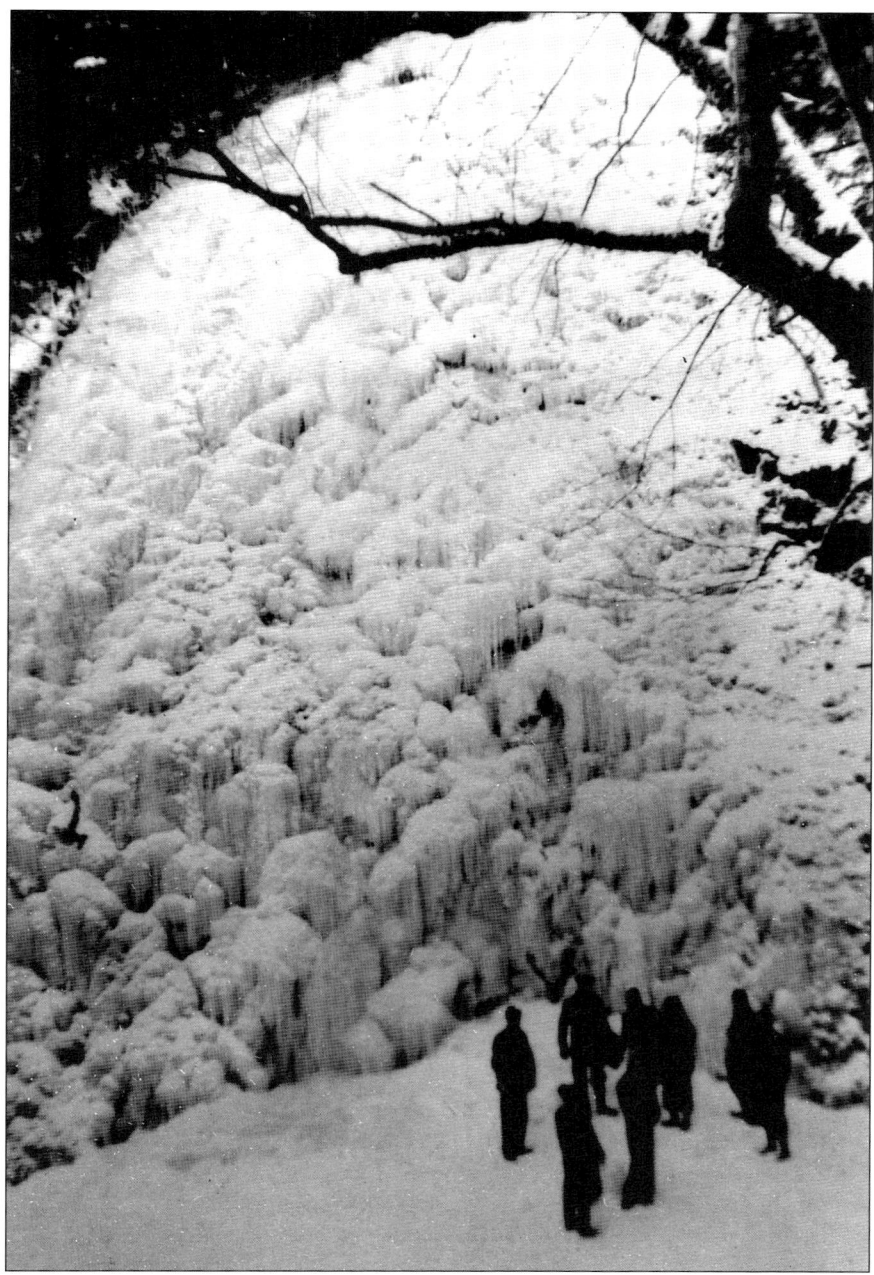

Crabtree Falls, located at milepost 339.5 on the Blue Ridge Parkway, cascades 70 feet over the Blue Ridge escarpment on its journey to the Toe River. A moderate hike from the trailhead in the Crabtree Meadows Campground, visitors delight in viewing the falls year-round. A part of the original land grant to the Penland family by the king, the falls are located where a thriving community once clustered around a gristmill owned by Billy Bradshaw and the Last Chance Baptist Church. However, locals know this falls as Murphy Falls, with Crabtree Falls being located on the Crabtree Creek Road that connects Little Switzerland with U.S. 19-E in the Estatoe community. (Courtesy of the U.S. National Park Service.)

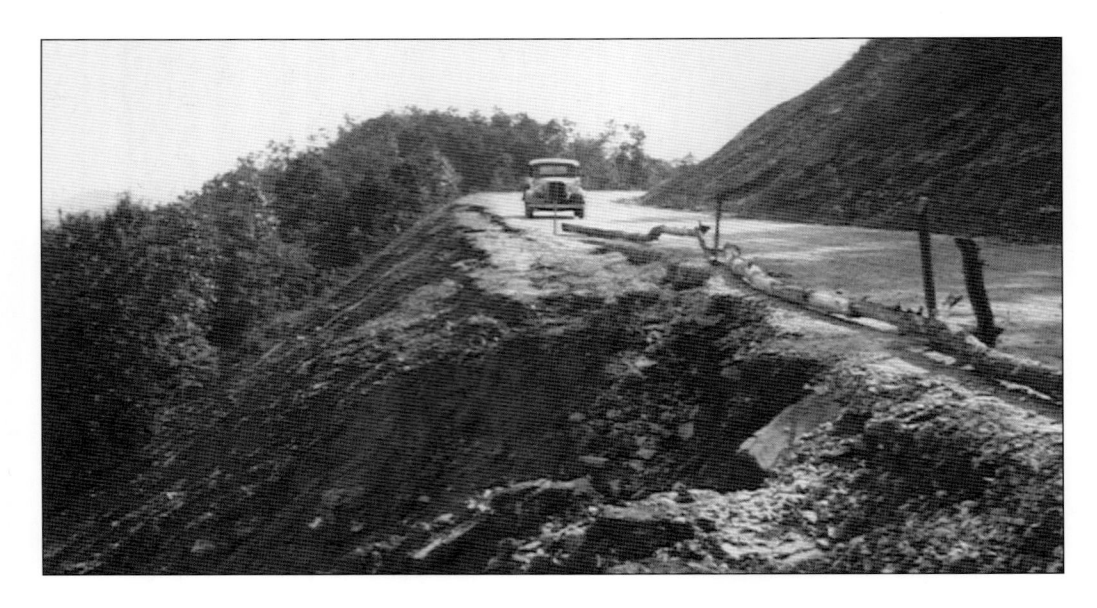

With its location along the heights of the Blue Ridge, the Blue Ridge Parkway is often subjected to the worst Mother Nature has to offer. Hurricanes and other storms have caused washouts of the highway and other damage. Above, on August 11, 1940, a hurricane washed out the road just south of Little Switzerland, and below, a rock slide closed the Blue Ridge Parkway near Crabtree Meadows in September 1953. More recently, Hurricanes Ivan and Frances forced closures of the road when they combined to wash out several sections near Little Switzerland in 2004. (Both courtesy of the U.S. National Park Service.)

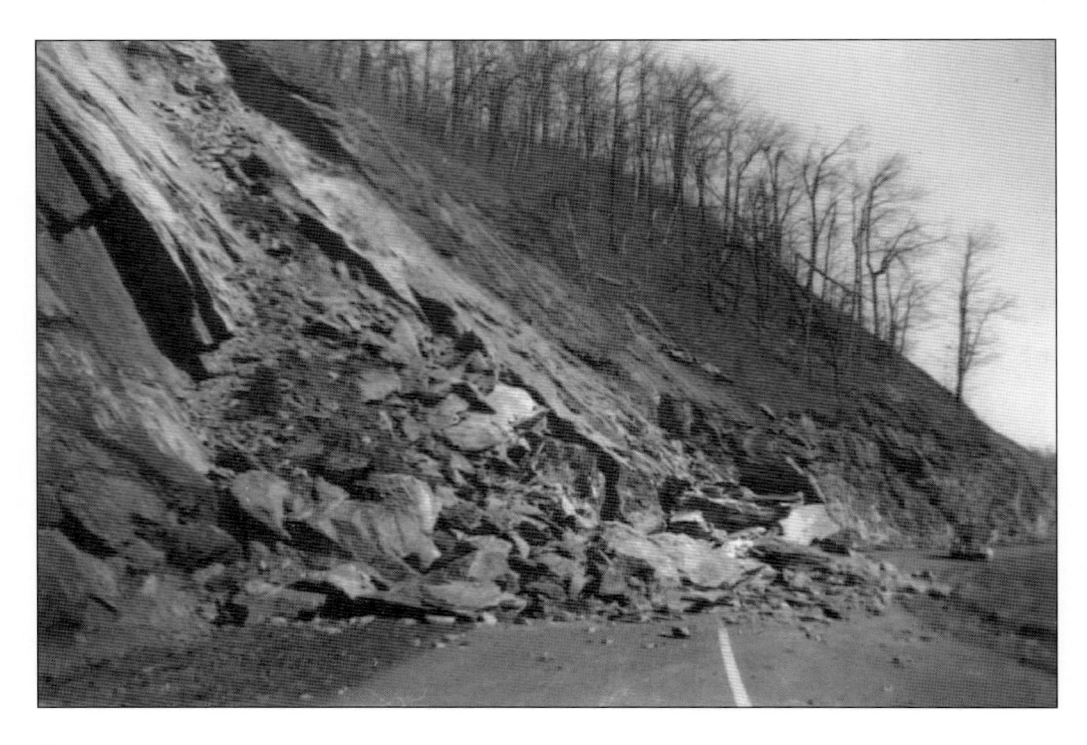

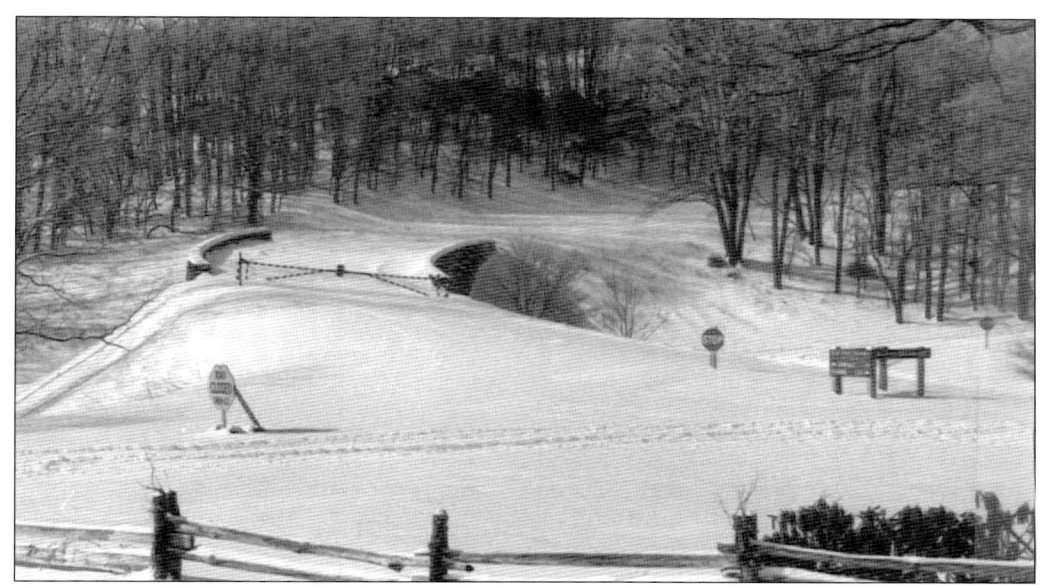

Wintertime can bring extreme weather conditions to Little Switzerland, forcing the closure of the Blue Ridge Parkway. In this photograph taken during the memorable winter of 1977–1978, the Blue Ridge Parkway was closed south towards Crabtree Meadows. That year, approximately 60 inches of snow fell in the region, forcing schools to be closed for most of January and February. Below, a photograph from December 2009 shows a similar scene at the same entrance. (Above courtesy of the U.S. National Park Service; below courtesy of Marsha Biddix.)

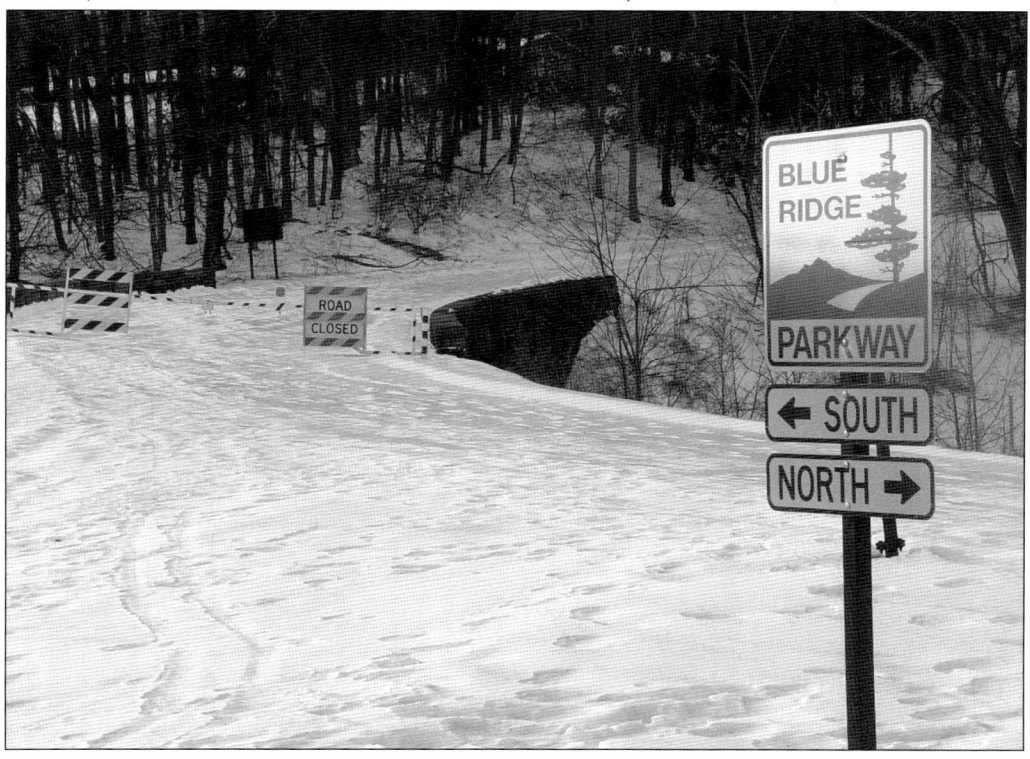

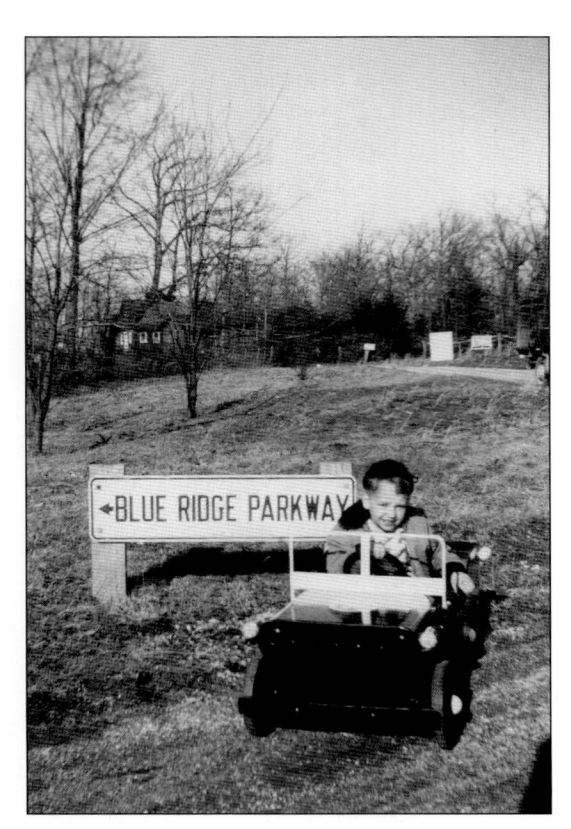

Local residents enjoy the Blue Ridge Parkway as much as visitors. Picnics, scenic vistas, treks to view natural wonders, and Sunday drives are popular pastimes. Spruce Pine native Phillip Buchanan takes his truck for spin on the road at the Little Switzerland intersection. (Courtesy of Ruby Buchanan.)

Two of the region's economic engines appear in this photograph. The Blue Ridge Parkway brings thousands of visitors to Little Switzerland each year, and the tunnel is a popular photograph spot on the highway. Frank Hollifield is a pioneer in the Fraser fir Christmas tree industry, having started his business in the 1960s. Christmas trees are a multi-million-dollar industry in North Carolina. (Courtesy of Frank Hollifield.)

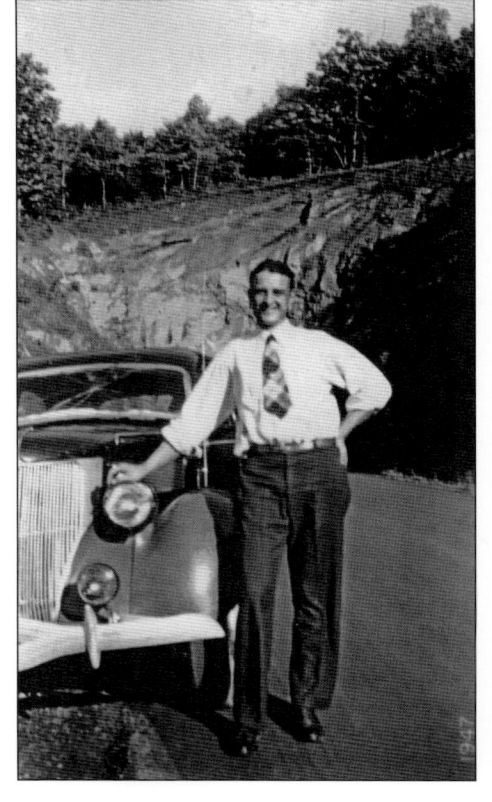

Four

Nature's Playgrounds
The Camps and Wildacres

Judge Clarkson wasn't the only person who had a vision for this magical mountain. In 1914, Charleston, South Carolina, resident Marie Gaillard Dwight started what many believe to be the oldest girls' camp in western North Carolina, As-You-Like-It, on the west side of Osborne Knob. Her goal was to provide approximately 100 campers each year with athletics, activities, and events designed to promote physical and mental well-being. For 31 years, she realized her dream of influencing the lives of girls through the camp.

Noted lecturer and writer Thomas Dixon, a native of Shelby, North Carolina, gained fame for his novel *The Clansman* and the resulting movie *Birth of a Nation*, and he longed to provide others with an environment for inspiration in artistic endeavors. He envisioned a mountaintop resort where artists could congregate and practice their craft with modern amenities provided. Using proceeds from his works, he purchased the top of a mountain near Little Switzerland and began building Wildacres in 1926. Unfortunately, his dream vanished with the stock market crash in 1929, and he lost the resort.

Charlotte businessman I. D. Blumenthal became aware of Wildacres in 1936 and purchased the property from a Texas bank. Like Dixon, he had a vision for the resort, but it was more encompassing. He felt the Lord had given him Wildacres for a special purpose, and he committed the property for the betterment of mankind.

In 1927, Charles S. Dwight Jr., decided to offer boys the same types of opportunities that his sister Marie offered girls through a summer camp. He leased 200 acres in the Lake Laurel section of Little Switzerland from the Boot McKinney family and opened Camp Alpine. Like the girls' camp, Alpine offered boys athletic and cultural activities during summer sessions, but as it had done to Dixon's ambitions, the Great Depression brought an end to Dwight's dream.

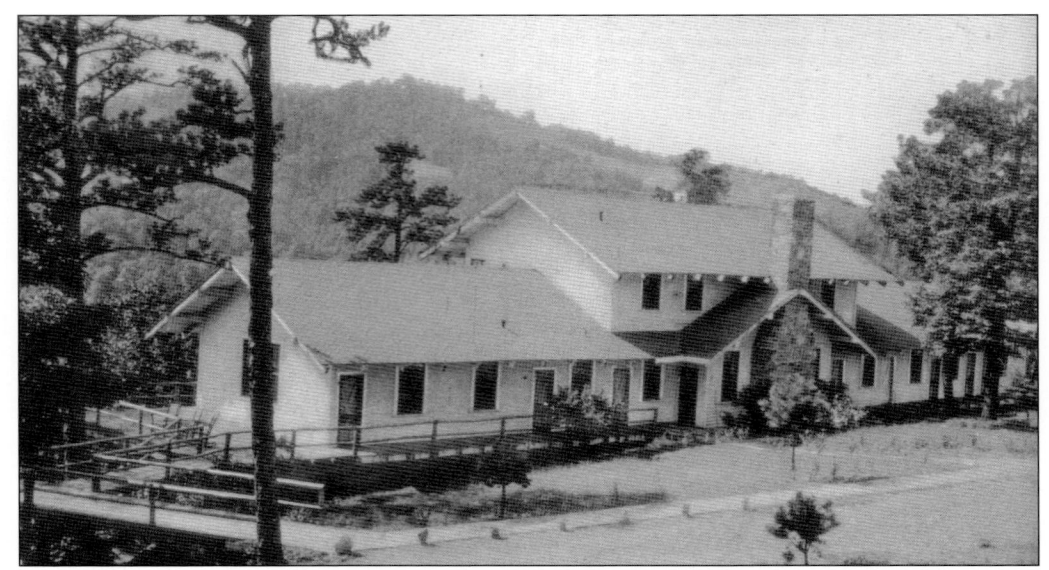

Thomas Dixon dreamed of a substantial resort atop Pompey's Knob featuring a large hotel, tennis courts, stables, a golf course, and swimming pools, but the Great Depression intervened, stopping construction of his dream. One building completed was this dining room and kitchen that was part of the hotel. It also featured an assembly hall and 20 additional rooms with baths. They were abandoned until 1936. (Courtesy of Wildacres.)

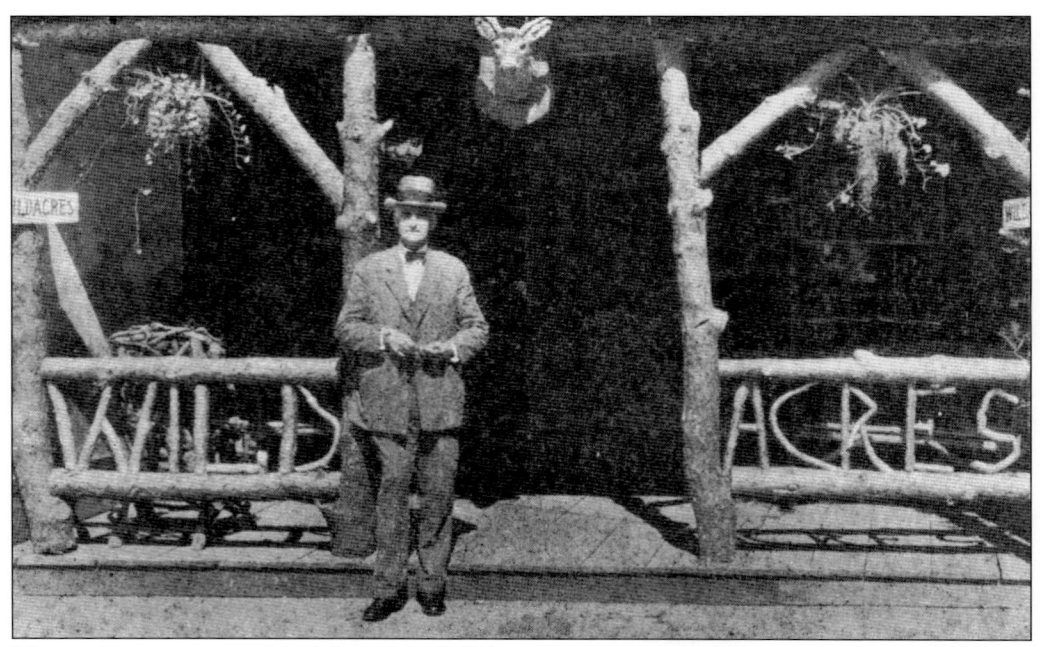

Thomas Dixon organized the Mount Mitchell Association of Arts and Sciences to develop Wildacres as a center for creative thinking and expression. He stands in front of the Wildacres Resort sales office in Asheville. The association's advisory board featured the presidents of UNC–Chapel Hill, NC State, UNC–Greensboro, Wake Forest, Duke, and Meredith College. (Courtesy of the North Carolina Collection, Pack Memorial Public Library, Asheville, North Carolina.)

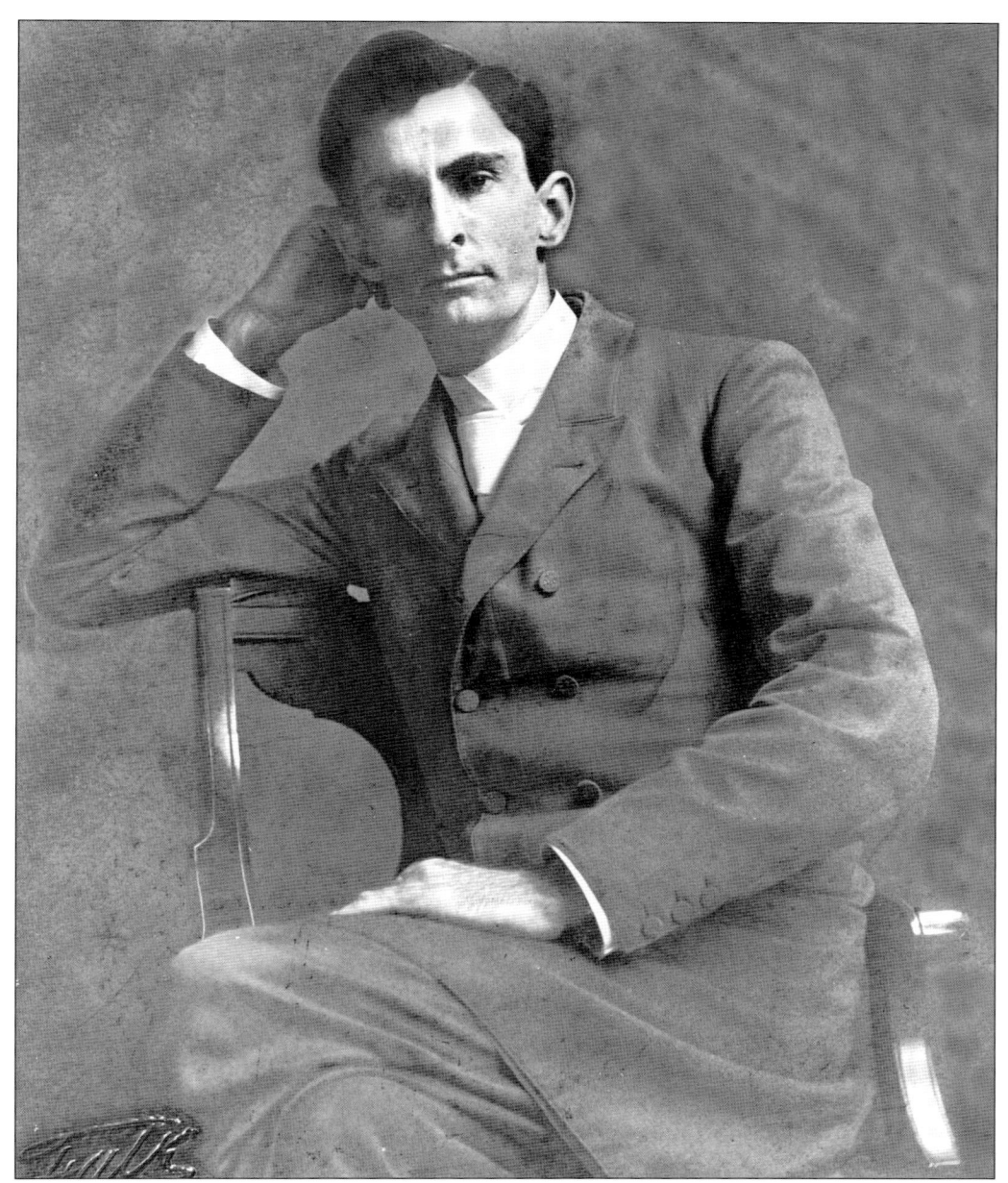

Shelby, North Carolina–born Thomas Dixon was a politician, lawyer, and minister who was educated at Wake Forest University and Johns Hopkins. He was a well-known lecturer who was in much demand after ministering at churches in Boston and New York City. He was close friends with future Pres. Woodrow Wilson and knew John D. Rockefeller and Theodore Roosevelt. However, he is best known for writing *The Clansman*, his seminal work on Southern Reconstruction. It was the inspiration for D. W. Griffith's film *Birth of a Nation* and made Dixon a millionaire. He took part of the proceeds and purchased the land for Wildacres and began its development. The stock market crash of 1929 cost him his fortune, and he lost Wildacres. He wrote one more novel (*The Flaming Sword* in 1939) before he died at age 82, serving as a clerk of court in Raleigh. (Courtesy the North Carolina Collection, UNC–Chapel Hill.)

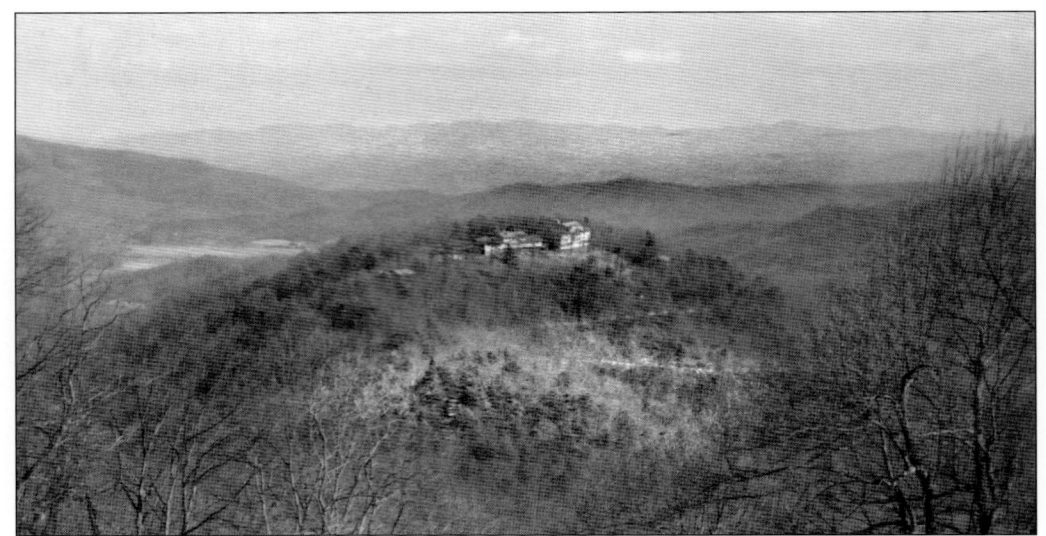

Wildacres is pictured from the Blue Ridge Parkway. A great fog descended on Pompey's Knob when I. D. Blumenthal accompanied a Texas banker to evaluate his bid for the property. The bank later accepted his offer of $6,500, even though it held a note on it for $190,000. Blumenthal considered the cloud a sign that the Lord had sent him to Wildacres for a special purpose. (Courtesy of the U.S. National Park Service.)

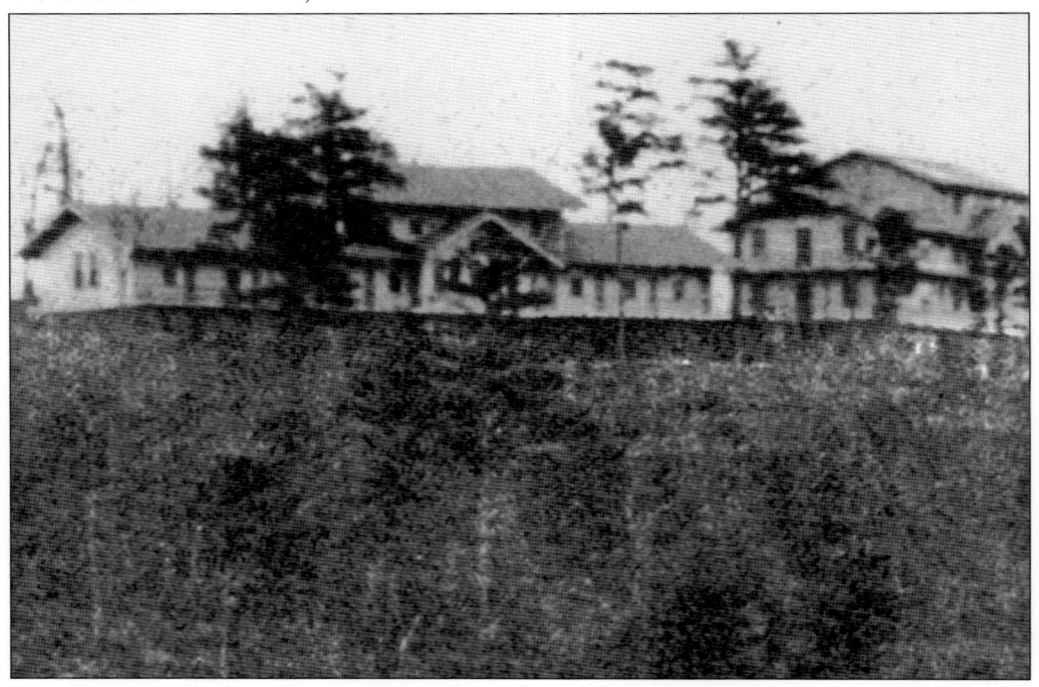

Atop Pompey's Knob southwest of Little Switzerland, Wildacres Resort was designed by founder Thomas Dixon to be "the nucleus of a refuge for creative thinking." His vision was to foster a community of writers, painters, and musicians, giving them the environment to nurture their work. The Wildacres campus can be seen and accessed from the Blue Ridge Parkway at milepost 336.8. (Courtesy of Wildacres.)

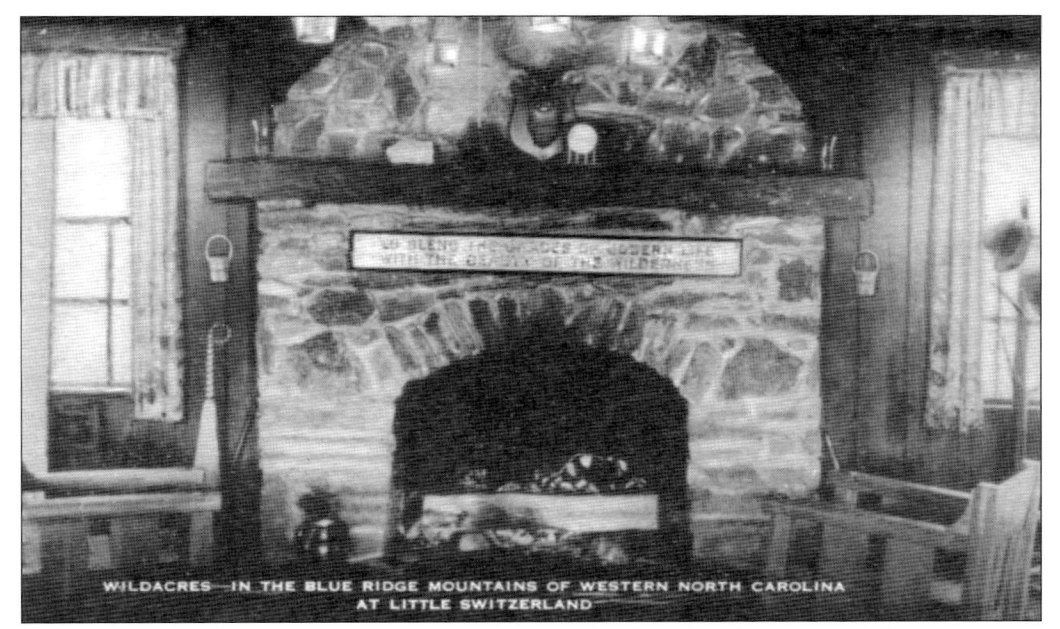

Pictured above in the original Assembly Hall at Wildacres, the fireplace contained an inscription that summarized Dixon's vision for the resort: "To blend the graces of modern life with the beauty of the wilderness." Today the old fireplace is gone, but the inscription, and Dixon's dream, lives on in the modern-day Assembly Hall, where attendees often gather for socializing. (Above courtesy of Davis and Jann Godwin; below courtesy of Wildacres.)

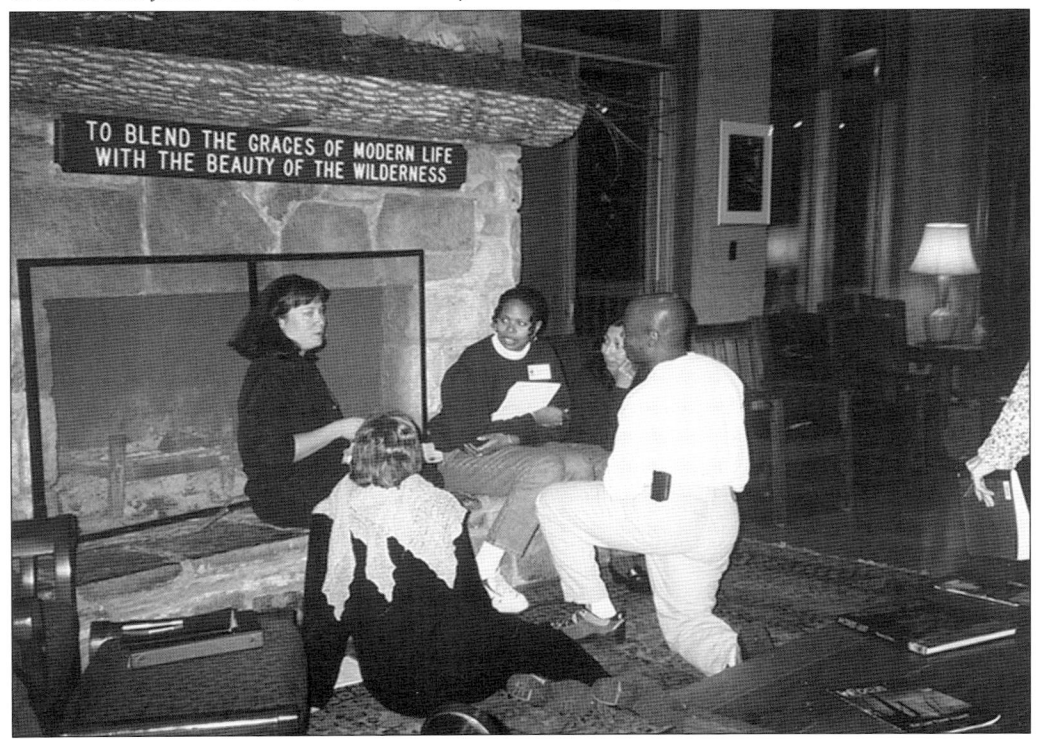

57

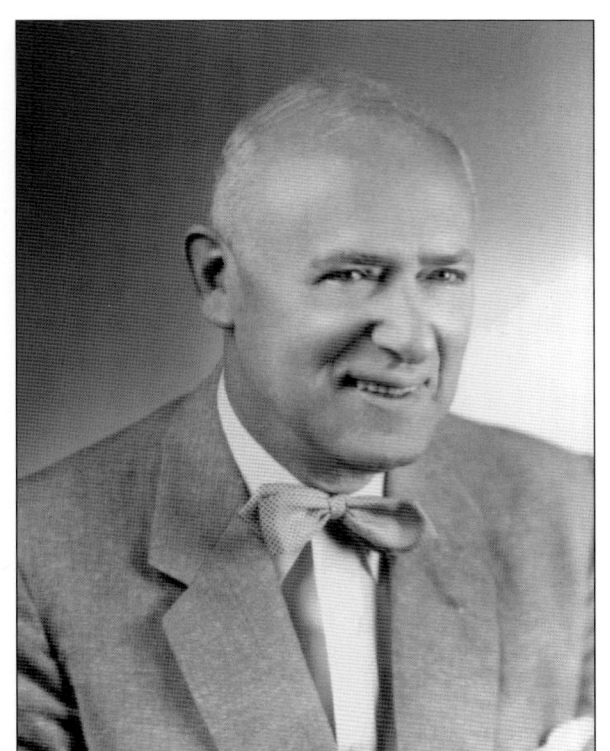

I. D. Blumenthal considered his 1936 purchase of Wildacres to be "a divine gift." A deeply religious man, his plans were to share his gift with others, providing a location where people could gather for conversations and enrichment to benefit mankind. Today Wildacres hosts a variety of workshops and events attended by individuals from around the world. (Courtesy of Wildacres.)

The Ringling School of Art and Design rented Wildacres from 1941 to 1945 for summer sessions. Students and faculty lived and studied together at the retreat as they painted from nature for three months each year. The Ringling School, began by circus promoter John Ringling, is one of the foremost art schools in the world. Here students head out for a painting class on the campus. (Courtesy of the North Carolina State Archives.)

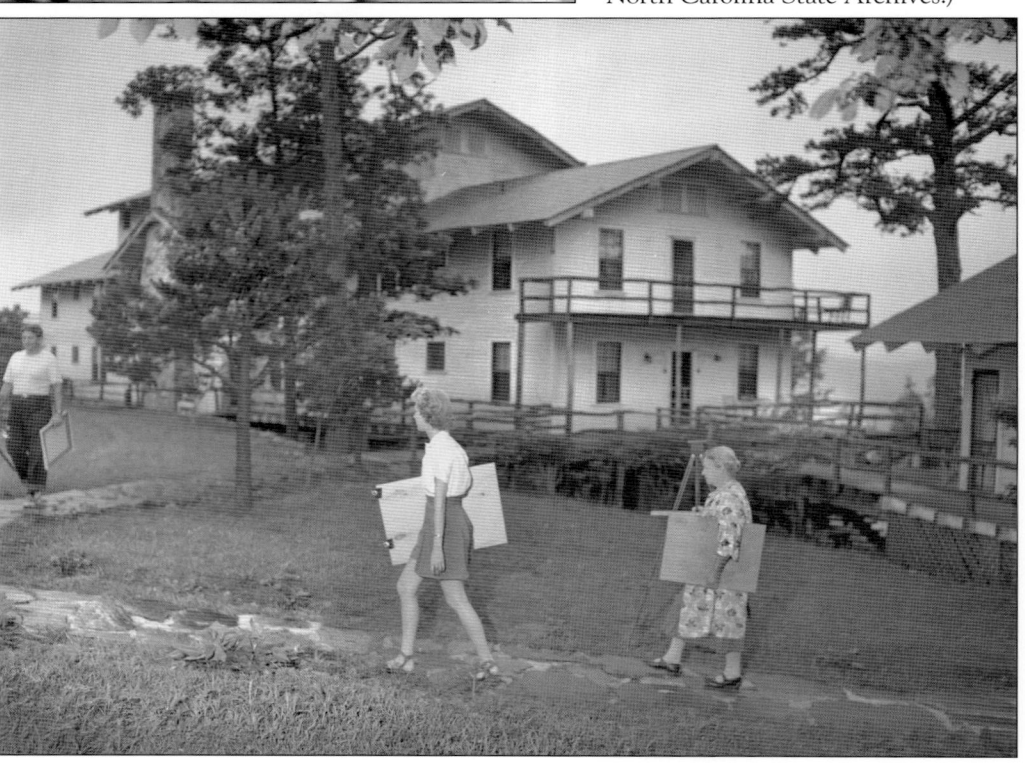

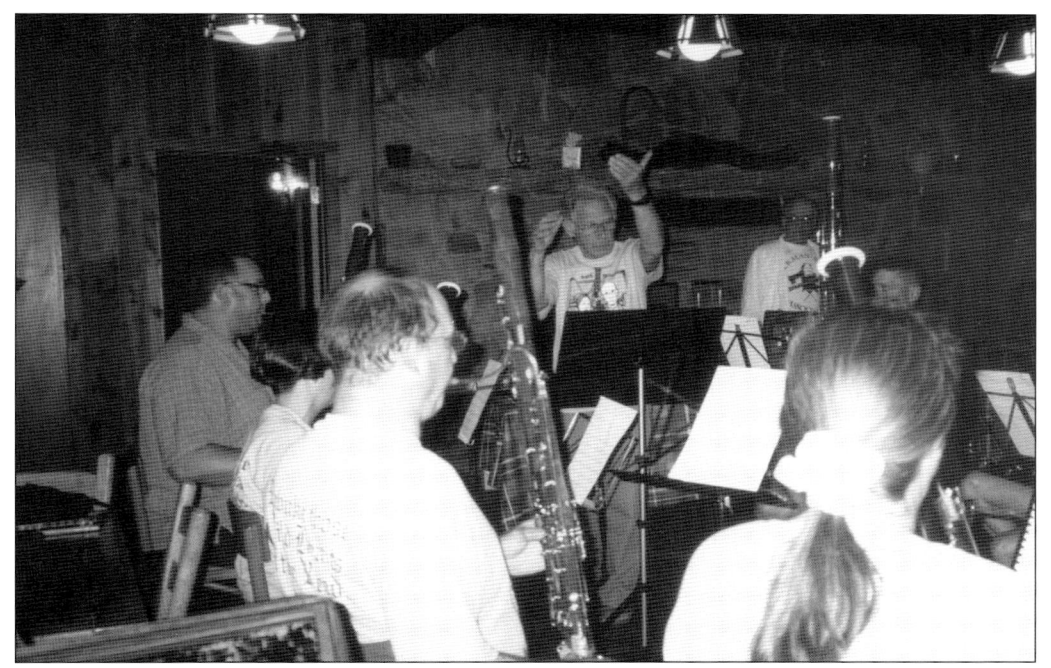

Wildacres hosts a variety of musical events each season from courses teaching an instrument to tune-ups for professional groups. Sessions typically last a week, with performances being open to the public. (Courtesy of Wildacres.)

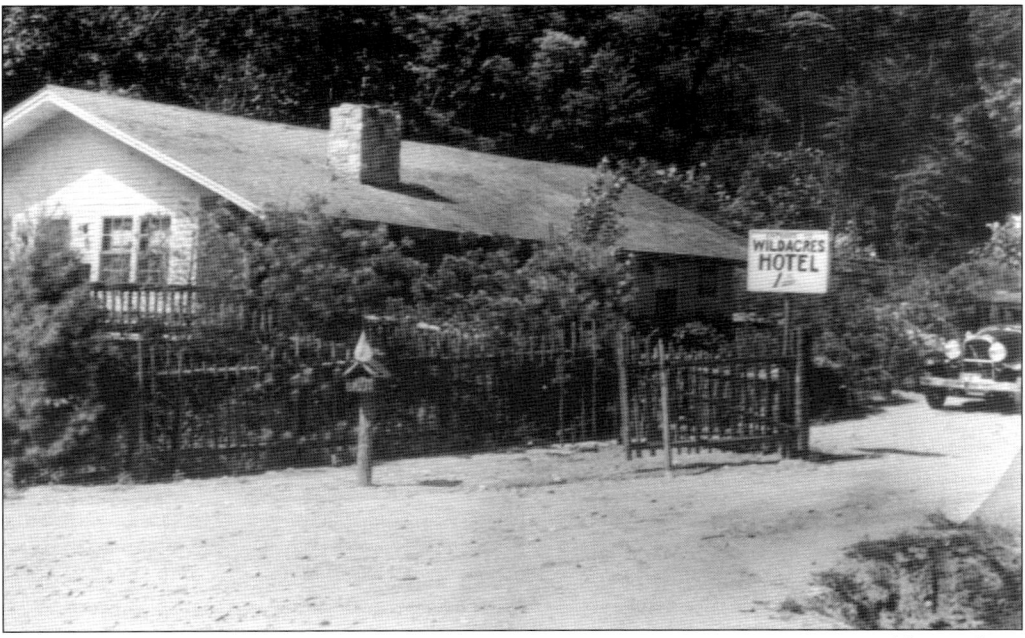

Spruce Pine innkeeper Ramey Beam rented Louise Dixon's former tearoom at Wildacres from 1938 through the early 1940s. He operated a tavern, selling sandwiches, coffee, and beer. Saturday nights, Beam's establishment hosted dances to jukebox music that were popular with locals and members of parkway construction crews. (Courtesy of Wildacres.)

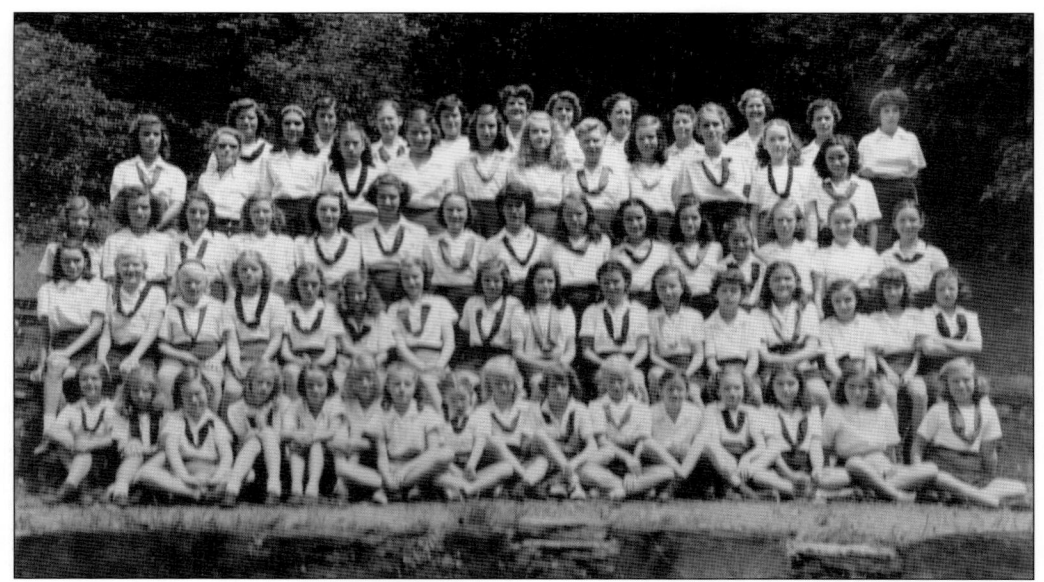

Each season, approximately 100 girls attended As-You-Like-It, enjoying activities from the years 1914 through its closure as Camp Glenlaurel in 1968. Community members were invited to plays, dances, and dinners, and the girls attended church services at the Church of the Resurrection and enjoyed ice cream courtesy of Pete Deal at the Switzerland Store. It was purportedly the first girls' camp in Western North Carolina. (Courtesy of Coles Jackson.)

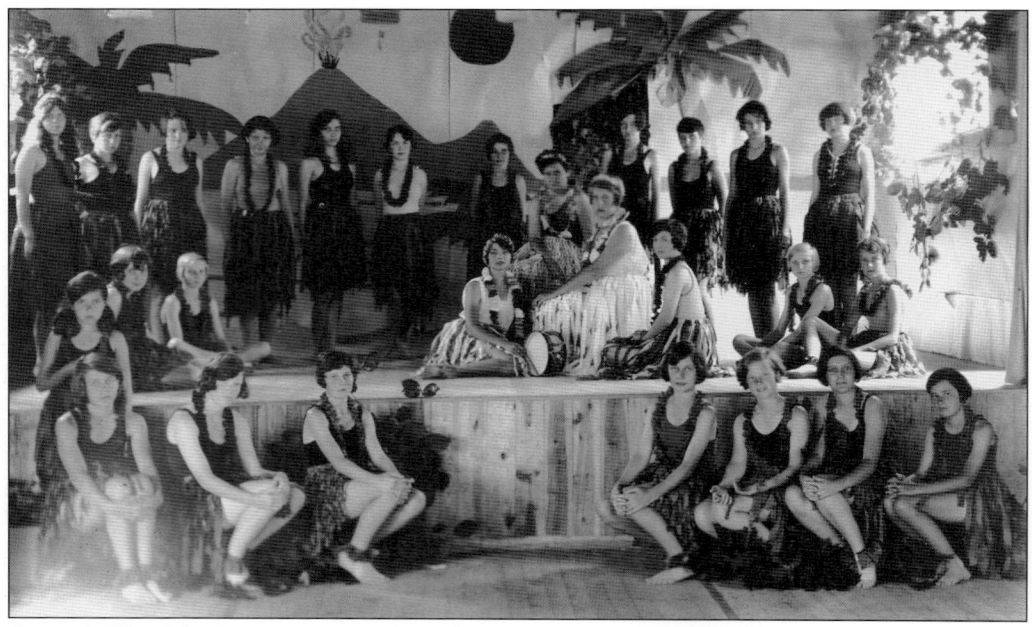

Camp As-You-Like-It's name comes from the Shakespeare play and was suggested by Ambrose E. Gonzales, editor of the *State* newspaper in Columbia, South Carolina. Dramatics were also one of the activities, with the girls performing plays each season. This photograph was taken in the 1920s before a performance in the playhouse. (Courtesy of Coles Jackson.)

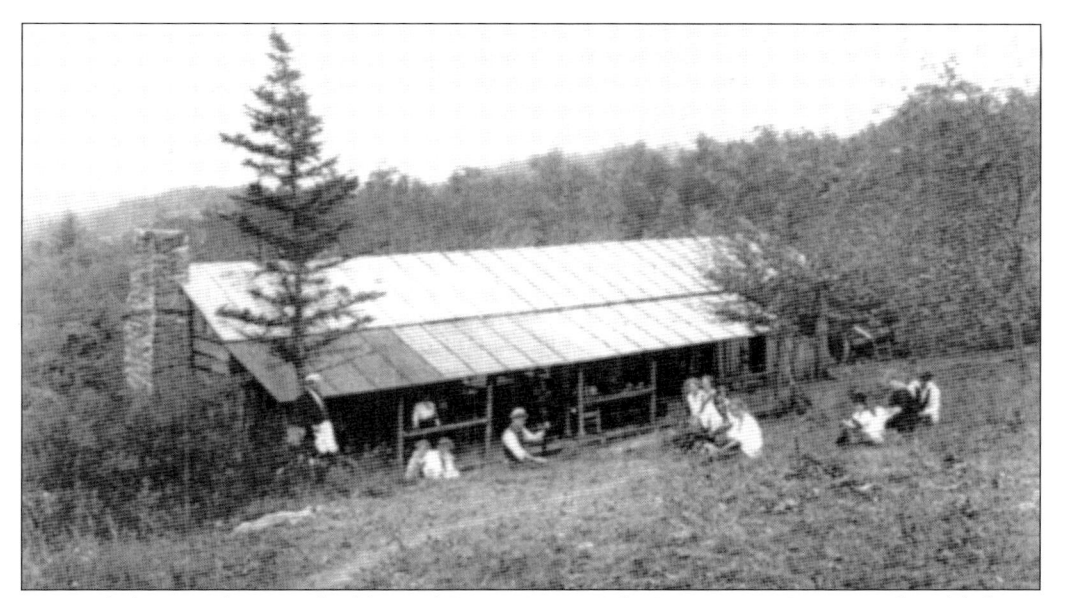

Pictured above is the main building of Camp As-You-Like-It in 1914. Marie Dwight added to a native cabin to make the structure when she opened in 1914. She operated it for 31 years, later selling to Jeanette Boone and Helen McMahon. They changed the name to Camp Glenlaurel and ran it until 1964. A series of owners then ran the camp until it closed in 1968. (Courtesy of Coles Jackson.)

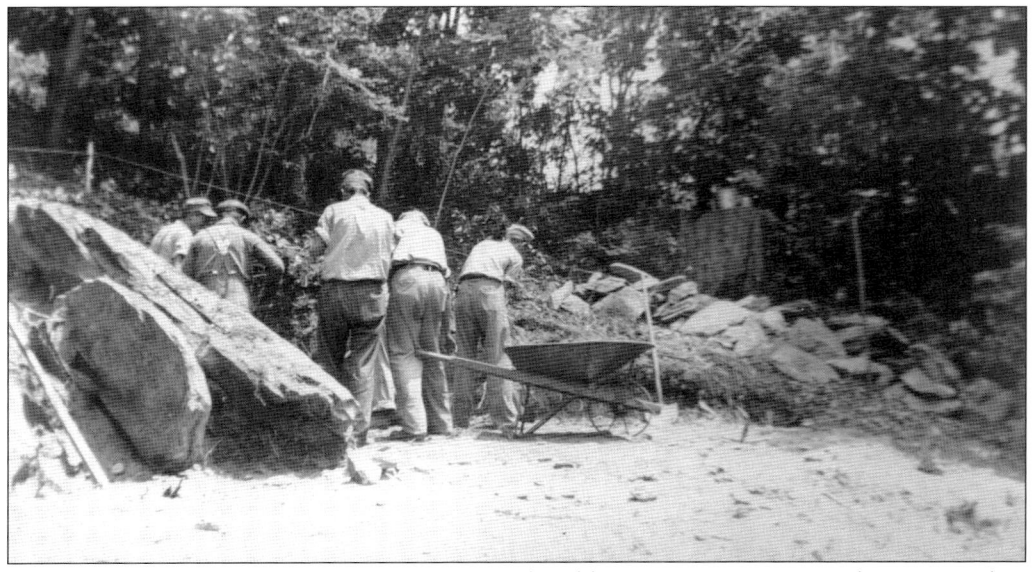

Local men, led by Lester McKinney, constructed and kept up Camp As-You-Like-It. Here they are building a wall with rocks gathered from the Linville Gorge and Grandfather Mountain. The quality of their work was outstanding, but vandals destroyed much of the stonework after the camp's closure. Some examples remain hidden deep in the woods. (Courtesy of Coles Jackson.)

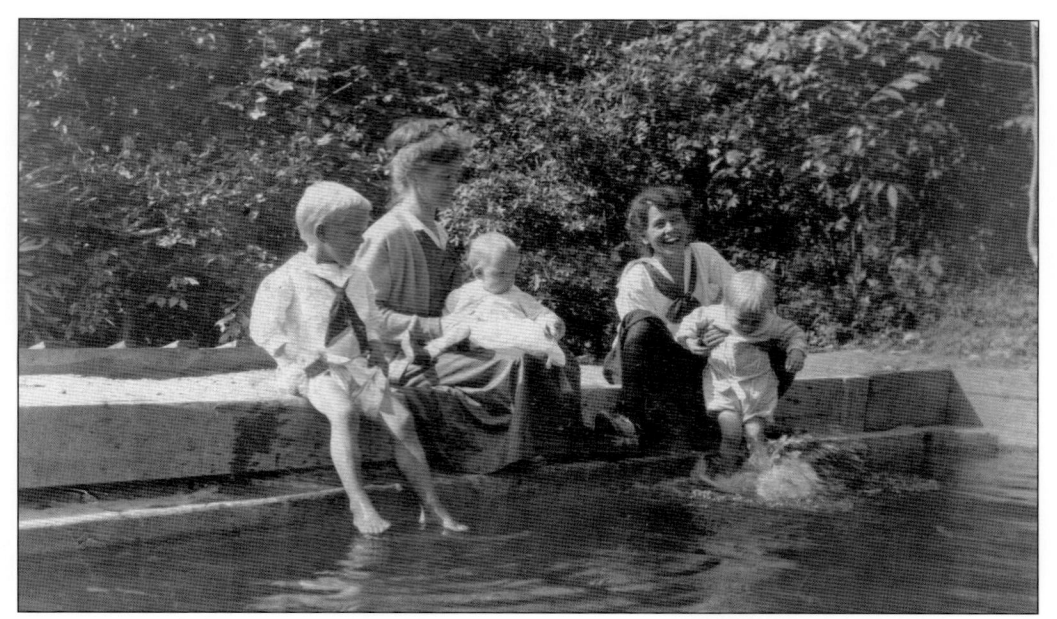

Enjoying a quick dip of toes in the pool at newly opened Camp As-You-Like-It in 1914 are, from left to right, Eugene Childs Cathcart Jr., Louisa Dubose Dwight Cathcart, Louise Dwight Cathcart, Marie Gaillard Dwight (owner of the camp), and Charles Dwight Cathcart. The Dwight and Cathcart families have long histories in Little Switzerland, starting with the camp and continuing today. (Courtesy of Coles Jackson.)

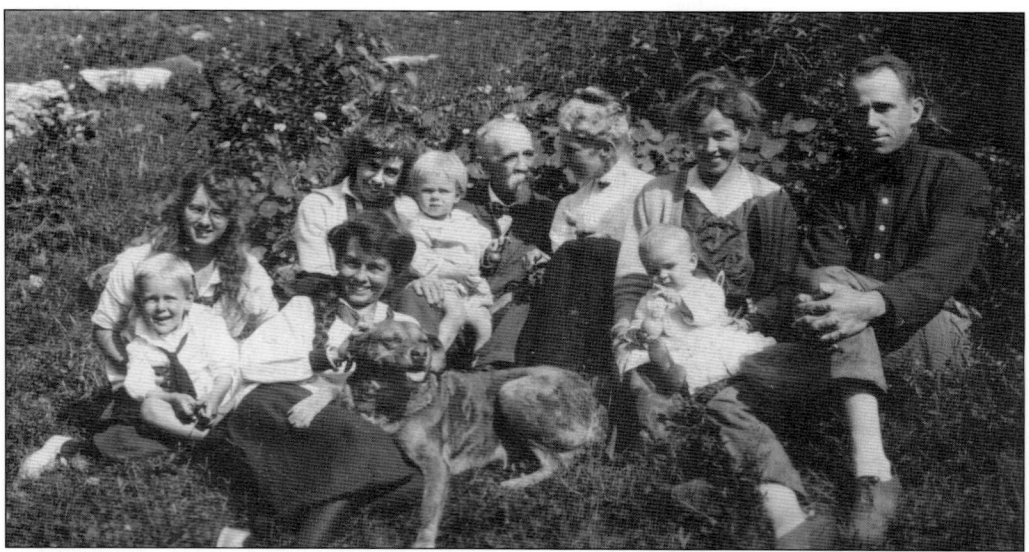

Mr. and Mrs. Charles Stevens Dwight (center back) are seen with their five children and three grandchildren at Camp As-You-Like-It in the summer of 1915. The Dwights traveled to Little Switzerland from their home in Winnesboro, South Carolina, to visit daughter Marie (front left), the owner of the camp. Her brother Charles (front right) owned Camp Alpine for three years in the late 1920s. (Courtesy of Coles Jackson.)

62

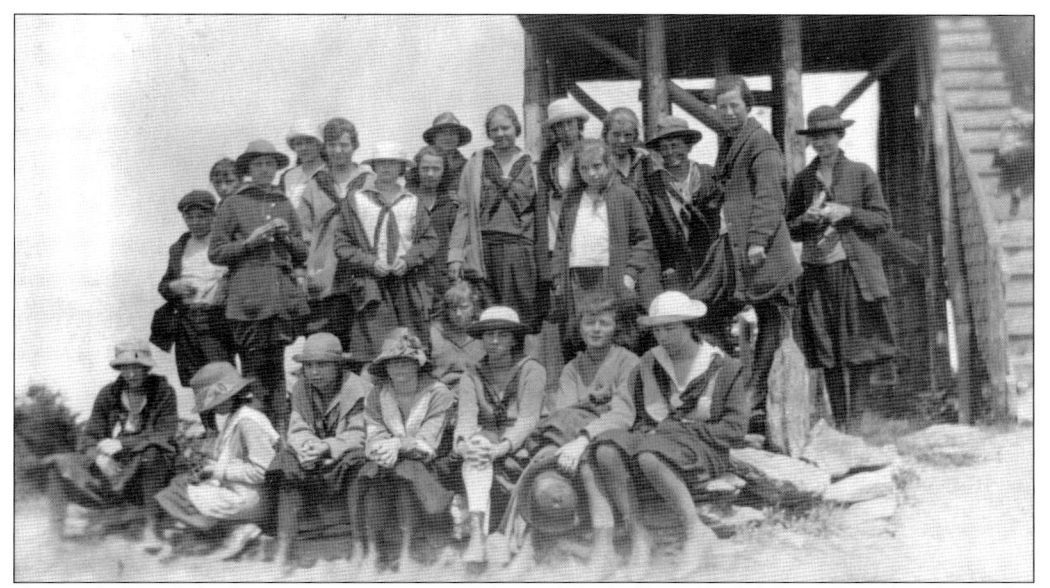

Camp As-You-Like-It campers pose atop Mount Mitchell in 1915. Marie Dwight planned a variety of activities, including visits to natural attractions in the region. The girls hiked 7 miles up eastern America's highest peak, camping in the ranger's cabin and visiting the newly opened observation tower. Access to Mount Mitchell was a far cry from today's paved highway and path to the summit. (Courtesy of Coles Jackson.)

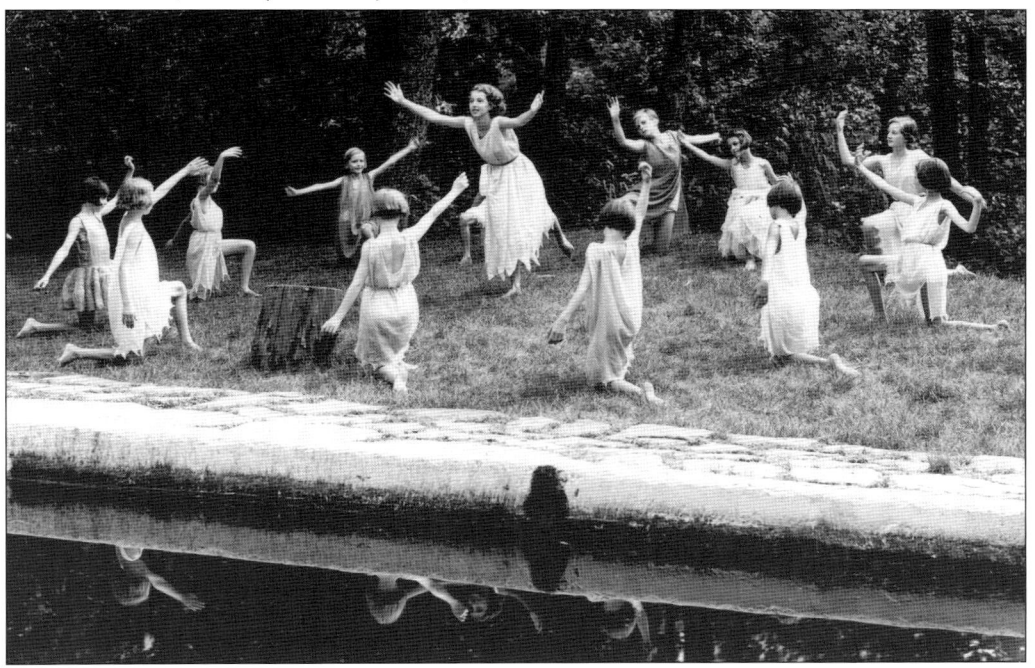

Dance and movement was another activity enjoyed by girls at the camp. In this photograph, they practice ballet poolside. Campers were to go home after their session "not only stronger physically, but with a better mental and spiritual balance," according to a camp brochure from 1942. (Courtesy of Coles Jackson.)

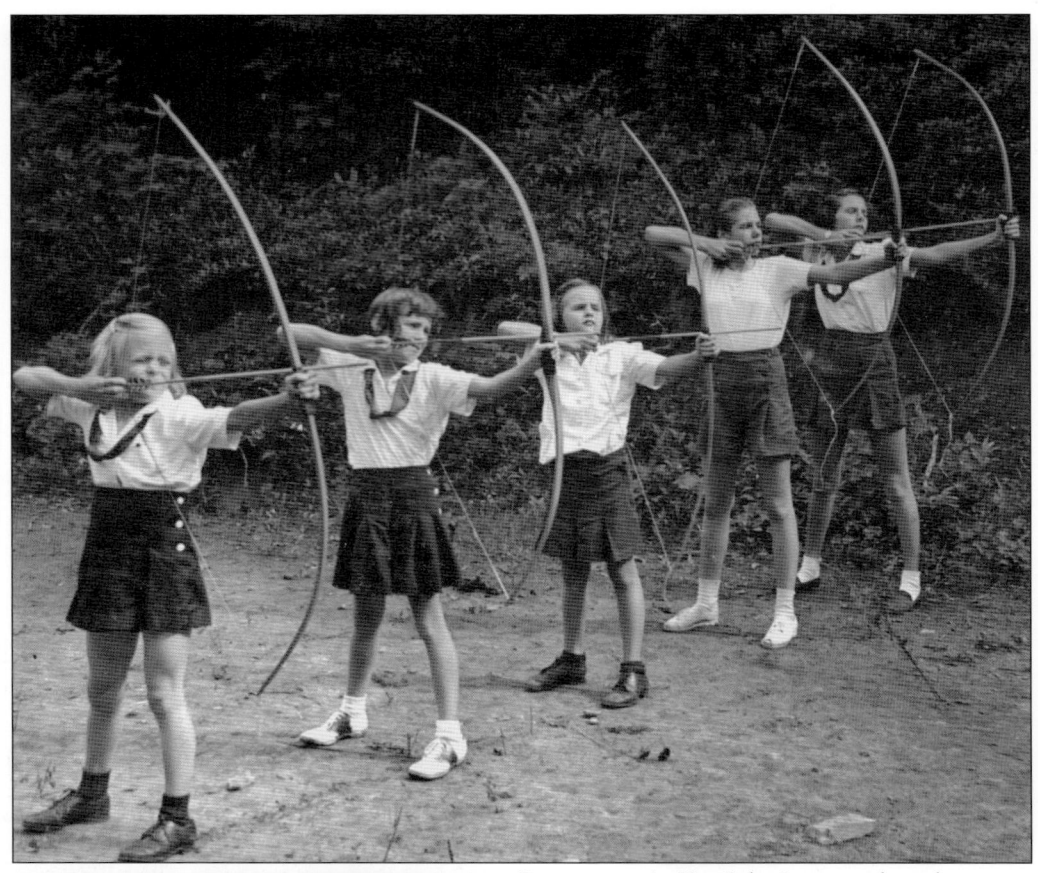

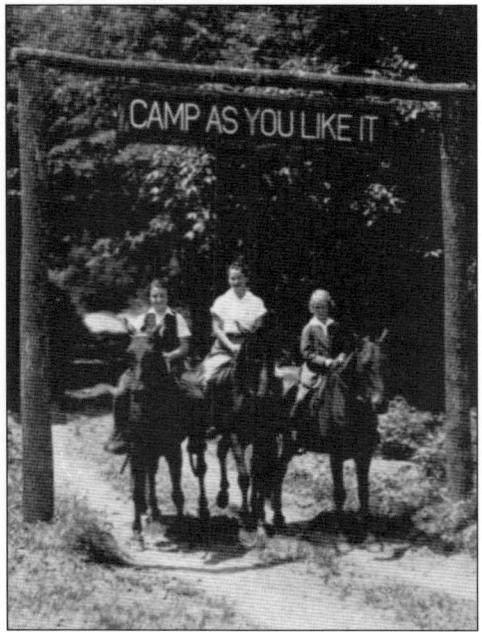

Campers at As-You-Like-It enjoyed outdoor activities such as hayrides, horseback riding, swimming, and camping. In this photograph, a young Coles Jackson (left) and friends take aim at the archery range. (Courtesy of Coles Jackson.)

Horseback riding was a popular attraction at the camp. The girls enjoyed a riding ring that the Blue Ridge Parkway threatened when it was constructed. Dwight successfully lobbied parkway officials for an access road to link the camp with the ring on an adjacent ridge. (Courtesy of Coles Jackson.)

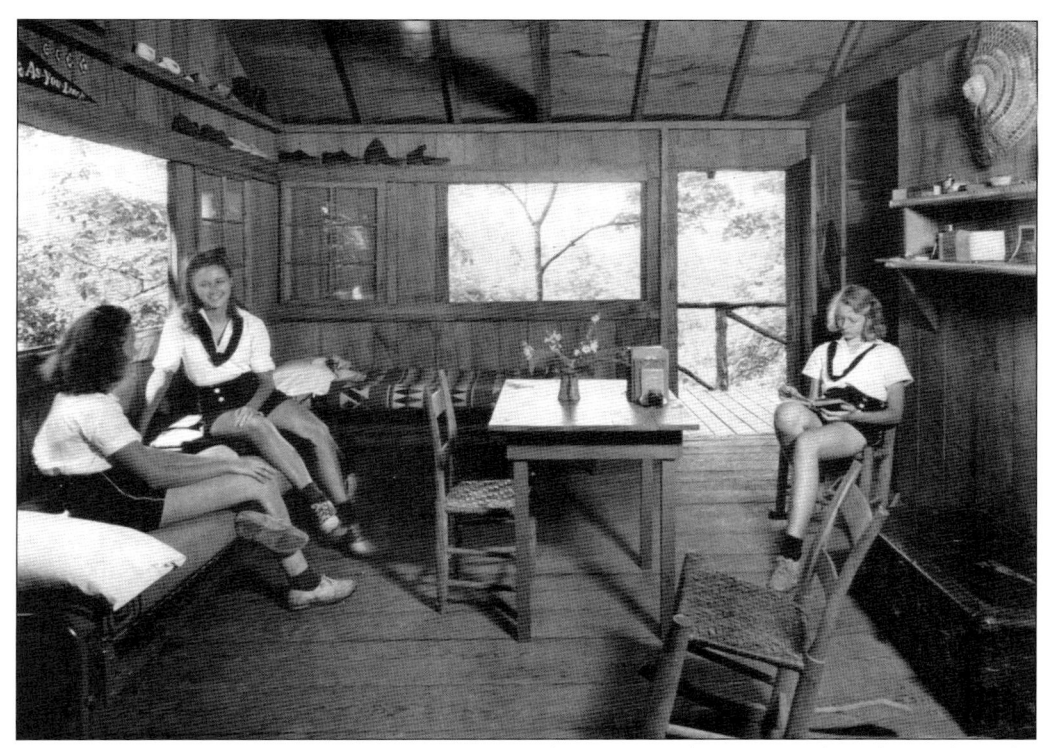

Girls at Camp As-You-Like-It enjoyed comfortable accommodations in cabins located on the mountainside. The cabins had colorful names like Squirrel's Nest, Tree Top, Owlette, and Trail's End. Amid transplanted wildflowers and ferns, lifelong friendships were made among the campers as they enjoyed activities during one of two four-week sessions each summer. Following the closure of the camp, buildings were burned or were vandalized. The remains of one of the cabins still stand in the woods where the camp was located. (Above courtesy of Coles Jackson; below courtesy of Marsha Biddix.)

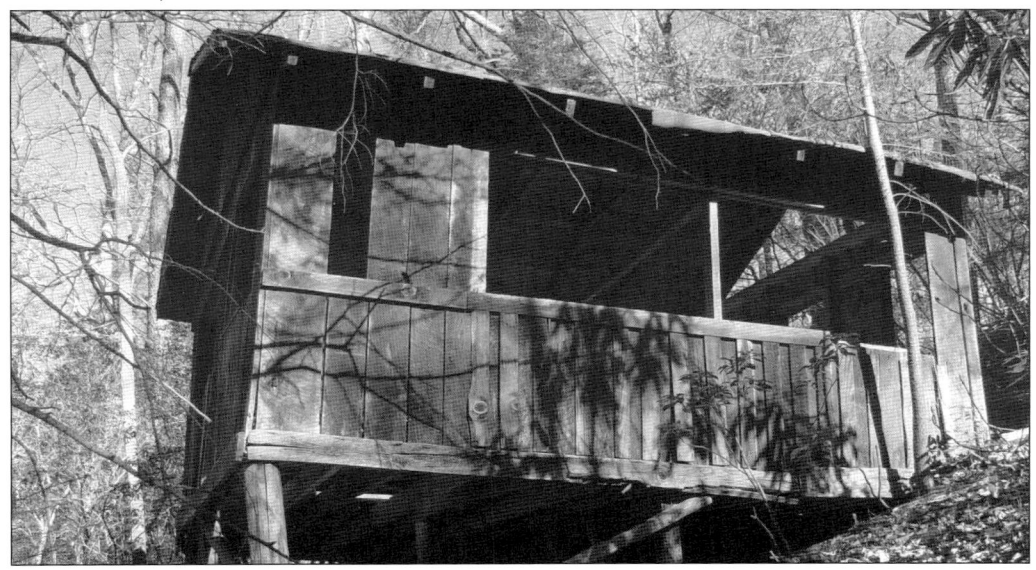

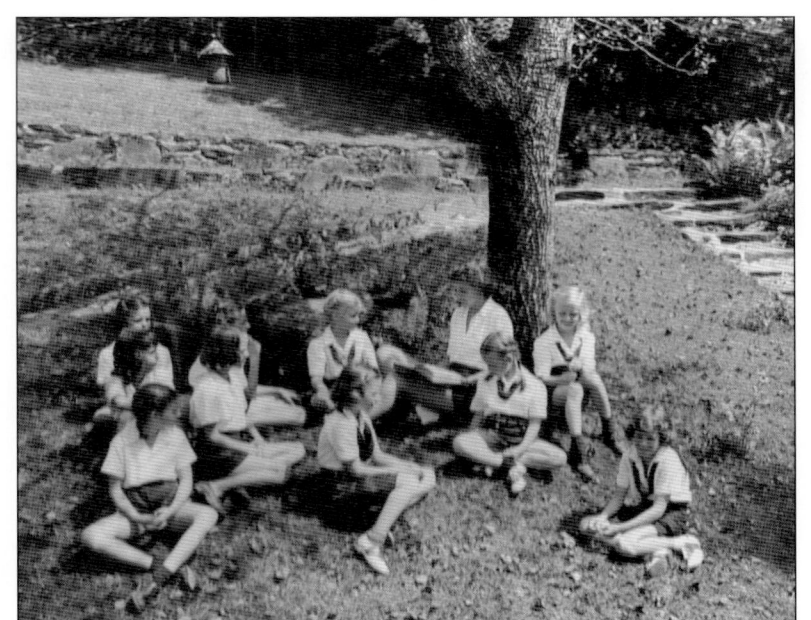

Counselors formed an integral part of the experience at Camp As-You-Like-It. Often former campers themselves, they led hikes, organized athletic events, took campers on excursions, and provided entertainment, like this story under a shade tree. (Courtesy of Coles Jackson.)

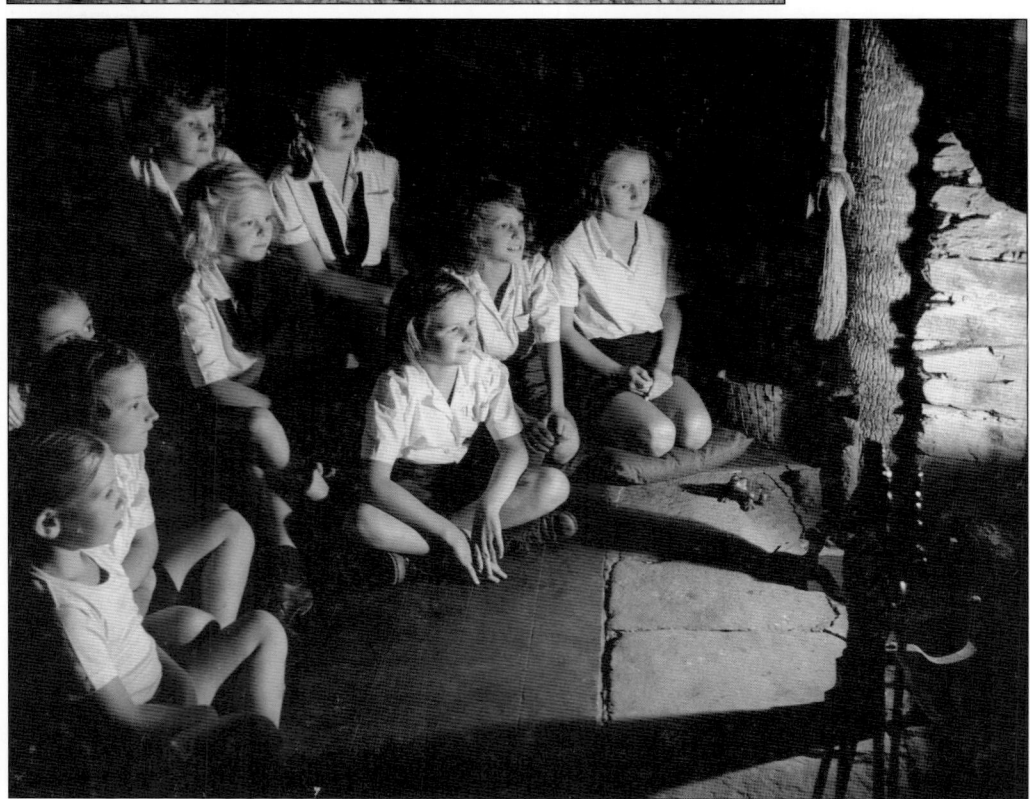

The end of the day brought quiet time in front of the fire. The girls relaxed following sessions of arts and crafts, dance, horseback riding, and other pursuits. Each four-week session was jam-packed with activities for the girls in a mountain paradise. (Courtesy of Coles Jackson.)

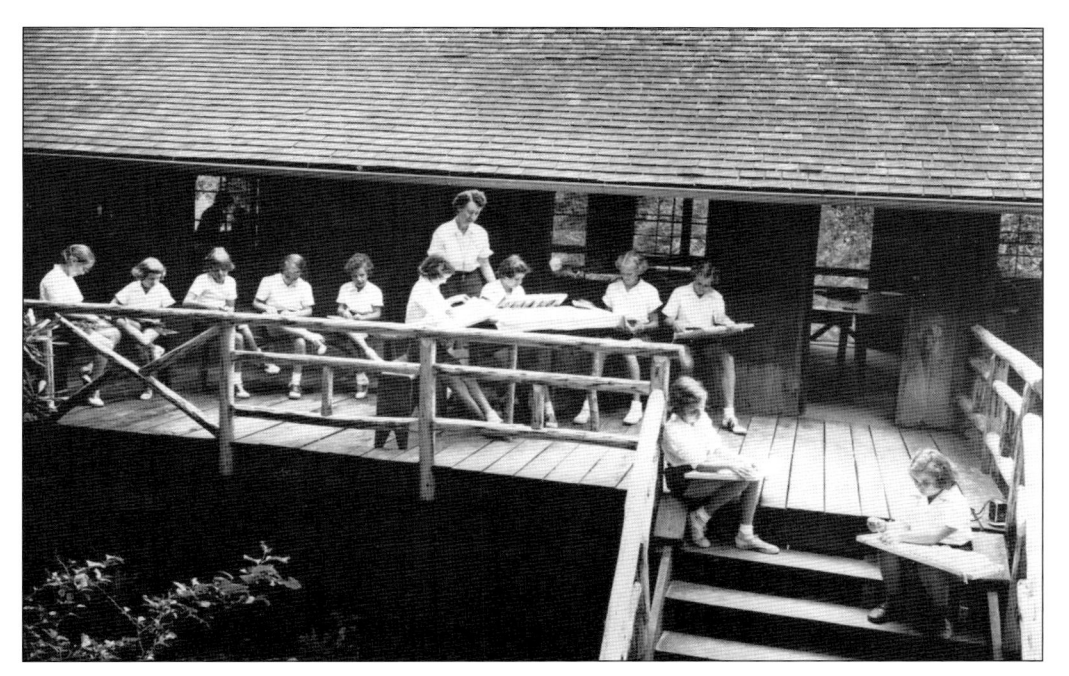

Camp Glenlaurel operated from 1945 to 1967 under two different owners. Initially the camp continued as it was with Marie Dwight serving in an advisory capacity. Facilities were maintained in top-notch condition, with buildings being modernized as needed and the famous swimming pool, opened in 1915, continuing to be an attraction. But changing times caused a decline in the popularity of summer camps in general, and Glenlaurel suffered from this fate. In 1967, the Western Carolina Development Corporation rented the camp to two ministers and their wives who tried to revive it as Glen Alpine (not to be confused with the boys' camp of the 1920s), but the endeavor failed. Next James E. Brannigan bought the property, and the camp closed. (Both courtesy of Coles Jackson.)

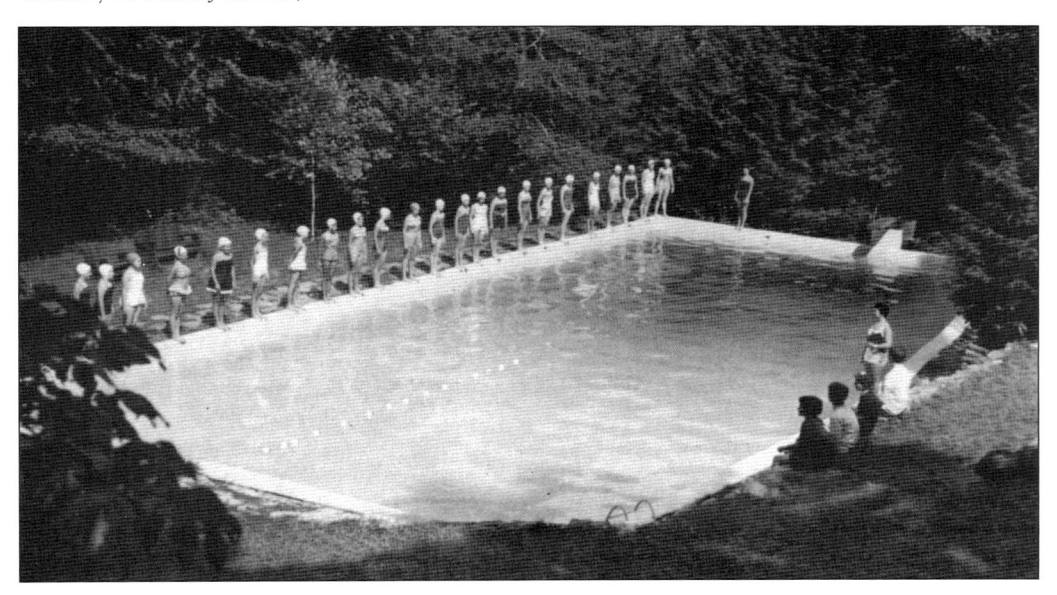

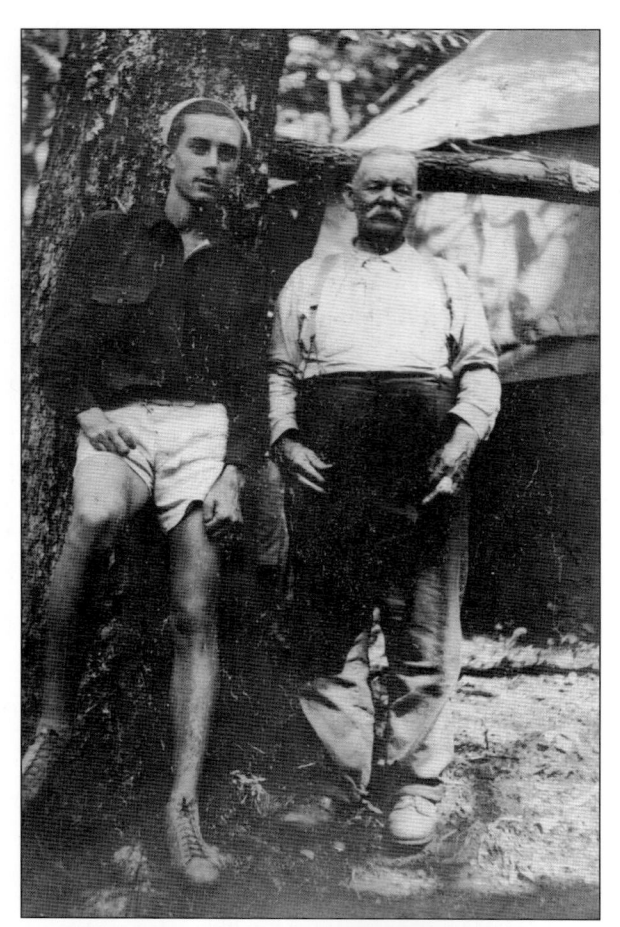

West Jacocks and Boot McKinney pose at Camp Alpine, the boys' camp. McKinney leased his family's property to Charles Dwight for the camp in 1927. It included a camp kitchen set in a Revolutionary War–era cabin. The property reverted back to McKinney following the 1930 session due to the economic conditions of the Great Depression. (Courtesy of Bill McKinney.)

Chow time was special at Camp Alpine, as the boys enjoyed a variety of nutritious meals. Brochures played up the quality of the food. Below, the guys relax with dinner on the grounds. In addition to enjoying the camp's kitchen, which was contained in the old log cabin, cooks traveled with the campers on excursions to local attractions. (Courtesy Jean Nydegger.)

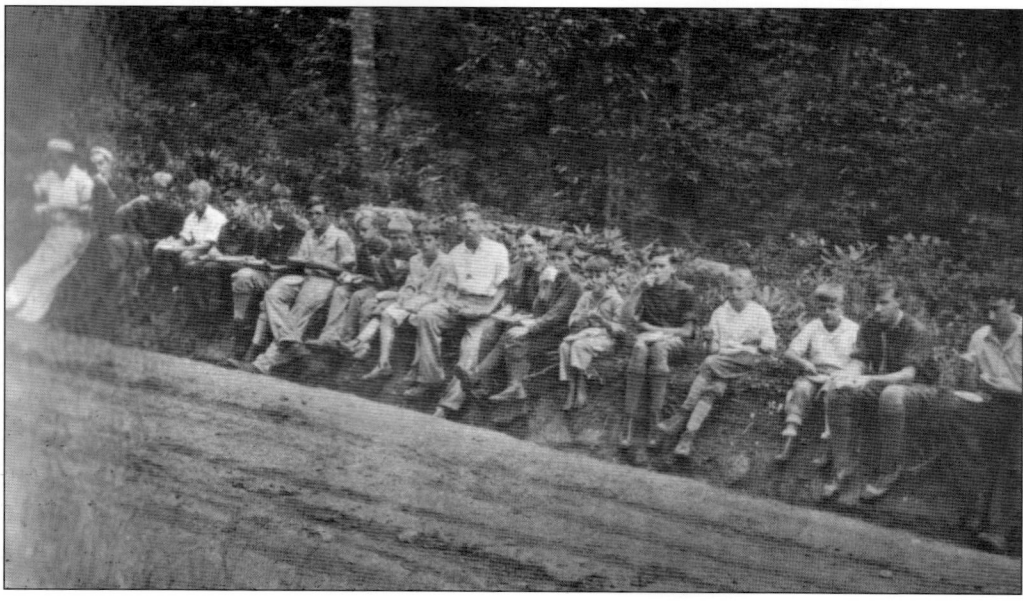

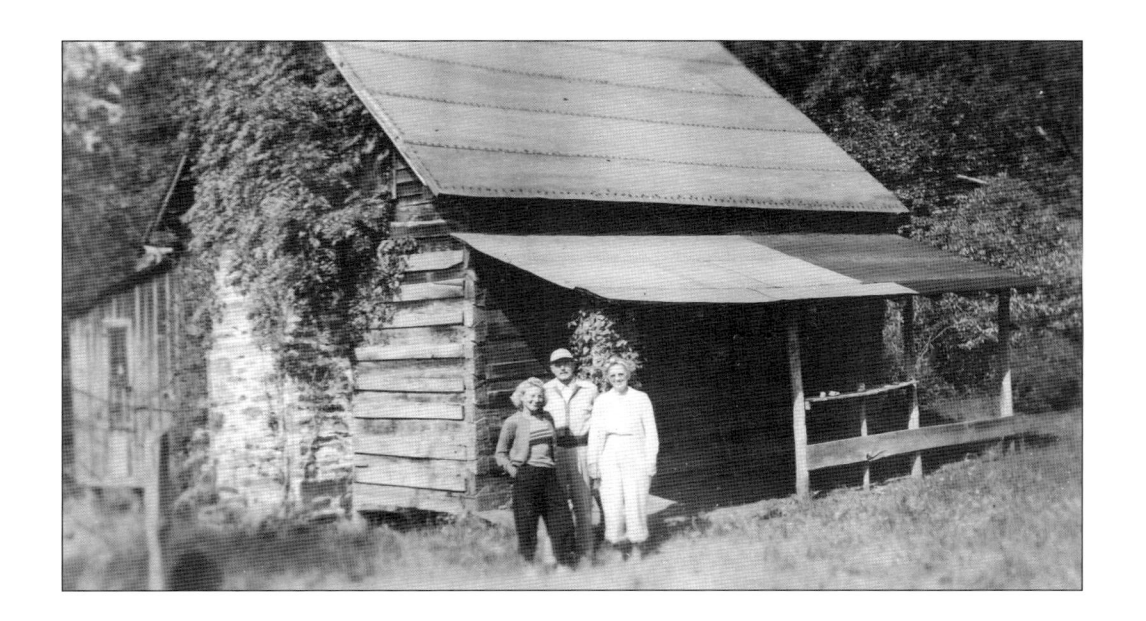

Camp Alpine was located on 200 acres in a clearing in the Lake Laurel section. It was owned by Charles S. Dwight of Charleston, South Carolina, and was operated by West Jacocks of Columbia, South Carolina, and Henry Strohecker of Charleston. The cabin, pictured above with Mr. and Mrs. Pete Brown and longtime owner Amy Nydegger, served as the kitchen of the camp. Amy's husband was Lester Nydegger, who is not pictured. It is one of the oldest structures in Mitchell County, built some time around 1800. The cabin is still in use as a residence. The lower view is of the archery range, facing the workshop and pool below. Camp Alpine operated for only three seasons, opening in 1927. (Both courtesy Jean Nydegger.)

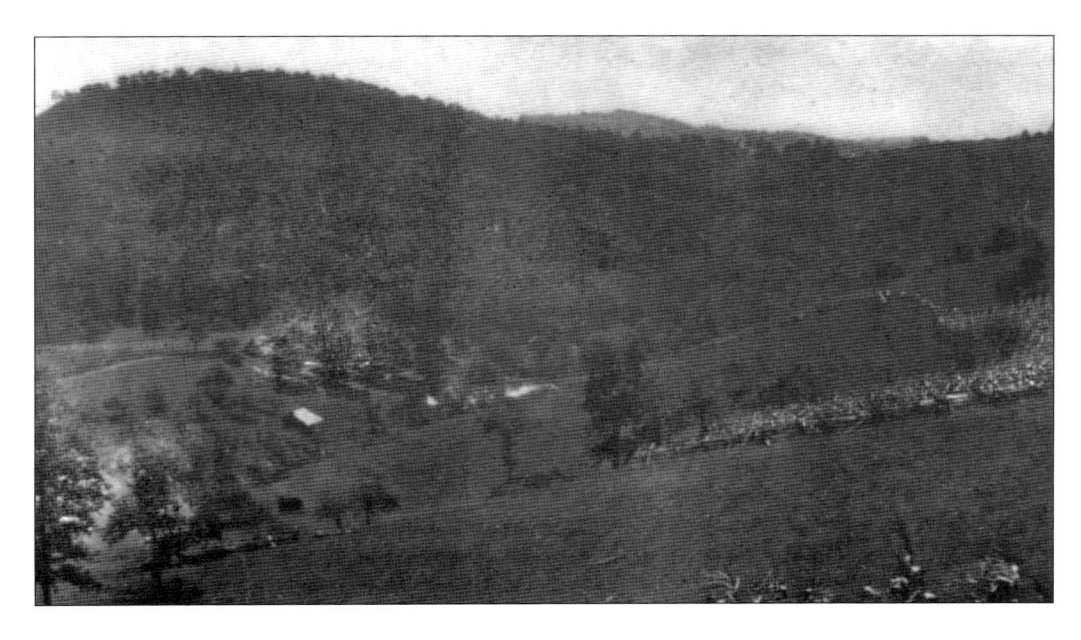

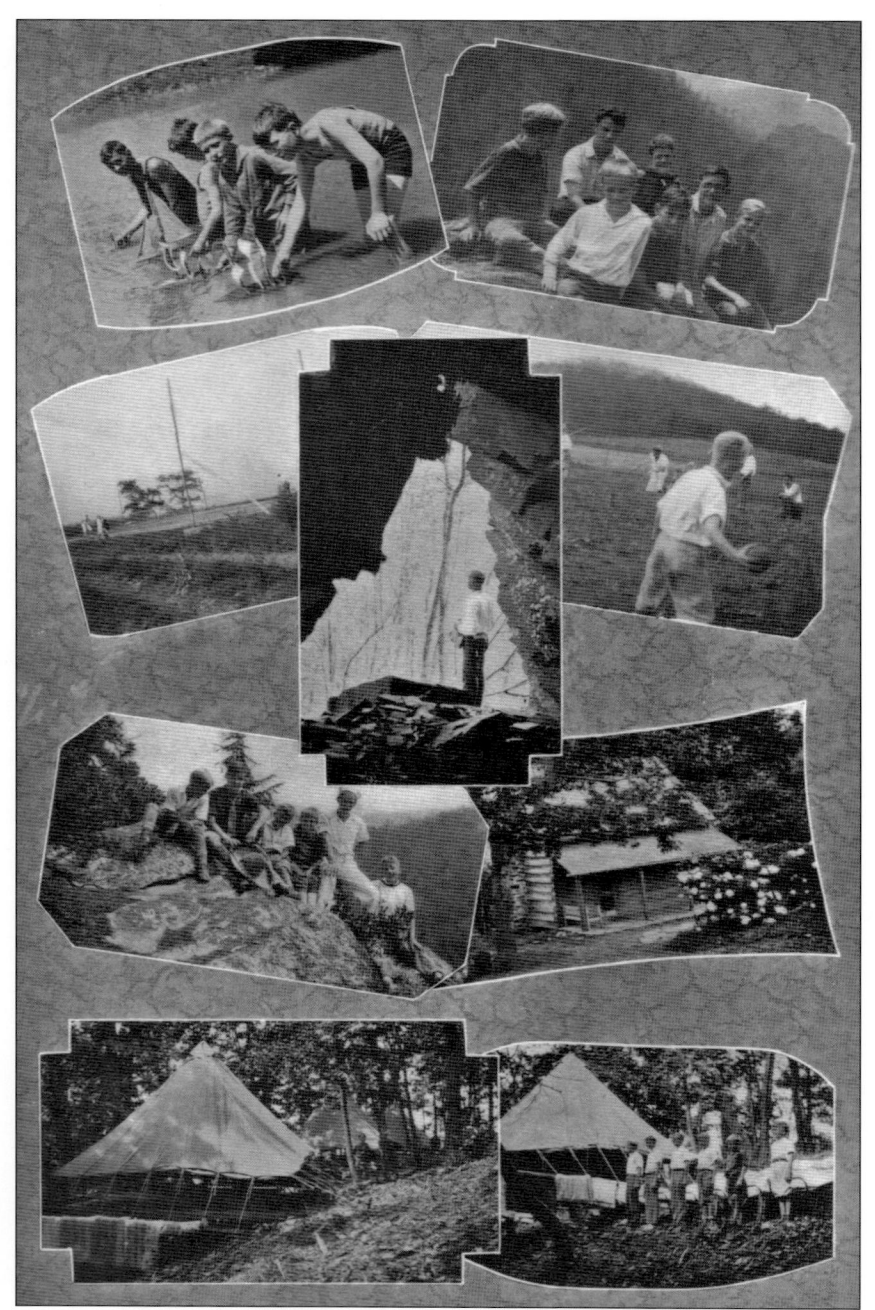

Between 25 and 30 boys attended each of the three summers at Camp Alpine. They enjoyed outdoor activities such as archery, tennis, lifesaving, horseback riding, and swimming. Overnight trips to nearby natural attractions by both automobile and horseback were common. The camp also boasted about its beautiful views and good food prepared by William, who apparently had a delicious fried chicken dinner. The cost to attend an eight-week session (July 3–August 28) was $125; a four-week session was $75. This collage of photographs from the 1929 camp brochure shows the boys engaged in several different pursuits. (Courtesy of Jean Nydegger.)

Five

Seasons on the Mountain
Faith, Family, Friends, and Fellowship

With its lofty position atop the Eastern Continental Divide at an elevation of 3,478 feet, Little Switzerland has long been the destination of those seeking someplace different. Contained in its unique landscape, a close-knit community developed where both natives and summer residents became involved in each other's lives. Geneva Hall and local churches, the Switzerland Store, and the post office were all places people gathered to visit, catch up on the news, and share a laugh.

Even today, life moves at a different pace in Little Switzerland. Its small-town charm and breathtaking scenery encourage visitors to slow down, relax, and enjoy their surroundings. As in any small community, characters abound, and their stories and legends help weave a rich tapestry of life on the mountain.

Gathered here are glimpses into the lives and events that have helped make the community special to those who call it home.

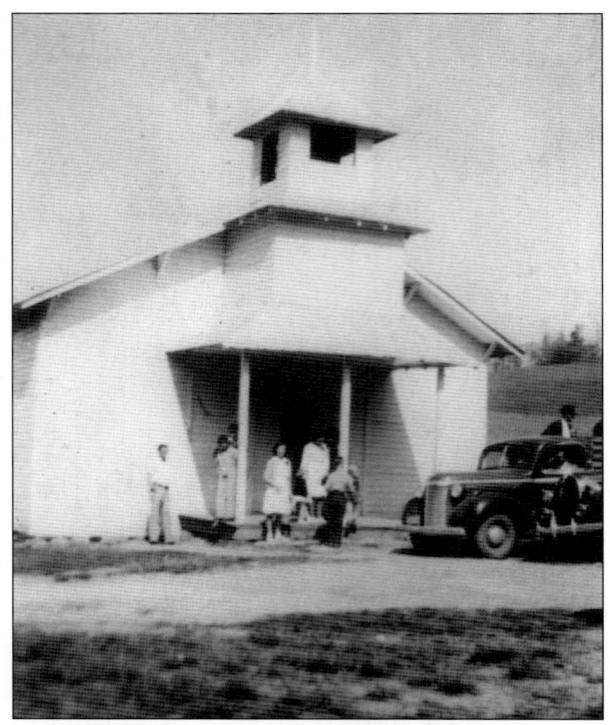

The Black Mountain Baptist Church started in 1882. Prominent families of the church included members of the McKinney, Glenn, McGee, and Ballew families. The church is still in its original building on Crabtree Creek Road. Sunday services are a joyous time of fellowship, as exhibited in this photograph. From left to right, pictured here are (first row) David McGee, Cindy Pendley, Glenda Buchanan, and Lynn Parsley; (second row) two unidentified men, Weldon Dale, Chesley Glenn, Boyd Parsley, Charlie Glenn, Allen Parsley, Rob McMahan, and Lawrence Buchanan. (Left courtesy of Ruth Parsley; below courtesy of Lloyd Glenn.)

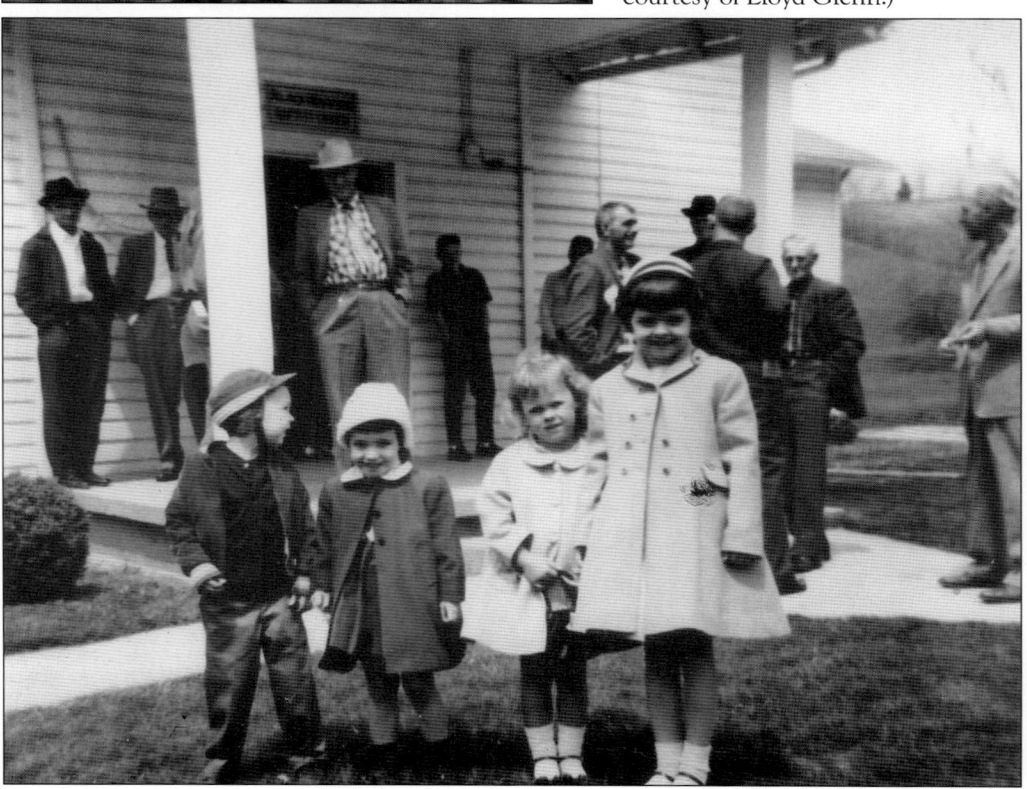

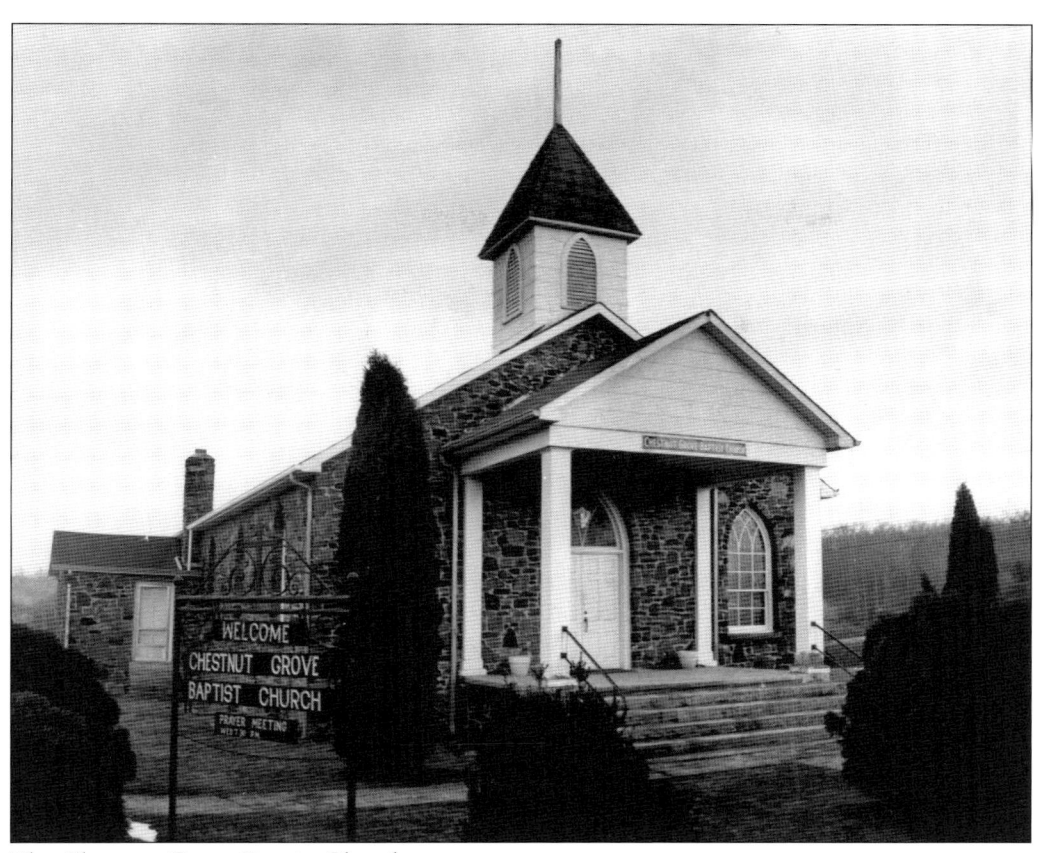

The Chestnut Grove Baptist Church traces its origins to meetings held in the home of John and Patty Collis around 1877. The first church, built around 1880, was located on Emerald Mine Road, with the second being constructed in 1900 in the Lake Laurel section. In the early 1920s, it was relocated to a new building on McKinney Mine Road, then it was moved to its present location on Chestnut Grove Church Road in 1945. The first pastor was James Collis, who served over 20 churches in the area. Rev. Jimmy Thomas, pictured at right, served as pastor in the 1920s. He delivered the invocation at the dedication of the Gillespie Gap monument on July 4, 1927, and presided at the dedication of Geneva Hall on August 1, 1928, in addition to his pastoral duties. (Above courtesy of Greg S. Burnette; right courtesy of Ruby Buchanan.)

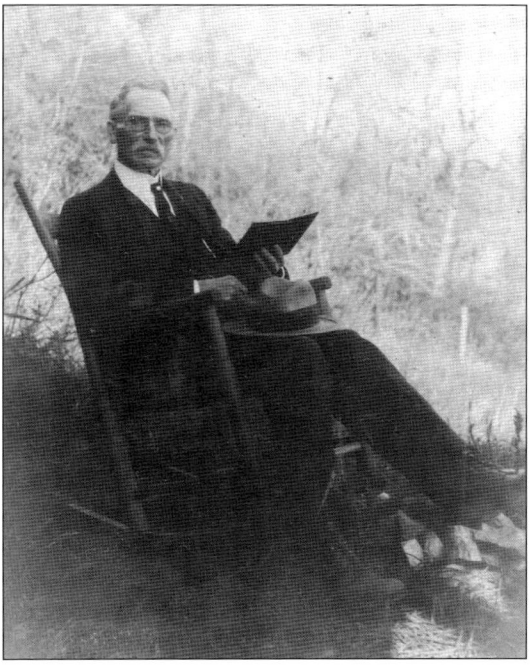

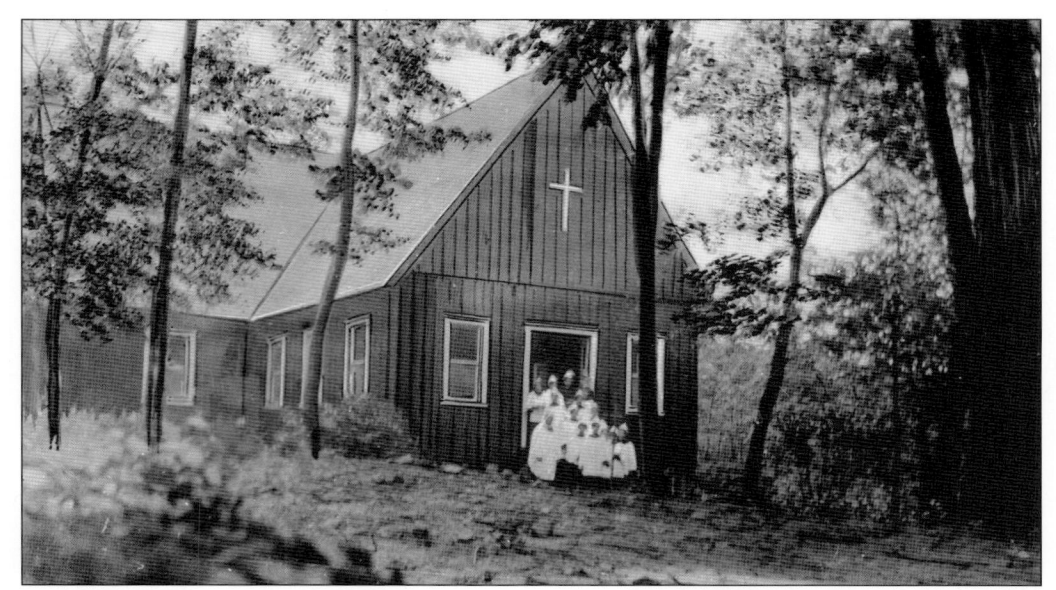

Judge Clarkson was a religious man, and he worked with Mrs. McNeely DuBose to establish an Episcopal church in Little Switzerland. It was originally planned as a memorial to DuBose's late husband. The Church of the Resurrection opened on June 13, 1913, with Rev. Francis M. Osborne, brother of Mary Clarkson, delivering the sermon. The building was designed by Adlai Osborne and was originally located on property later acquired for the Blue Ridge Parkway. It was then moved 100 yards up the hill to its present site. Services are still held there for six months during the year. It is listed on the National Register of Historic Places. (Both courtesy of the North Carolina Collection, UNC–Chapel Hill.)

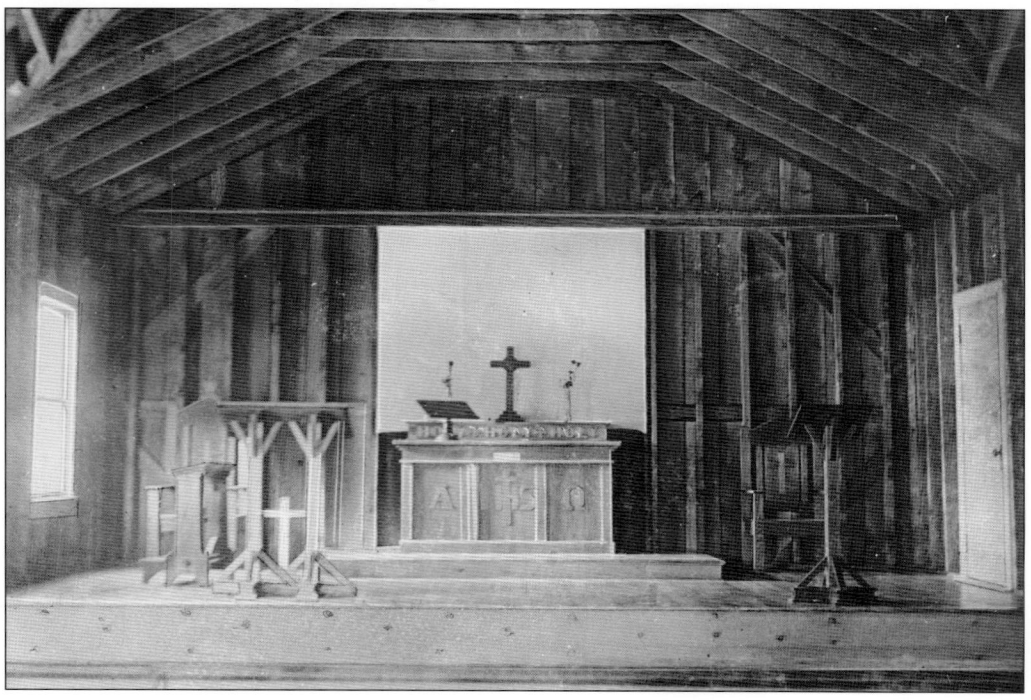

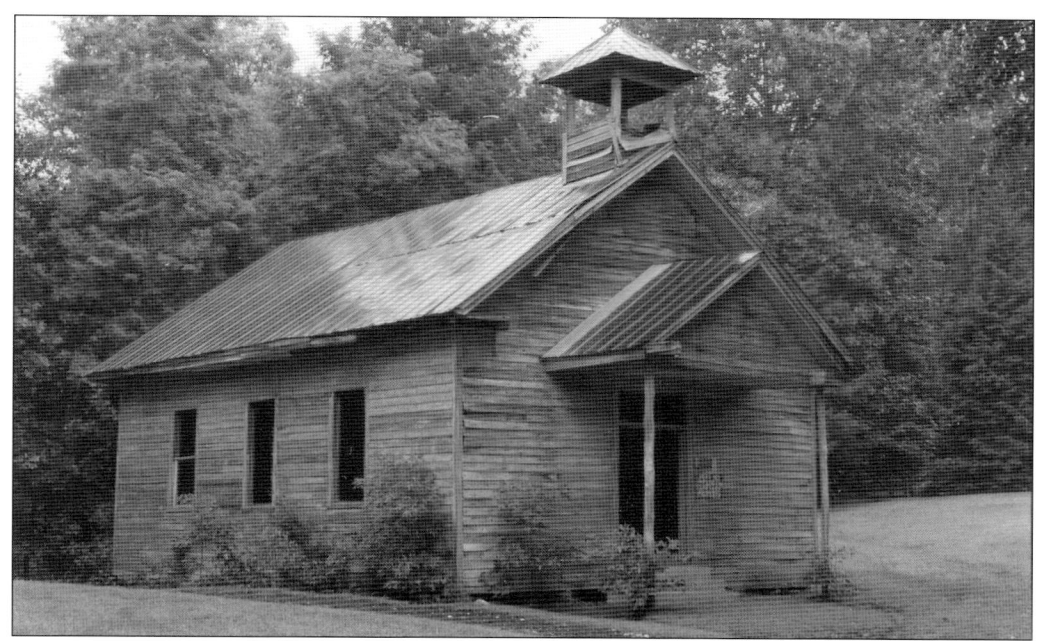

David M. Glenn constructed the Glenn Church, a nondenominational meetinghouse located in the Glenn community near Black Mountain Baptist Church, as a memorial after his son Plato Glenn was killed in a factory accident. David Glenn moved to the region after the Civil War, buying 1,500 acres along Crabtree Creek and establishing a settlement with a gristmill, sawmill, general store, and post office. David Glenn's great-grandson Chesley Glenn, assisted by brothers, cousins, nephews, and friends, started restoring the structure in 1998, with work continuing today. (Both courtesy of Lloyd Glenn.)

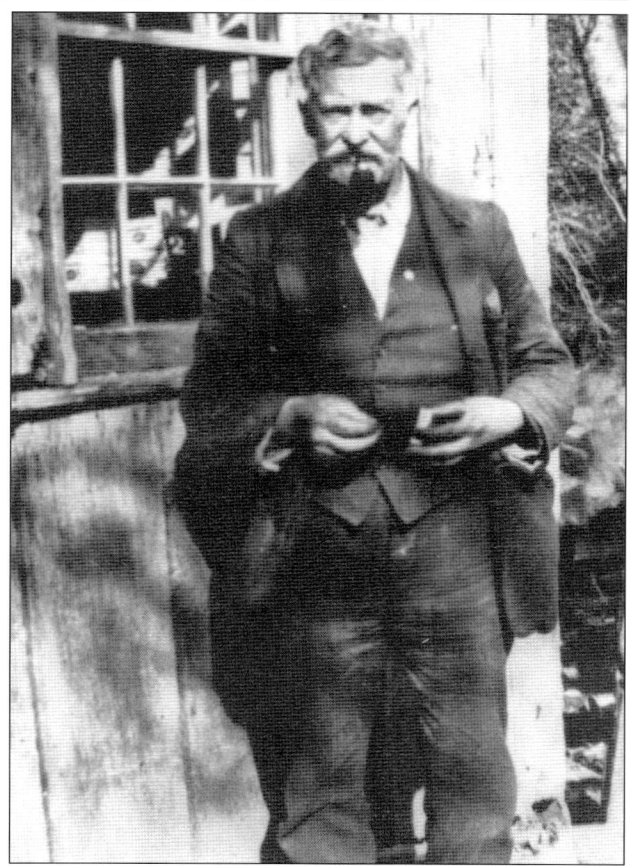

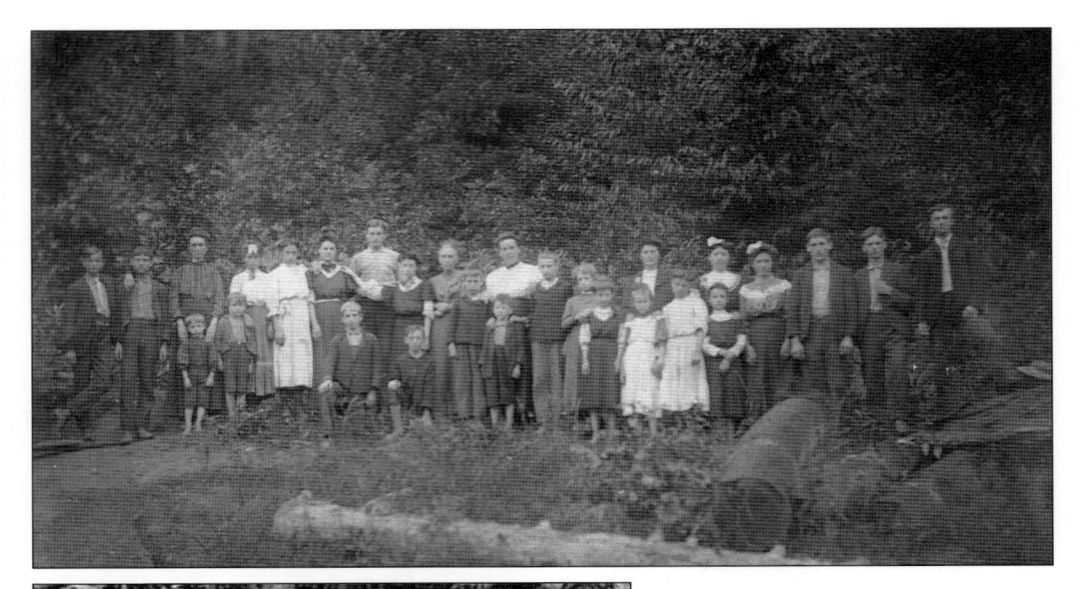

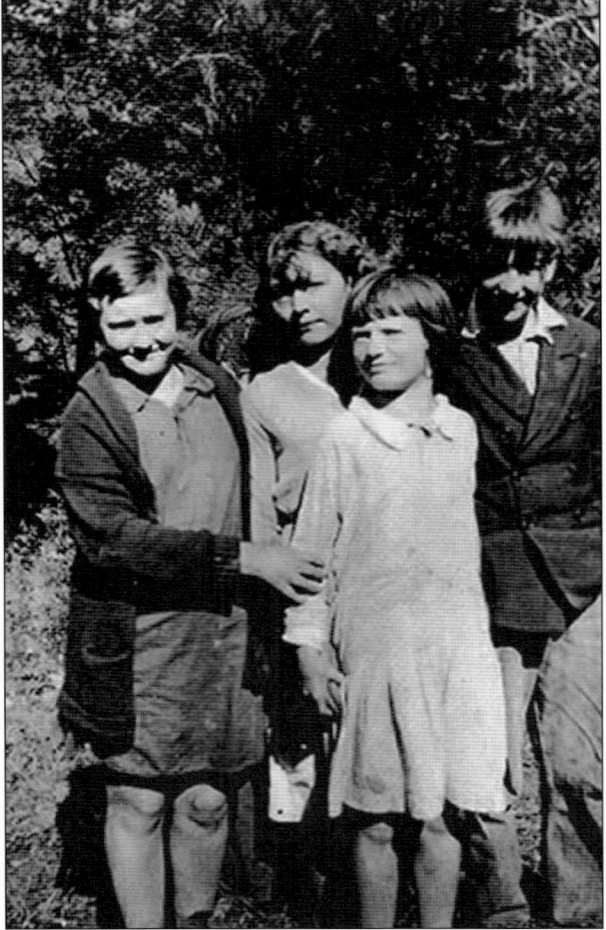

The children of Turkey Cove School pose for a portrait around 1886. Early settlers of Little Switzerland came through the Armstrong and Turkey Cove sections of McDowell County to settle the hills. Several of these children are related to Cyrus and Fed Burnette. Cyrus was a pioneer settler of Little Switzerland. (Courtesy of John McKinney.)

Seen here from left to right are sixth-graders Pauline Ballew, Minnie McGee, Lois Mace, and Claude Williams. Rural schools like Black Mountain and Chestnut Grove gave children the opportunity to get an education, since transportation was limited. Up through the 1930s, students in Little Switzerland attended these schools before completing high school in Spruce Pine. (Courtesy of Minnie Hoilman.)

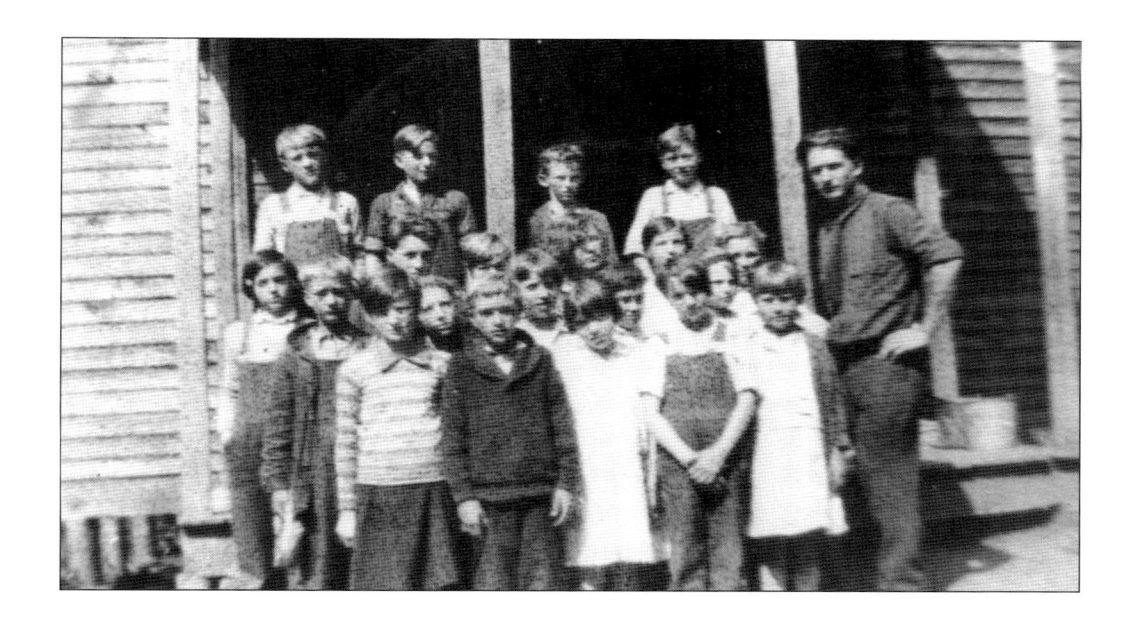

Conley Hollifield and his class at Chestnut Grove School gather on the front porch in the 1920s. The school hosted grades one through seven, with students attending high school in Spruce Pine. Pictured below, it was located just off the McKinney Mine Road and served the Little Switzerland area until the late 1930s, when it burned down. The Black Mountain School, located across from the Black Mountain Church near the Glenn community, held grades one through six. It was closed in 1927. (Above courtesy of Bernice McKinney; below courtesy of Bob Young.)

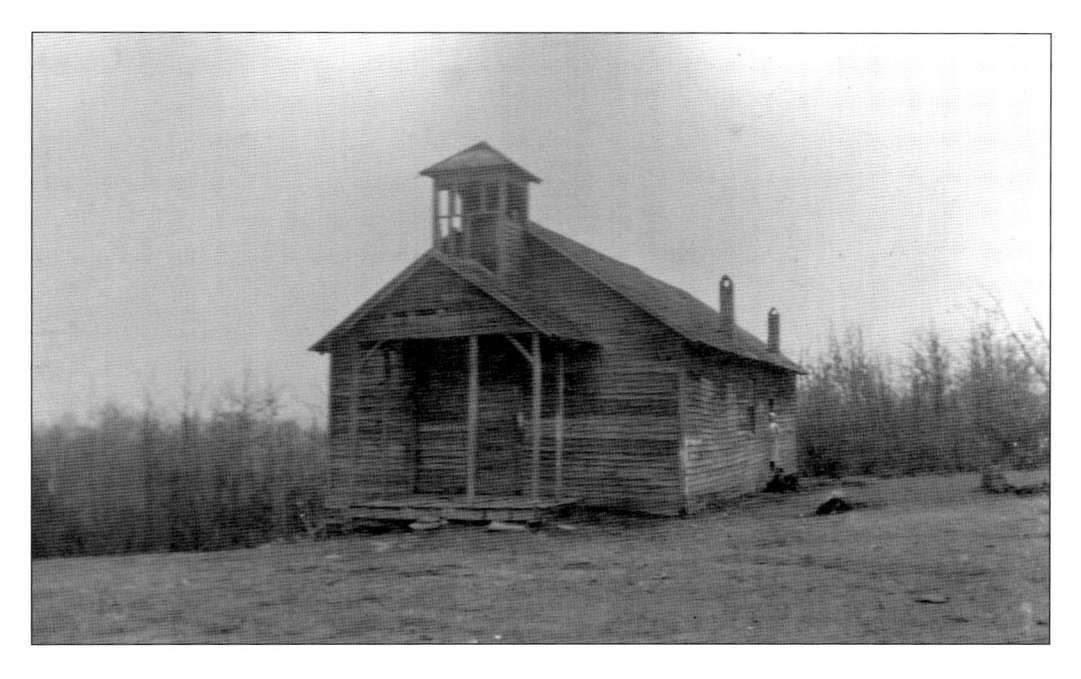

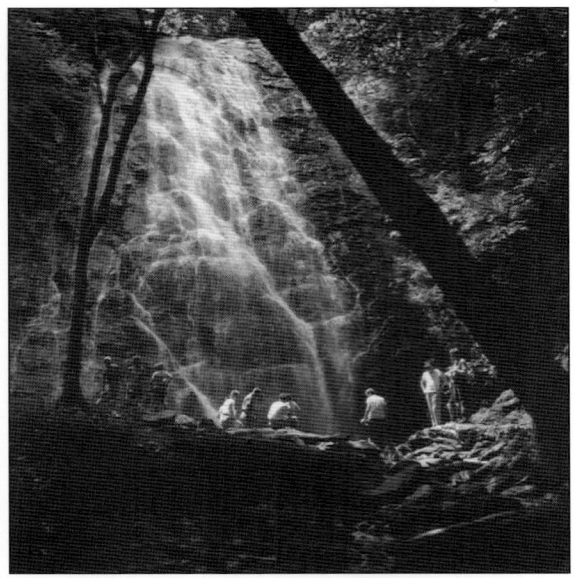

Crabtree/Murphy's Falls is a popular destination during the summer. The cool, moist environment is a refreshing respite from the heat. Parkway officials inexplicably changed the name of the falls when Crabtree Meadows opened to visitors. Originally, the area was known as Blue Ridge Meadows and may have been fire-cleared by Cherokees prior to settlement by whites. Below, a young boy and his dog prepare for the journey to the falls from the parking area adjacent to the Crabtree Meadows campgrounds. Murphy's Creek continues from the falls to join Crabtree Creek and empty into the Toe River near Wing. (Both courtesy of the U.S. National Park Service.)

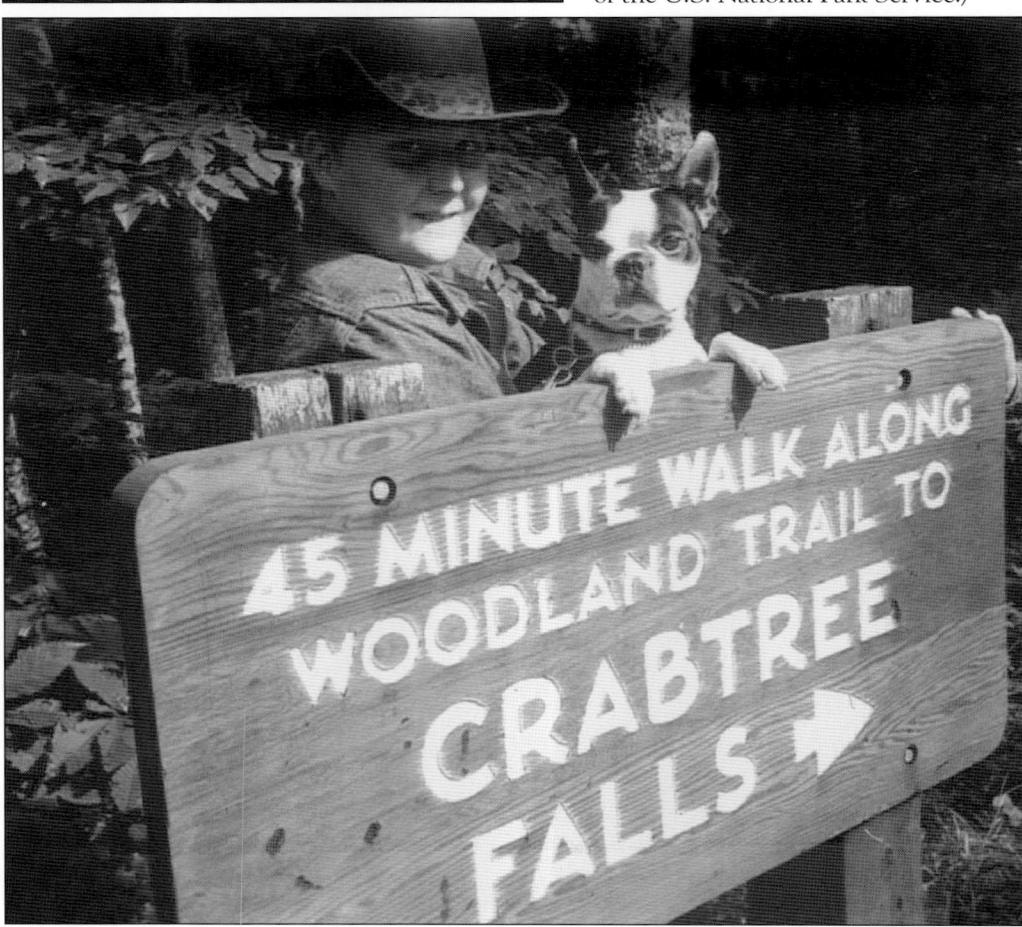

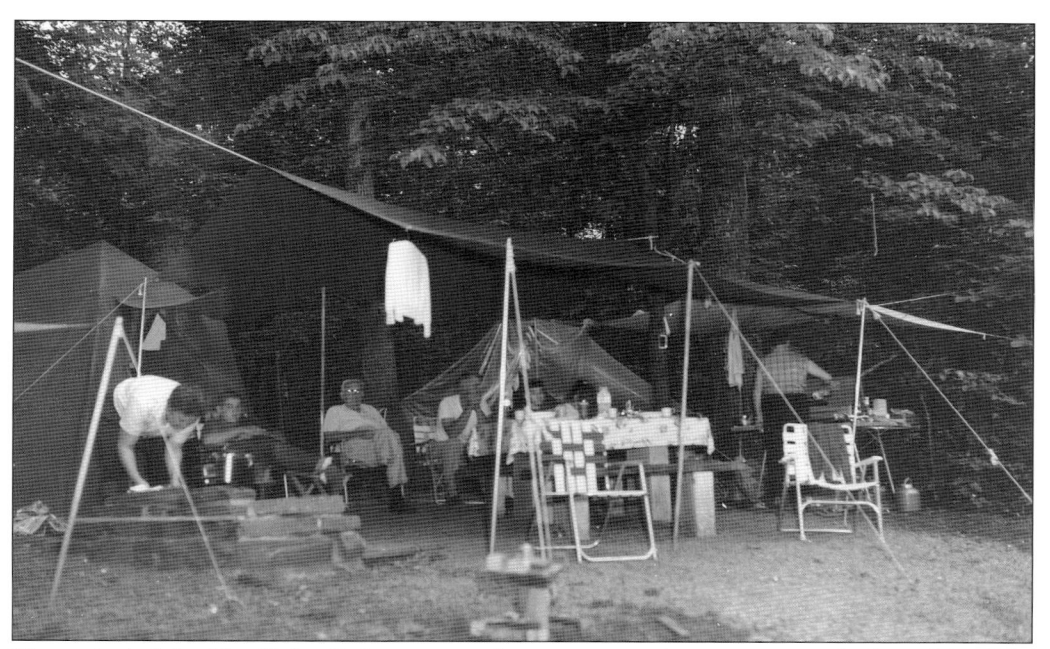

The arrival of the Blue Ridge Parkway opened up recreational opportunities. Crabtree Meadows was one of the original planned service areas to add to visitors' enjoyment. A campground for both tent and trailer camping, along with a picnic area, enticed travelers to stop and relax. Originally Crabtree Meadows boasted a camp store, restaurant, gas station, and souvenir shop, but changing economic times and readily available gas near the Blue Ridge Parkway forced the closure of the gas station. The restaurant was later replaced with vending machines. (Courtesy of the U.S. National Park Service.)

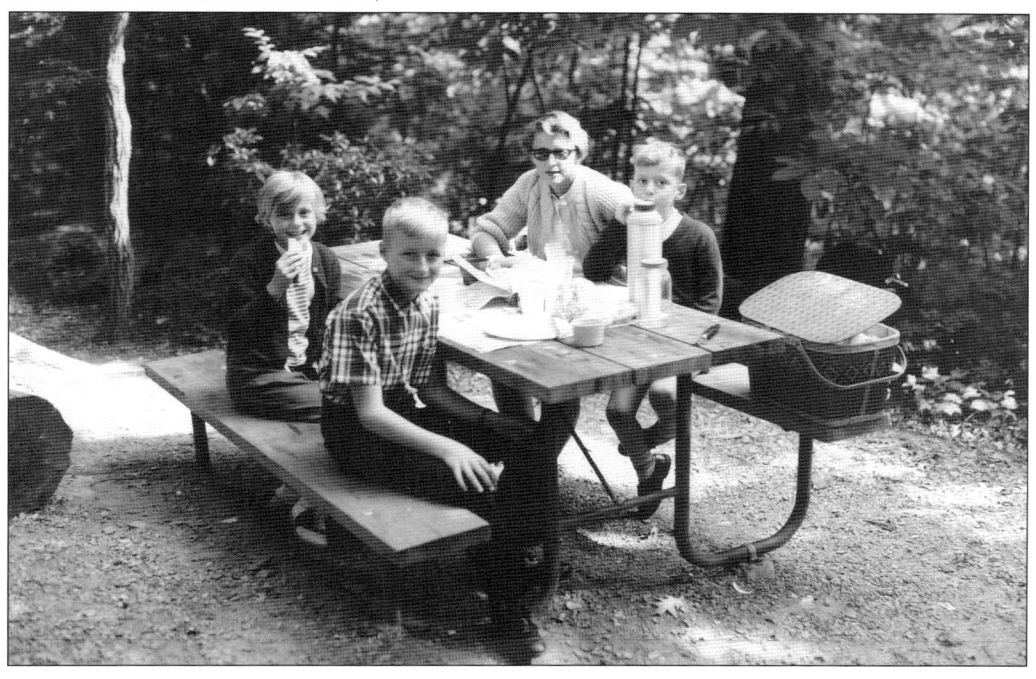

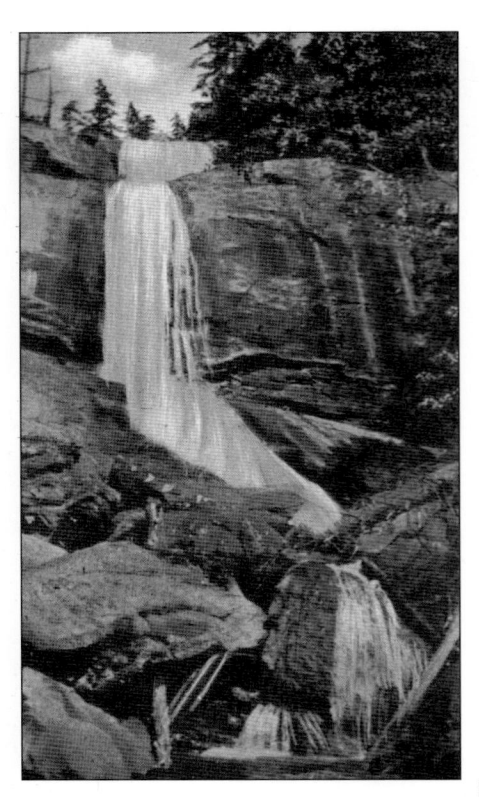

Crabtree Falls, located on Crabtree Road, is 4 miles from Little Switzerland. It has always been an attraction for both locals and visitors, providing scenic views, fishing, and wading at its base. An upper and lower falls make up this beautiful stretch of water. (Courtesy of Davis and Jann Godwin.)

The waters of Grassy Creek Falls, located near the Switzerland Inn on Grassy Creek Falls Road, flow into the Toe River near Spruce Pine. It is made up of three stages and has been a favorite destination for summer residents and locals alike for over a century. (Courtesy of David Biddix.)

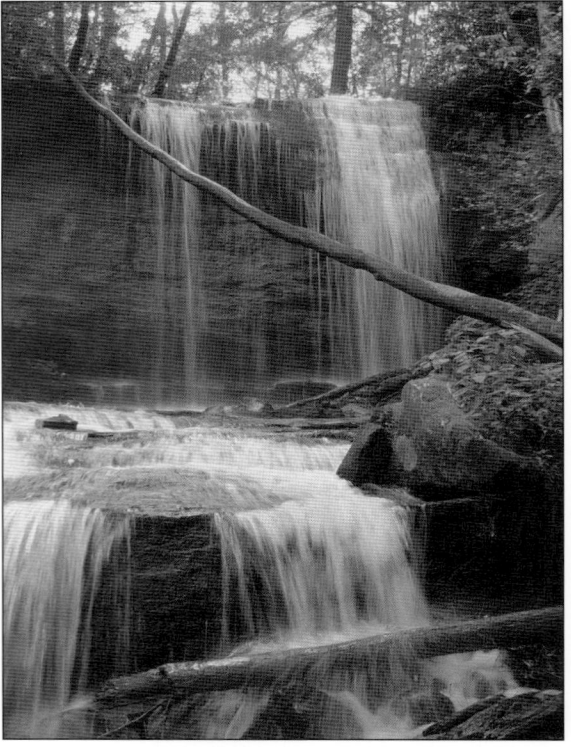

The Marrying Tree stood at the entrance of the Big Lynn Lodge. It was 75 feet tall, with a circumference of 13 feet. Members of the Overmountain Men camped there and hanged British sympathizer Nathaniel Riddle from its branches before continuing to Kings Mountain. It was the scene of marriages, as it stood on the Mitchell/McDowell County line, where irate parents couldn't stop the ceremonies. The Little Switzerland tollgate stood under it until 1921. Age, disease, fire, and weather took a toll, causing the tree to endanger nearby buildings. In 1949, parkway officials planned to cut it down, but a campaign saved it. In 1965, the 500-year-old tree could stand no more and was cut down. Two sprouts from it grow today. (Right courtesy of the North Carolina State Archives; below courtesy of the U.S. National Park Service.)

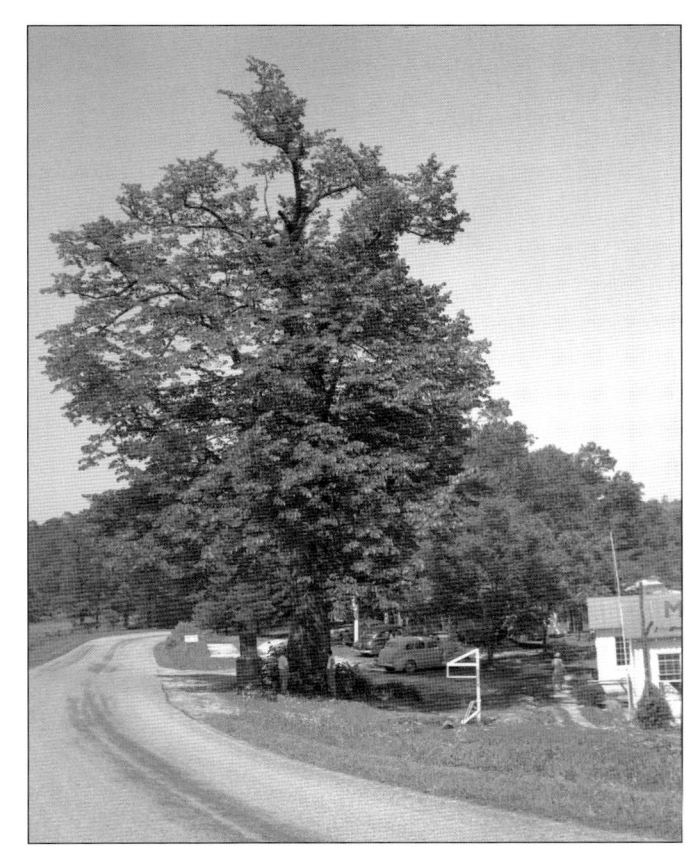

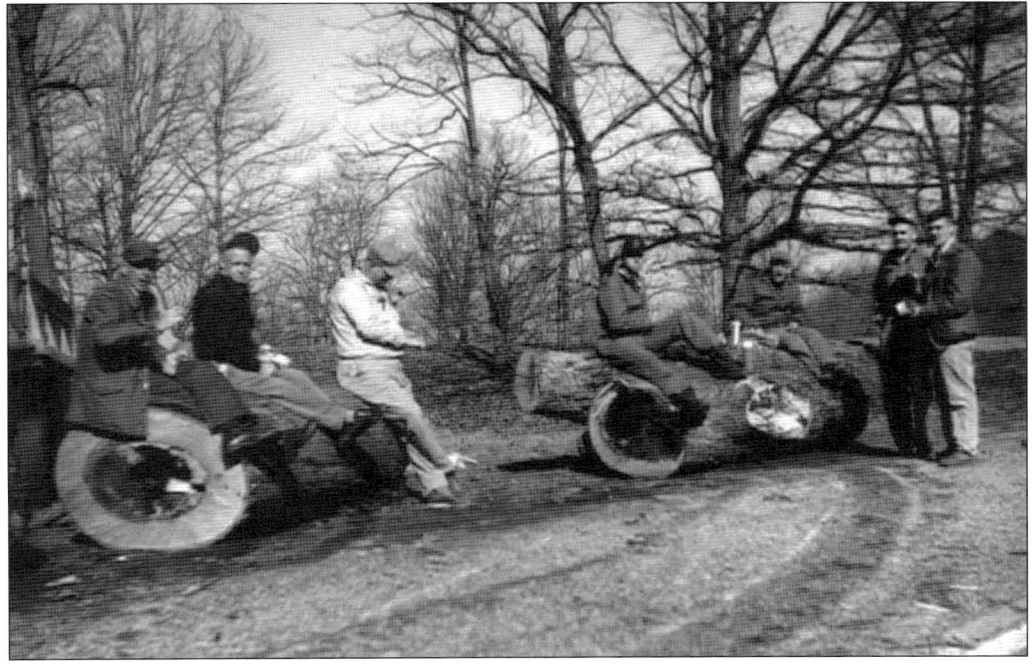

81

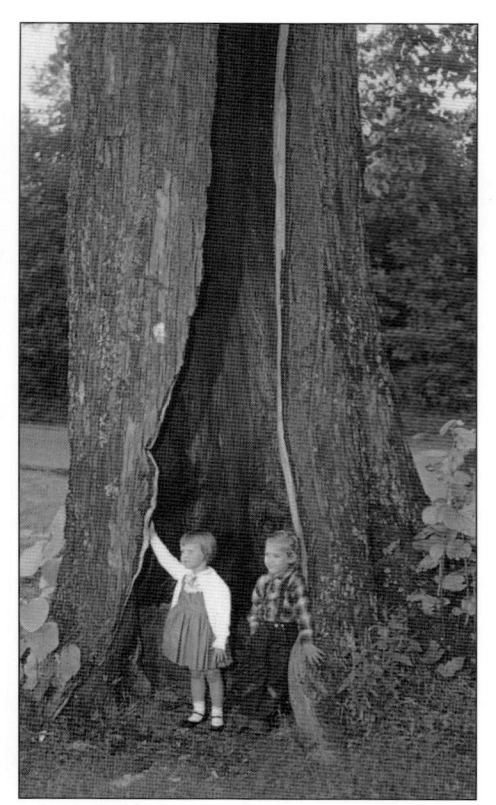

The extent of damage to the Marrying Tree is evident in the photograph at left of Martha Ann Johns, daughter of Big Lynn Lodge owners J. P. and Lucille Johns, with a summer guest playmate standing at its base. Some have claimed that a horse could fit inside the trunk. Age and disease brought down the linden tree in 1965. (Courtesy of Davis and Jann Godwin.)

Below, the Fons and Jane McKinney family pose for a portrait in 1946. From left to right are (first row) Jerry McKinney, Mildred McKinney, Betty McKinney Mace, Phillip Buchanan, Pat Turner Mitchell, and Rodney Burleson; (second row) Fons McKinney, Lewis McKinney, G. E. "Shorty" Burleson, Ila Gail Burleson, Ruby McKinney Buchanan, Ida McKinney Burleson, Edith McKinney Turner, Effie Snipes McKinney, Jane Buchanan McKinney, Thelma McKinney Sparks, and Lawrence Sparks. (Courtesy of Davis and Jann Godwin.)

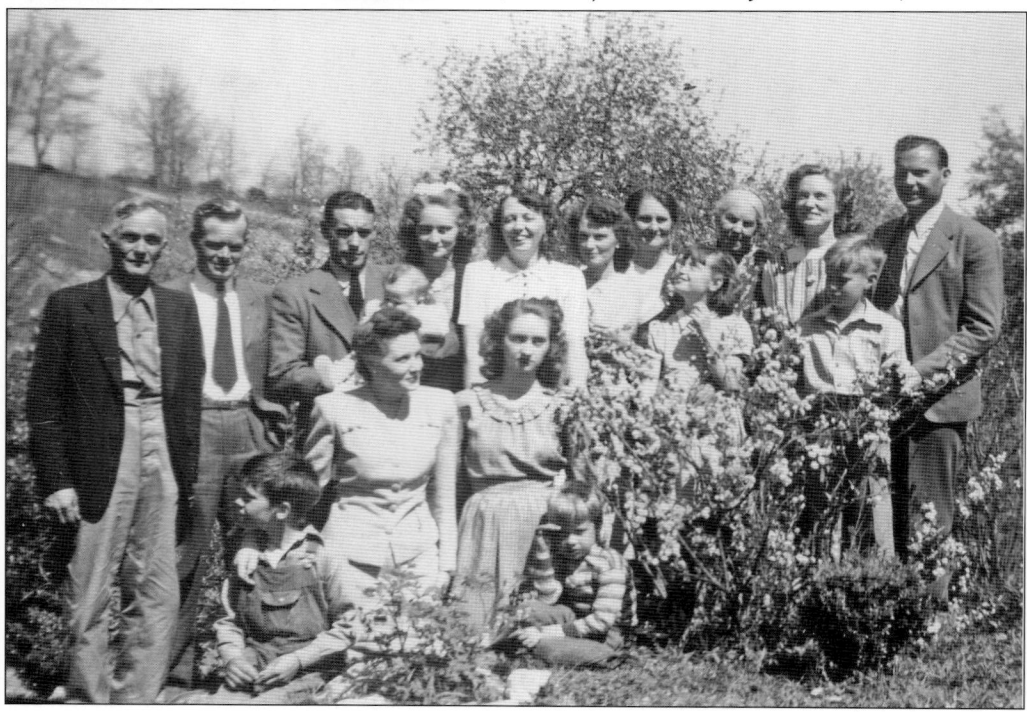

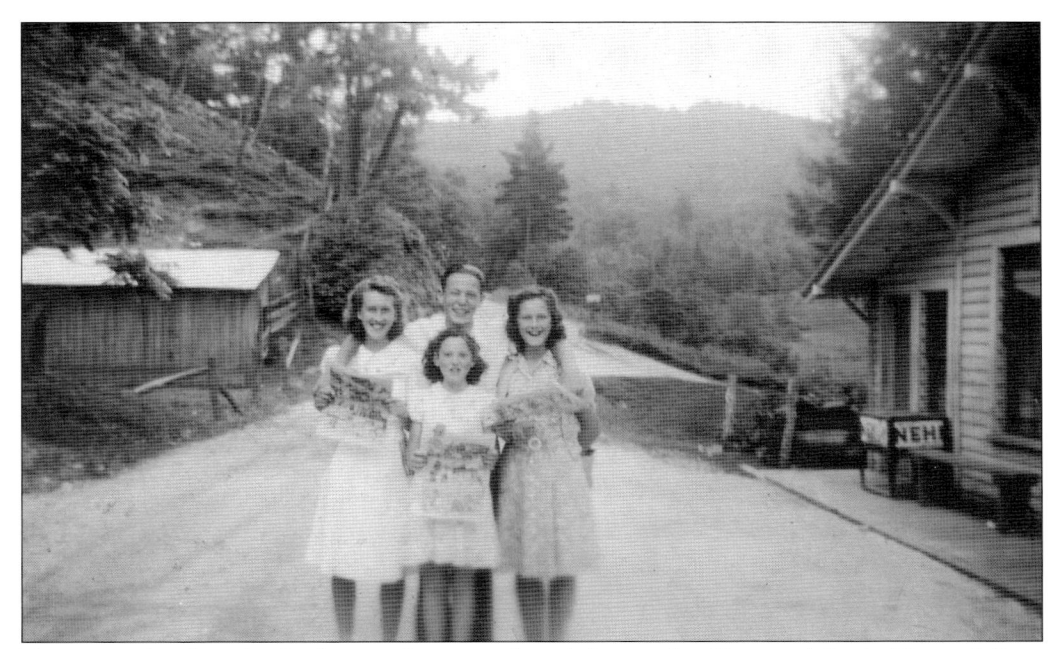

Enjoying a laugh with the funnies here are, from left to right, (first row) Ruth Glenn, Lillian Ballew, and Elva Glenn; (second row) Sherrill Ballew. Lillian and Sherrill's father Barney ran the store in the right of the photograph. Country stores like this one were a staple of rural life. They provided products that could not be grown or made at home. Ballew's store was located on Crabtree Road. (Courtesy of Tommy and Lillian Hollifield.)

The McKinney children enjoy an afternoon visit with pony "Billy Sunday" in the 1920s. Children played ball and games and made their own fun on Sunday afternoons. Posing with their horse and wearing their Sunday best are, from left to right, Thelma, Ruby, Ida, Mildred, Lewis, and Edith. (Courtesy of Ruby Buchanan.)

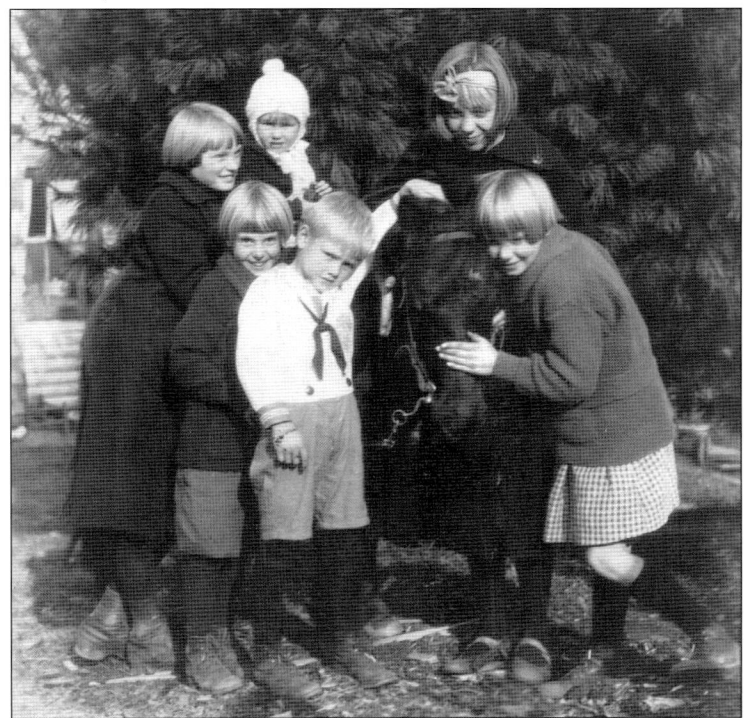

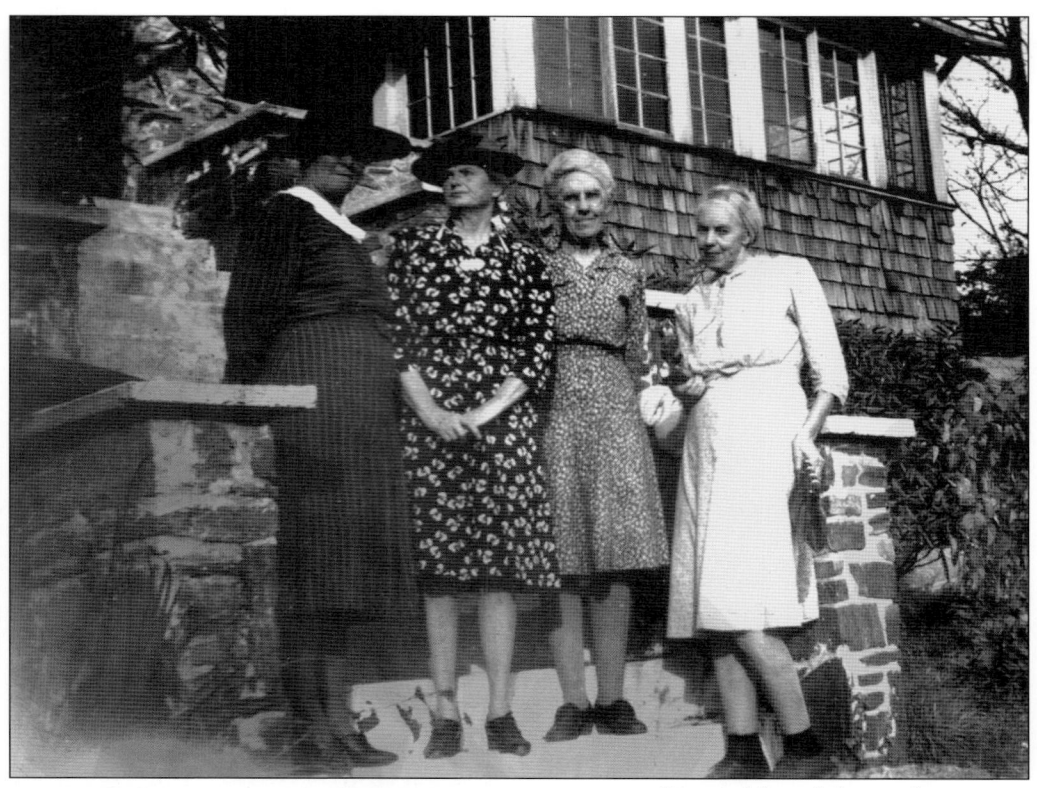

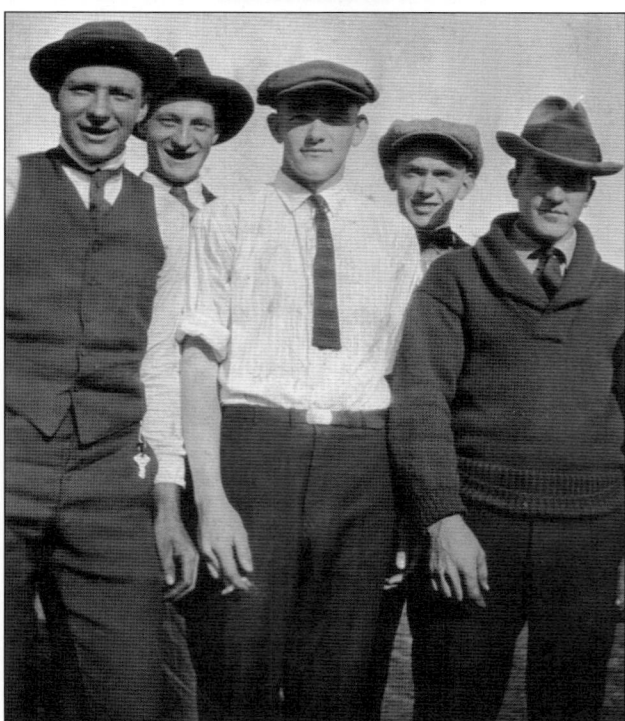

Pictured from left to right are friends Maude Hollifield, Emily Butler, Ethel Hakes, and Jane McKinney. Hakes came from Winter Park, Florida, and she is shown with Maude, who was Nancy Buchanan's granddaughter; Emily, Nancy's daughter-in-law; and Jane, Nancy's daughter. Emily Butler was well known for her delicious buttermilk. (Courtesy of Greg S. Burnette.)

Sporting their Sunday best, the local boys seen here from left to right are Jack Burnette, Pete (Plato) Burnette, Warner McKinney, Ine Burnette, and Lester McKinney. They held many positions in the community, with Jack and Pete serving as deacons at the Chestnut Grove Baptist Church. (Courtesy of Greg S. Burnette.)

84

Pictured are Ethel Hollifield (left) and Effie Snipes McKinney as young women. These two cousins spent nearly a century in Little Switzerland, living in the Chestnut Grove Church area. Each was well known to summer residents. Effie was a devoted, lifelong member of Chestnut Grove Baptist Church. (Courtesy of Betty Mace.)

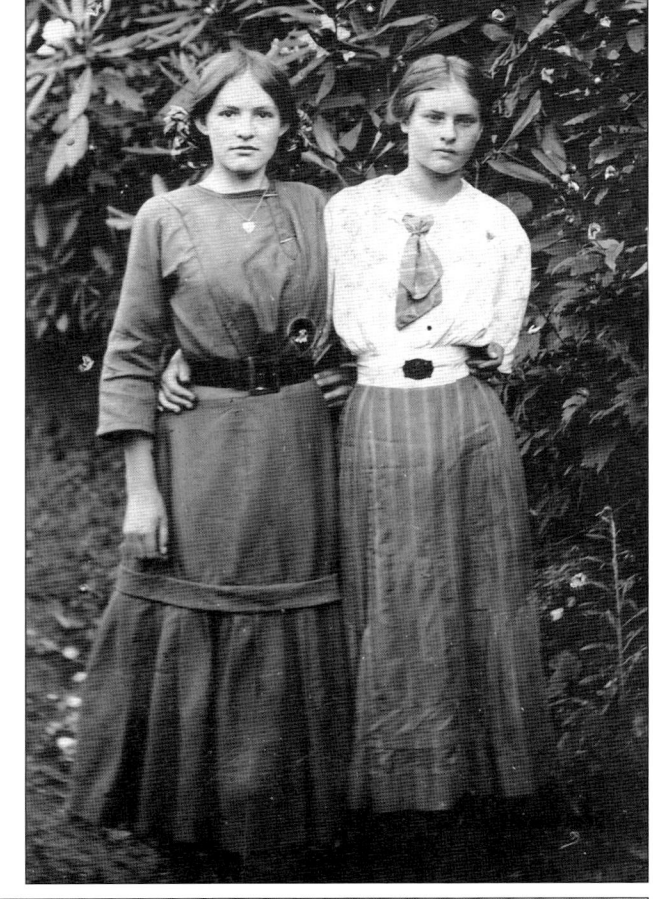

Below, the McKinney and Hakes families enjoy an outing at Wiseman's View with Hawksbill Mountain in the distance, overlooking the Linville Gorge. Summer residents and local families often enjoyed outings to nearby natural wonders together. Pictured from left to right are Ruby McKinney, Elise Hakes, Earl, Effie, and Betty McKinney. (Courtesy of Ruby Buchanan.)

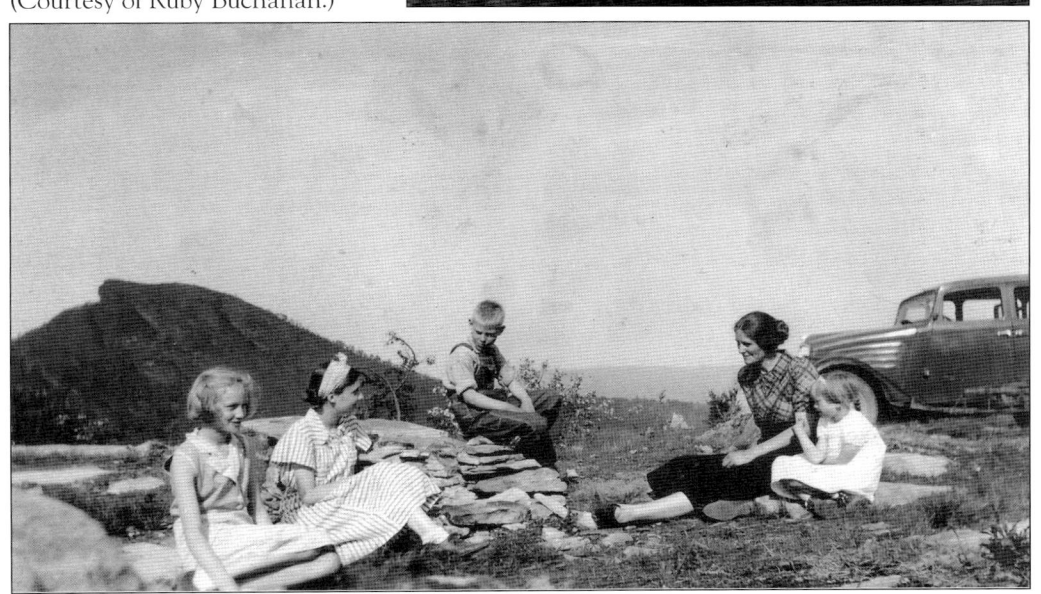

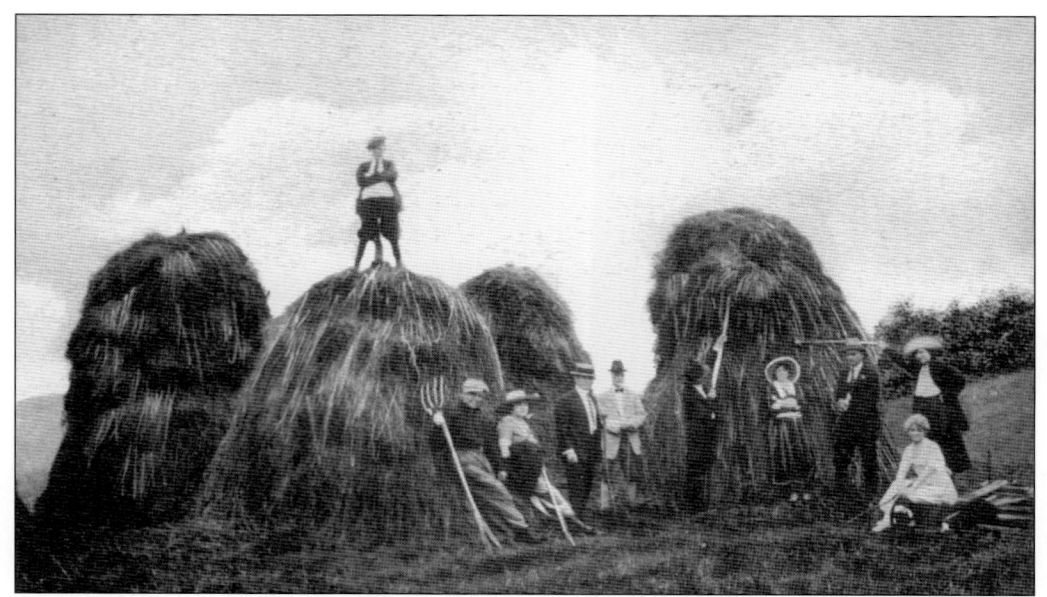

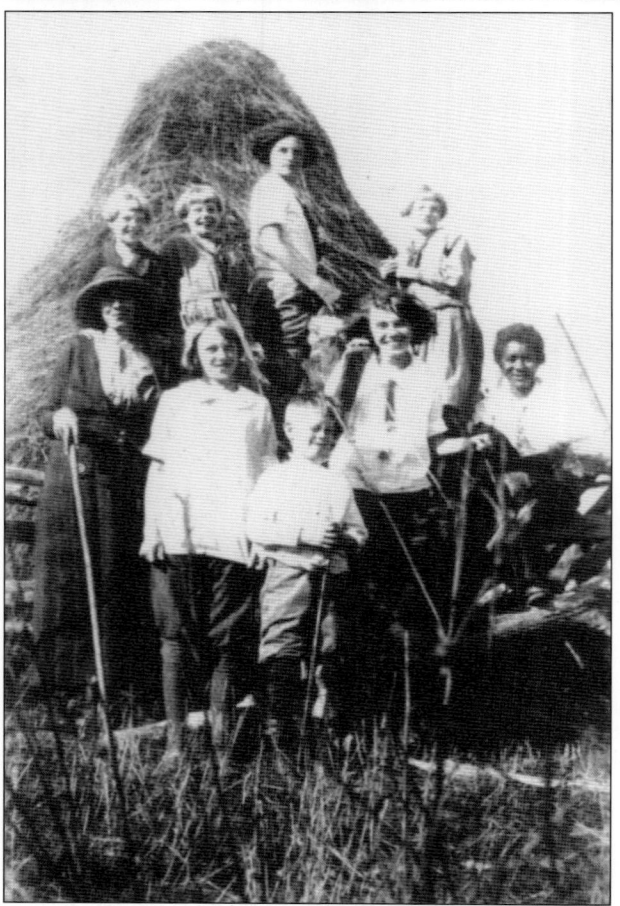

A common scene each autumn was the harvesting and storage of hay in great shocks in the field. Using sickles, the hay was cut and dried. Then, using pitchforks, the stacks were created. Neighbors and friends gathered to help put up the hay, which was used for animal feed in the winter. At left, a group of local and summer residents gather in the hay field for a photograph. Pictured here are, from left to right, (first row) Jane McKinney, Ida Jones McKinney, Buddy Hand, Dot ? and Tobitha ?; (second row) Edith Rae McKinney, Mildred McKinney, Harriet Hand, and Thelma Ann McKinney. (Above photograph courtesy of Davis and Jann Godwin; left courtesy of Pat Mitchell.)

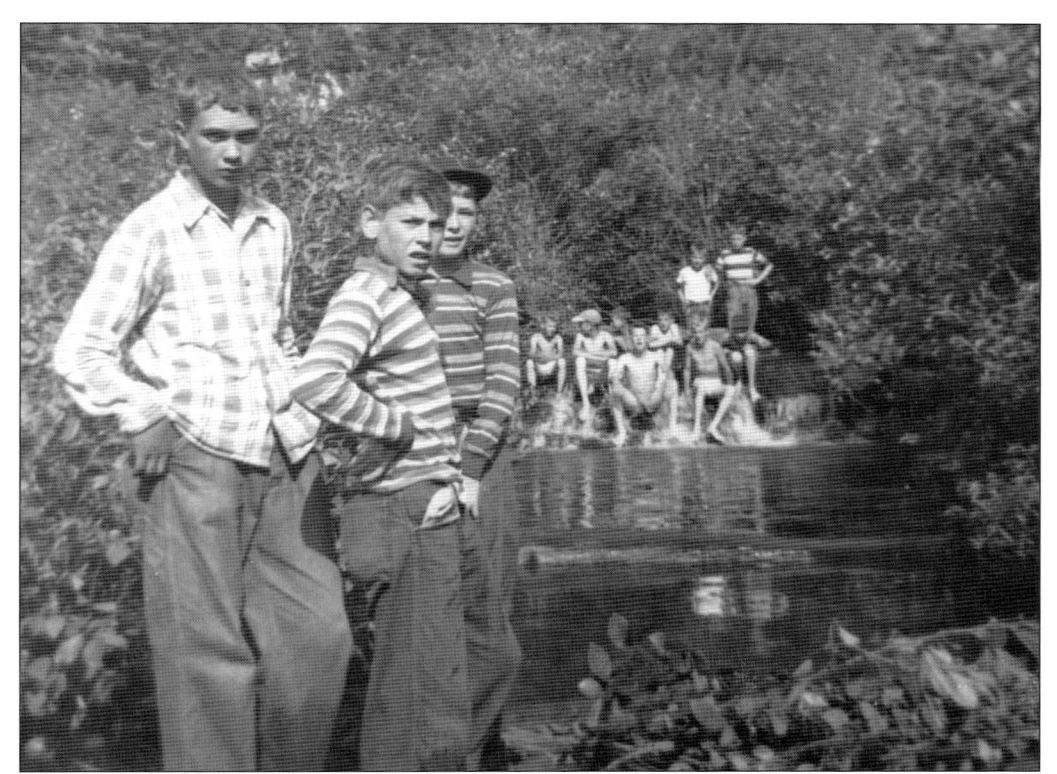

From left to right, Walter Self, Eddie Hollifield, and Fred Ray Self join other boys at the old Mill Pond, located where Lake Laurel is today. An afternoon swim was the perfect way on warm summer days to relax and cool off. (Courtesy of Hugh Glenn.)

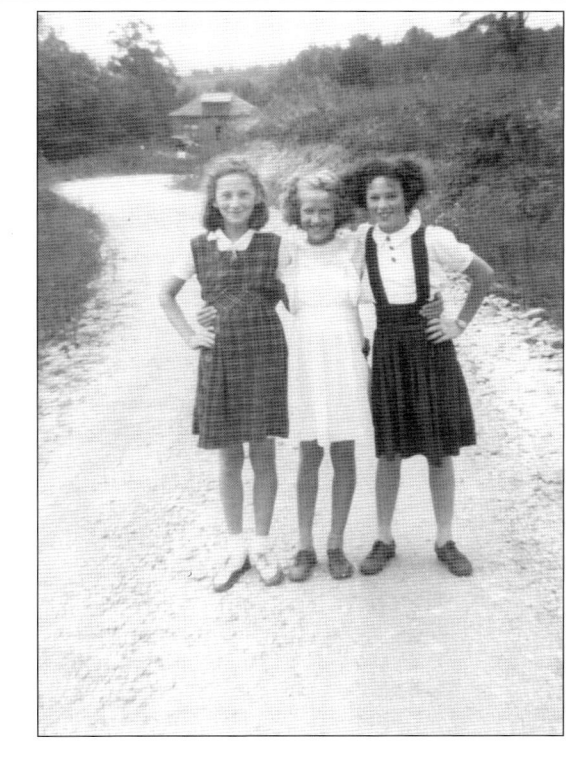

From left to right, Margie Mace, Betty Glenn, and Lillian Ballew enjoy a walk down a country road, seeking out fun and adventure on a lazy summer afternoon. Childhood friendships form lasting bonds that stand the test of time. (Courtesy of Tommy and Lillian Hollifield.)

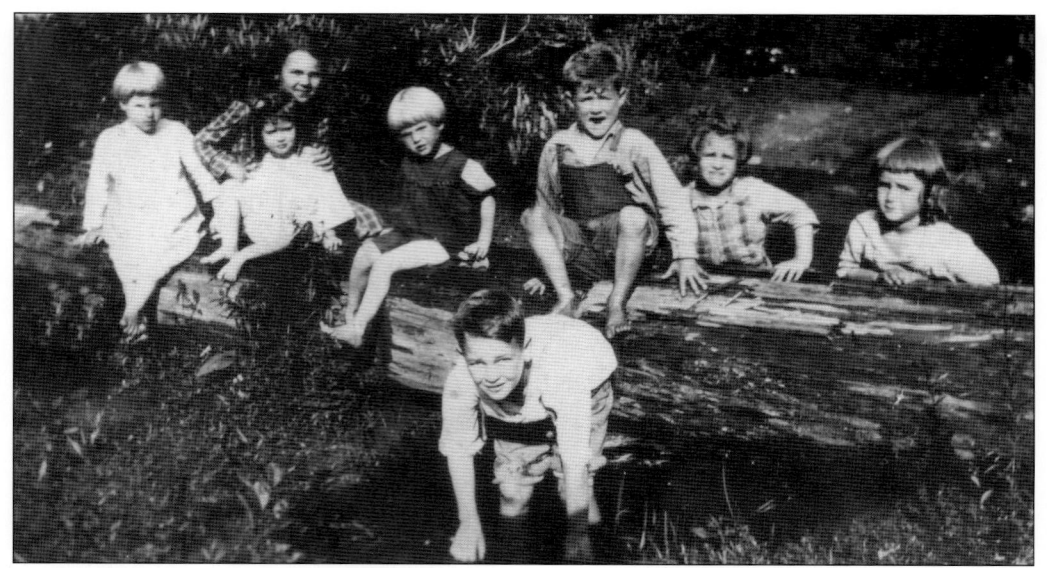

Children of both summer residents and local families often gathered for playtime in the creek and the woods. Pictured here from left to right are Mildred McKinney, Rosalie Avery, an unidentified child, Edith Rae McKinney, Dubose Avery, Isaac Avery, and two more unidentified children. (Courtesy of Pat Mitchell.)

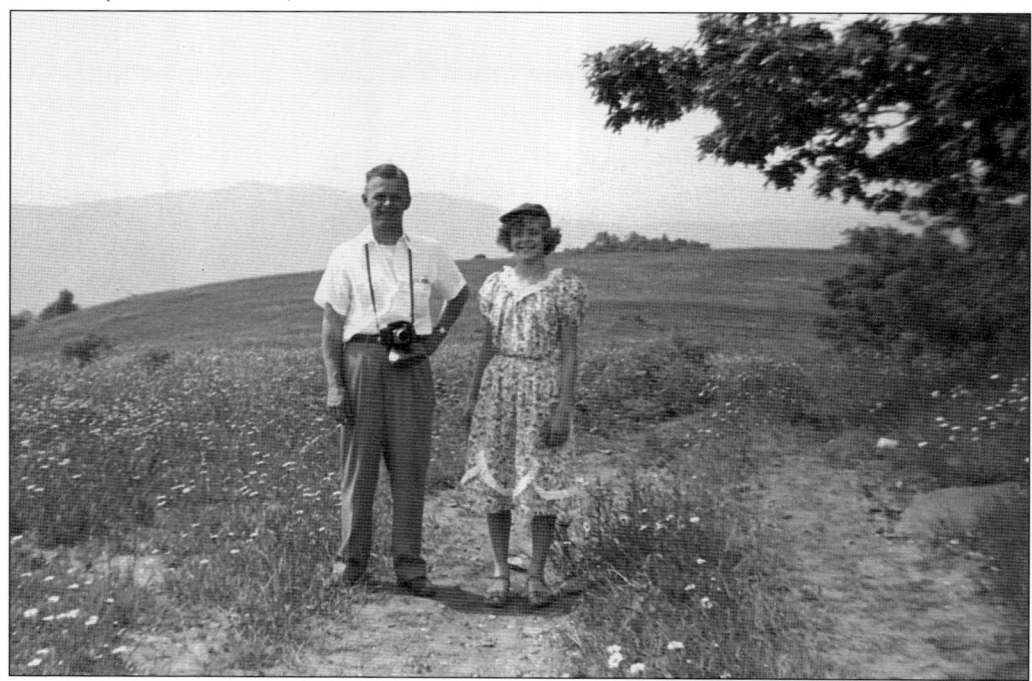

Grassy Mountain was a popular destination in the summers, when cool breezes wafted through the meadows. It was renamed Clarkson's Knob in Judge Clarkson's honor, and the Kilmichael Tower was constructed at its summit. Charles Dwight Cathcart poses with his daughter Coles Heyward Cathcart on the road to the top. Today much of the meadow has been overgrown by trees. (Courtesy of Coles Jackson.).

Nellie Waycaster felt the call of patriotism when her brother Nick left for World War II, and she volunteered for service in the U.S. Navy WAVES. Seeing tours of duty in World War II and in Korea, Nellie later worked in the Pentagon, then entered the Naval Reserves while working for the U.S. Postal Service in Charlotte. She penned several historical documents about Little Switzerland. (Courtesy of Chris Hollifield.)

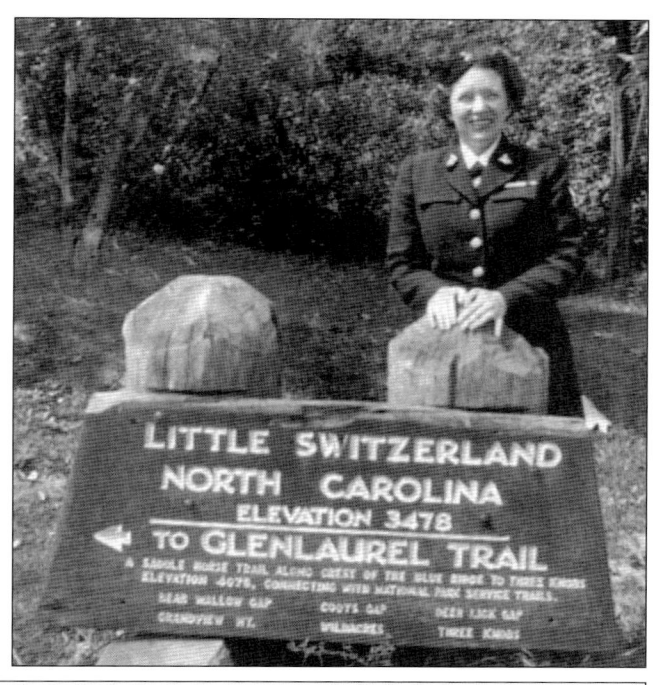

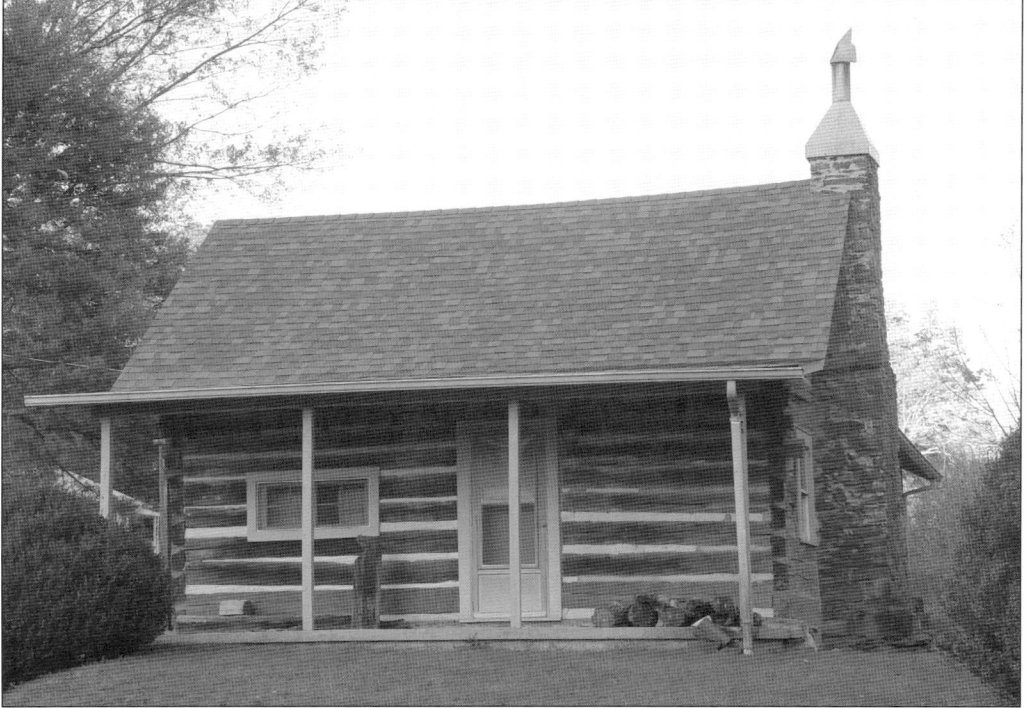

The John Collis cabin, built in 1877, stands near Lake Laurel. John was wounded, captured, and imprisoned in the Civil War. He was a mild-mannered farmer. Great-granddaughter Nellie Waycaster renovated the cabin in the late 1980s. Chestnut Grove Baptist Church traces its roots to a meeting in this cabin. (Courtesy of David Biddix.)

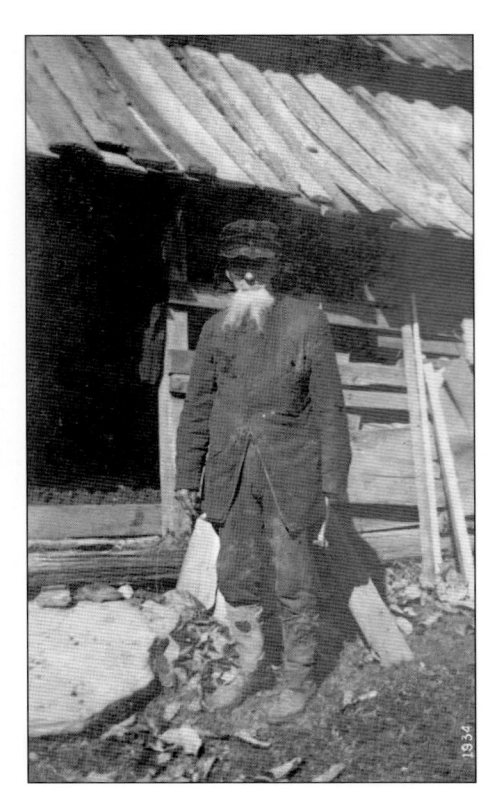

Sam Cresawn was known locally as the Snake Man. He concocted and sold a cure-all for tuberculosis made of rattlesnakes that he caught and cut up, mixing the parts with whiskey. He was a hermit who wouldn't use paper money, preferring a small stash of gold. He lived off of black walnuts in a small cabin pictured below, 9 miles from Little Switzerland on the Marion Road. (Both courtesy of Robert and Cama Merritt.)

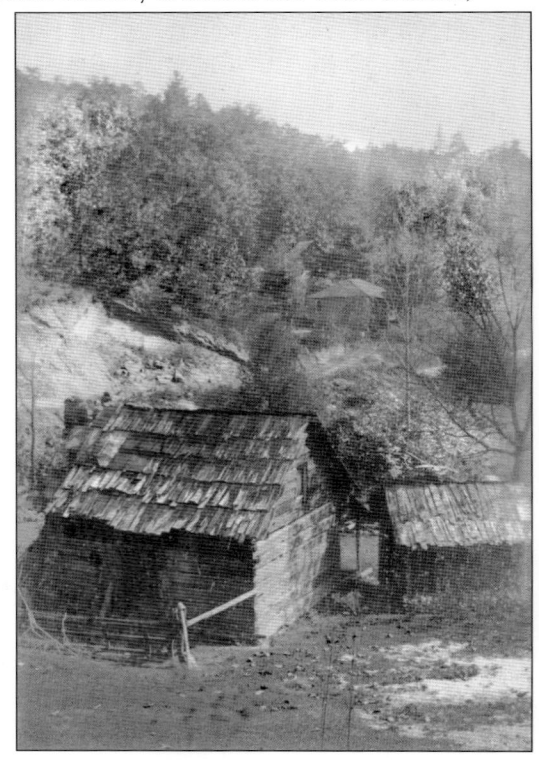

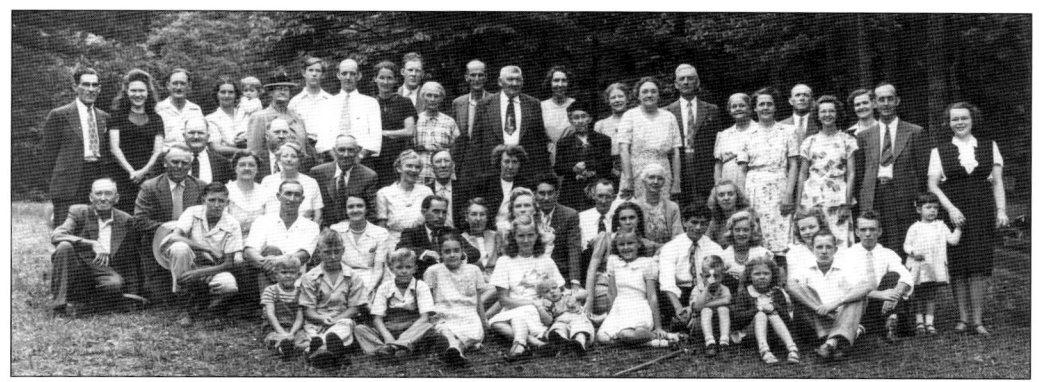

Decoration days are held each year at the various family and church cemeteries. In this mountain tradition, relatives meet to remember departed family members and to enjoy fellowship, preaching, singing, and dinner on the grounds. This photograph from the 1940s shows a gathering at the Collis Cemetery, held each year on the first Sunday in August. Today decorations continue to be an important part of family life in the mountains. (Courtesy of Lloyd Glenn.)

The men of the summer colony embarked on a camping trip to Mount Mitchell July 24–26, 1913. They pose by the monument to Elisha Mitchell atop the mountain. They are, from left to right T. J. Davis, J. B. Cannon, O. B. Robinson, Edward Scholtz, William A. Avant, J. R. Van Ness, S. W. Davis, M. R. Davis, Francis Clarkson, Clark Jones, and W. D. Perry. (Courtesy of Mike Queen.)

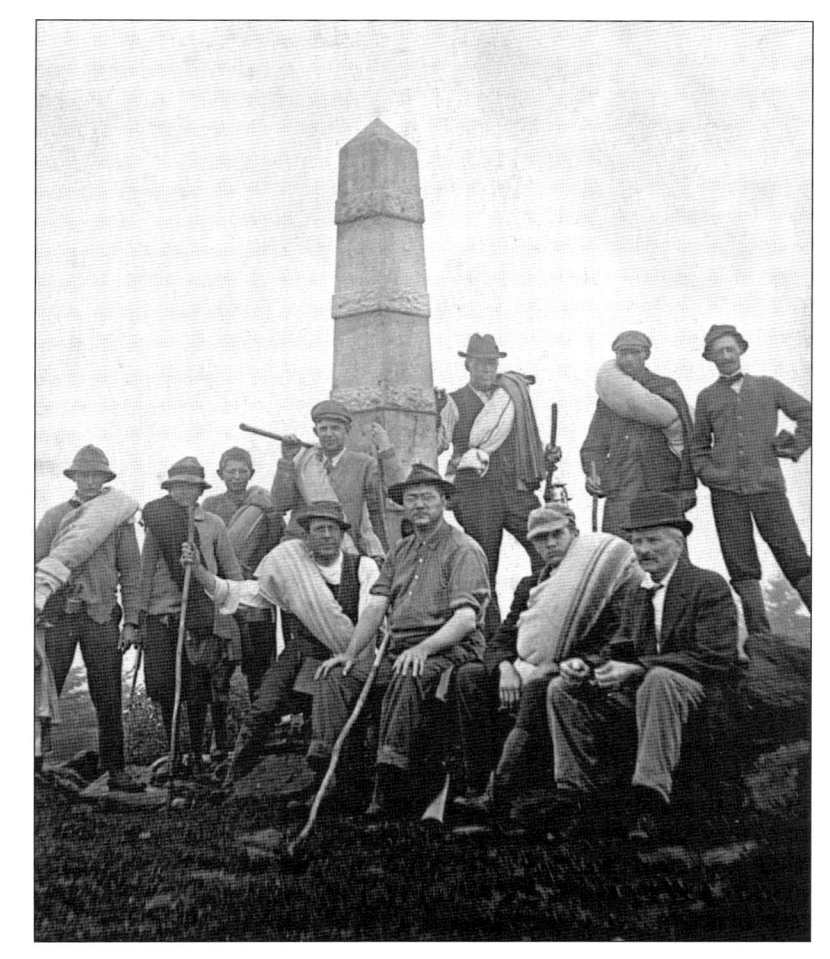

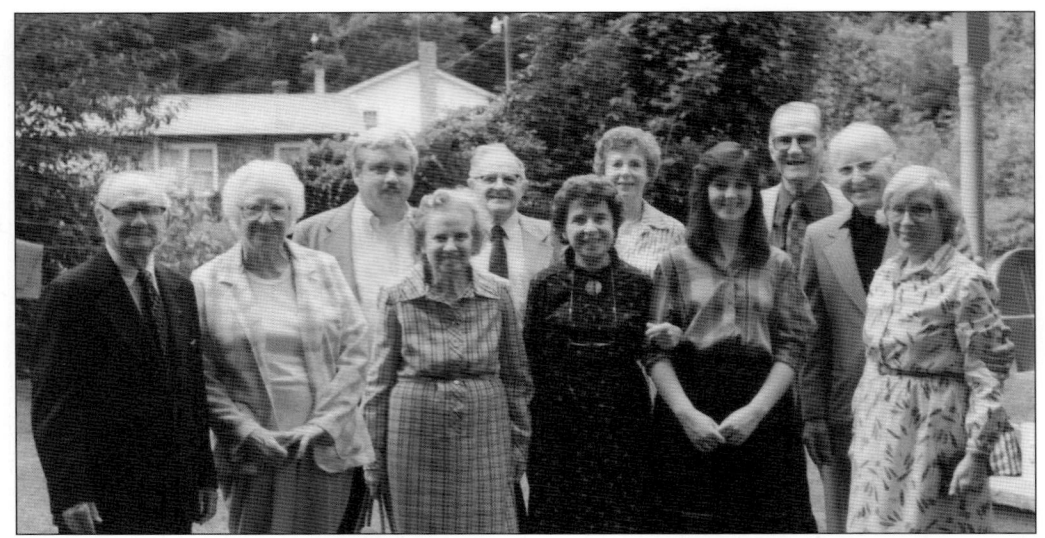

Residents of Laurel Lane gather for a portrait on a summer afternoon in the early 1980s. From left to right are (first row) Judge Francis Clarkson, Kathleen Fink, Cama Clarkson, Betty Ball, Helen Lane, Arthur Fink, and Betty Baird; (second row) Eugene Lane, Ken Ball, Patsy Miller, and Bud Miller. (Courtesy of Dr. Stan Black.)

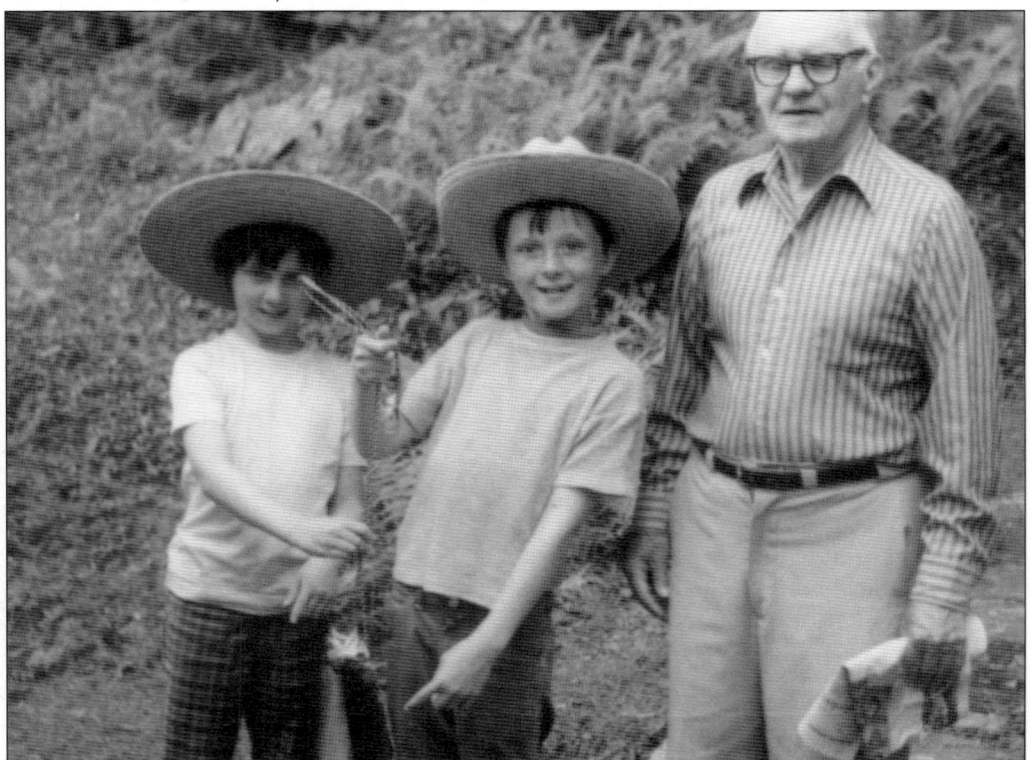

Judge Francis Clarkson and Helen and Michael Lane enjoy an afternoon of fishing. Clarkson was an avid fly fisherman and could be found frequenting the local fishing holes whenever he had the chance. (Courtesy of Dr. Stan Black.)

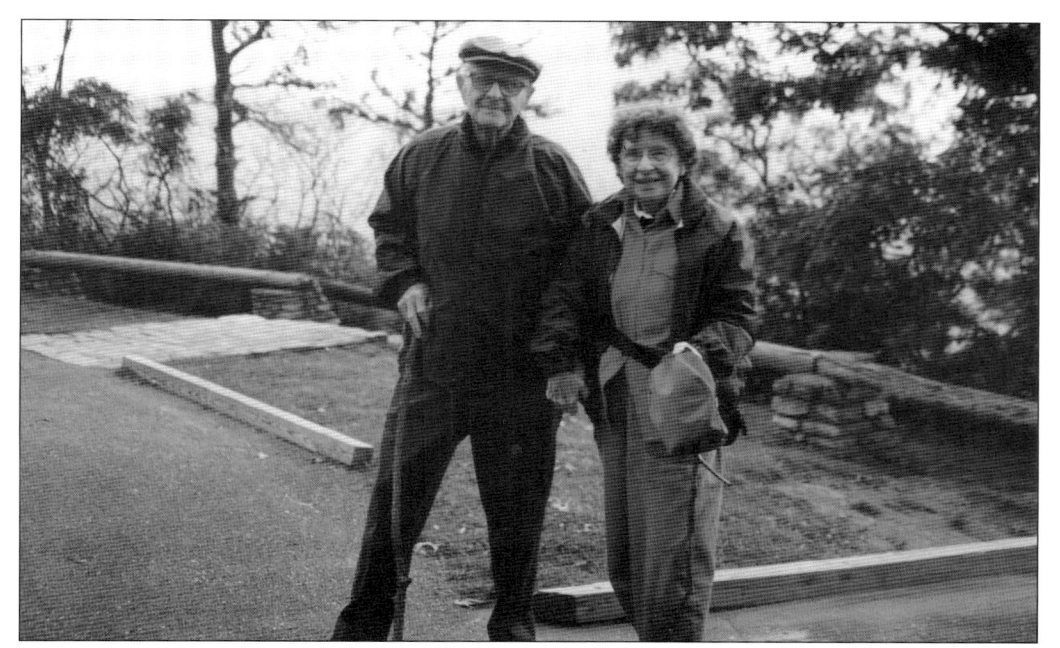

Ken and Betty Ball were well-known summer residents. Ken was a retired park ranger and was legendary for his presentations on wildflowers. He also served on the board of directors for the Switzerland Company. He lived to be 102 years old. Betty is an active member of the Church of the Resurrection. (Courtesy of Dr. Stan Black.)

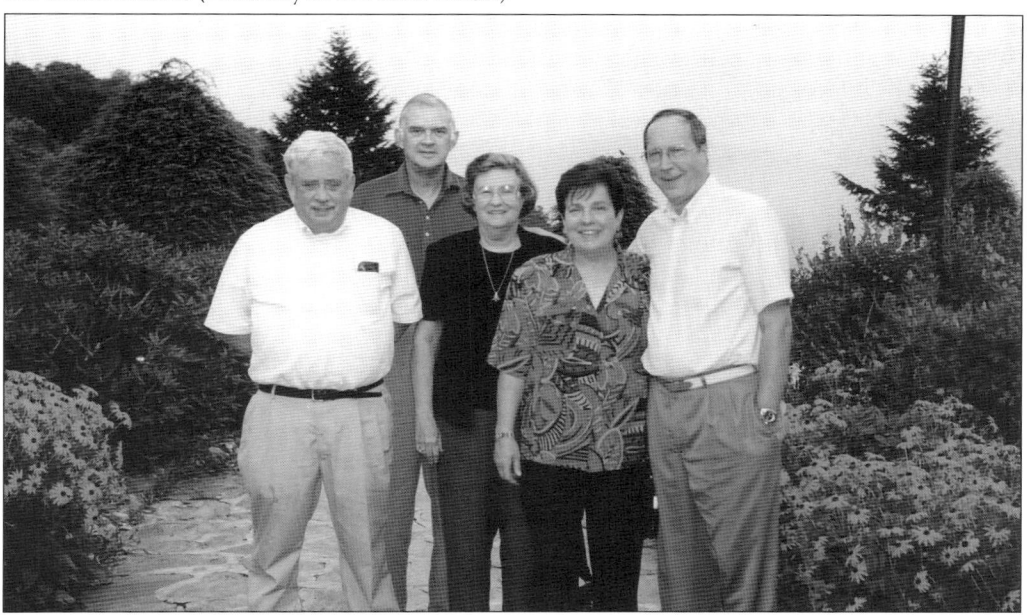

Little Switzerland has close ties with UNC–Chapel Hill. Harriet Morehead Berry, who worked at the university, built Laurel Ledge Cottage, which her sister Mary Brown and husband Dr. Kent Brown inherited. Other UNC professors followed the Browns to Laurel Lane; several live there today. Pictured from left to right are Eugene Lane, Charles Dickinson, Bev Dickinson, Roberta Black, and Stan Black. (Courtesy of Dr. Stan Black.)

93

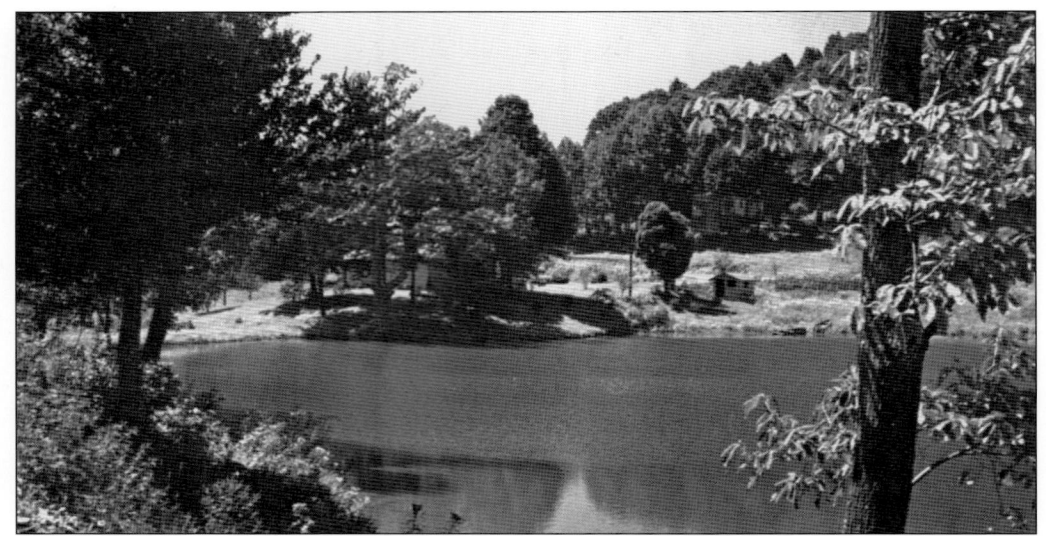

Lake Laurel is on Chestnut Grove Road near the location of the original Phenoy Post Office, which served the region in the late 1800s. Robert McKinney's gristmill was also located nearby. Quince Collis began as a housing development in 1959. Fishing, swimming, and canoeing are popular pastimes. (Courtesy of the North Carolina Collection, Pack Memorial Public Library, Asheville, North Carolina.)

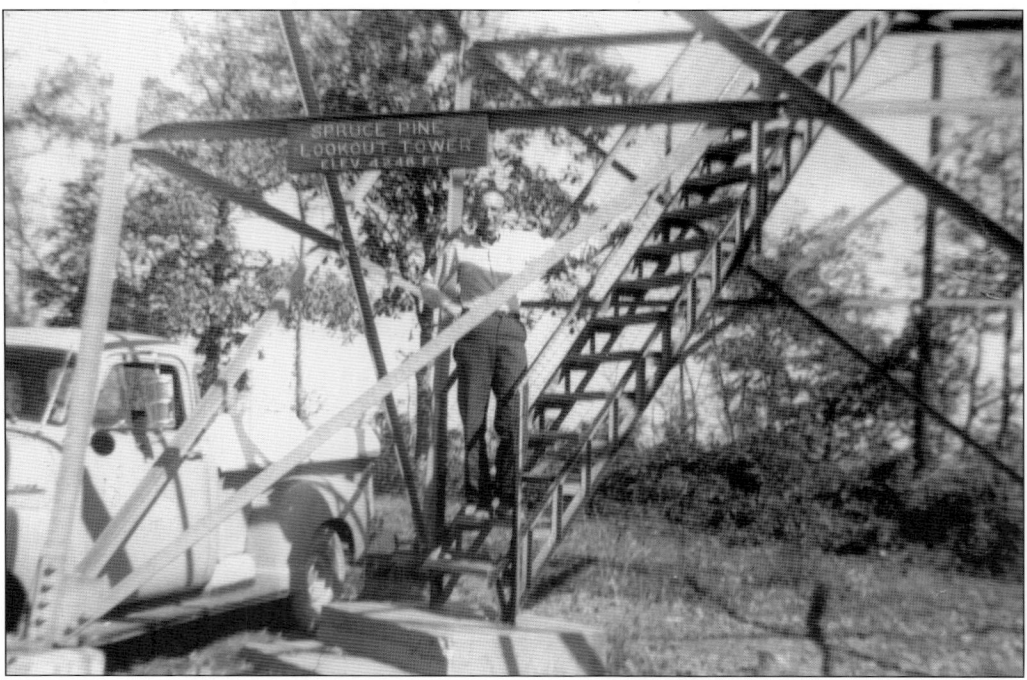

The Spruce Pine Lookout Tower was constructed in 1958 on Woody's Knob (Charlie Woody Mountain) as part of the Forest Service's efforts to detect woodland fires. It was manned from April to October by observers who lived on the mountain. Eddie McGee is pictured ascending to the observation deck shortly after the tower opened. Today it is unmanned but serves as a communications transmission facility. (Courtesy of Chris Hollifield.)

Summer residents and locals often visit each other, and many become lifelong friends. Here, Coles Jackson (rear left), visits with Frank Smith (rear right), Bessie Smith (front left) and Verdie Mae Cox (front right). Verdie Mae is well known for her flower gardens, which summer residents make a point of visiting each year. Below, Judge Francis Clarkson enjoys a laugh with Bessie Smith. Bessie was known for her quilting and quality canned foods. (Right courtesy of Coles Jackson; below courtesy of Robert and Cama Merritt.)

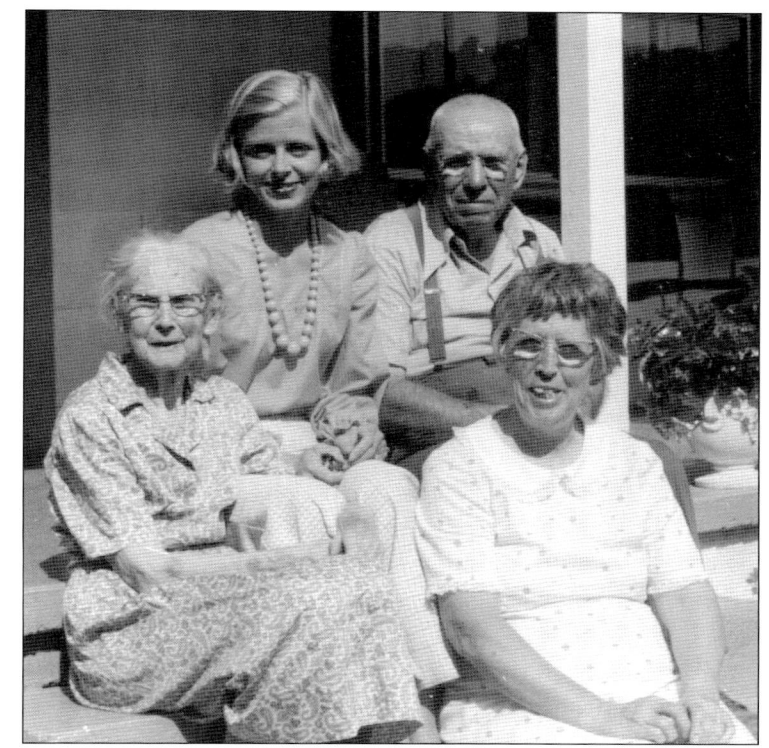

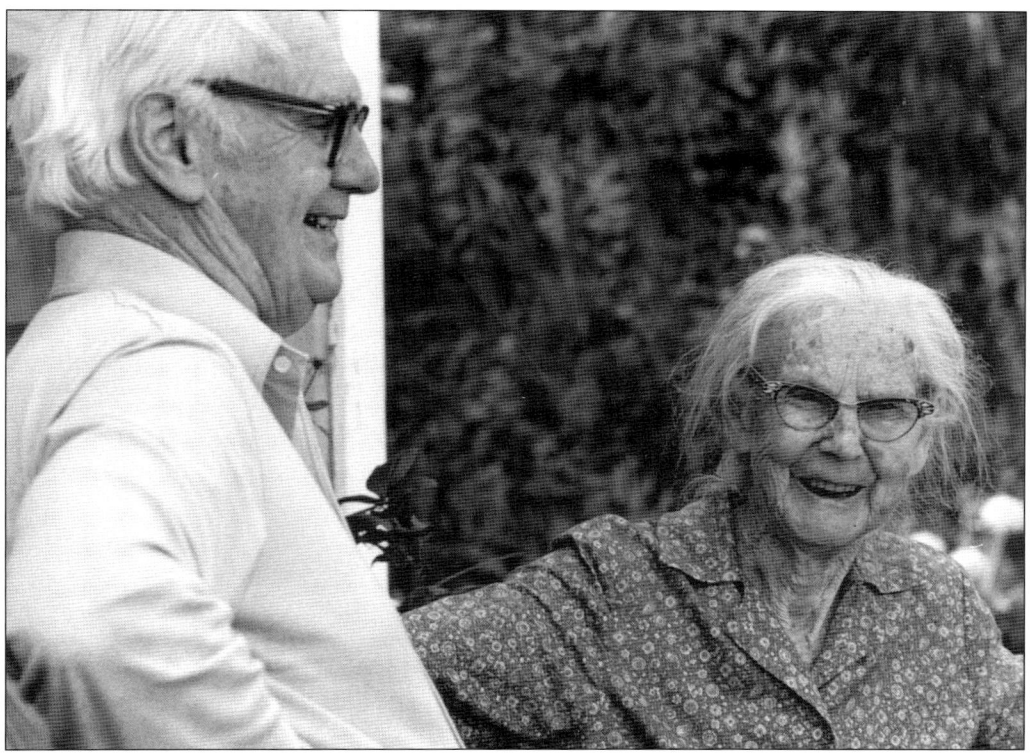

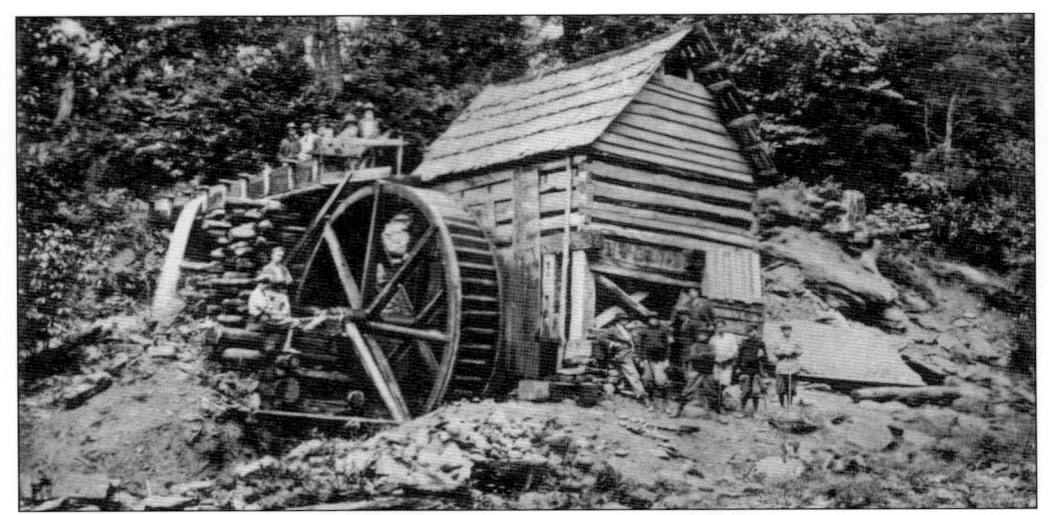

The gristmill was the social center of many communities in the 1800s and early 1900s. Residents would catch up on news and socialize while waiting their turn. The miller would normally keep a portion of whatever was milled as payment for grinding the corn. Robert McKinney owned this mill, located near current Lake Laurel in Little Switzerland. (Courtesy of Ruby Buchanan.)

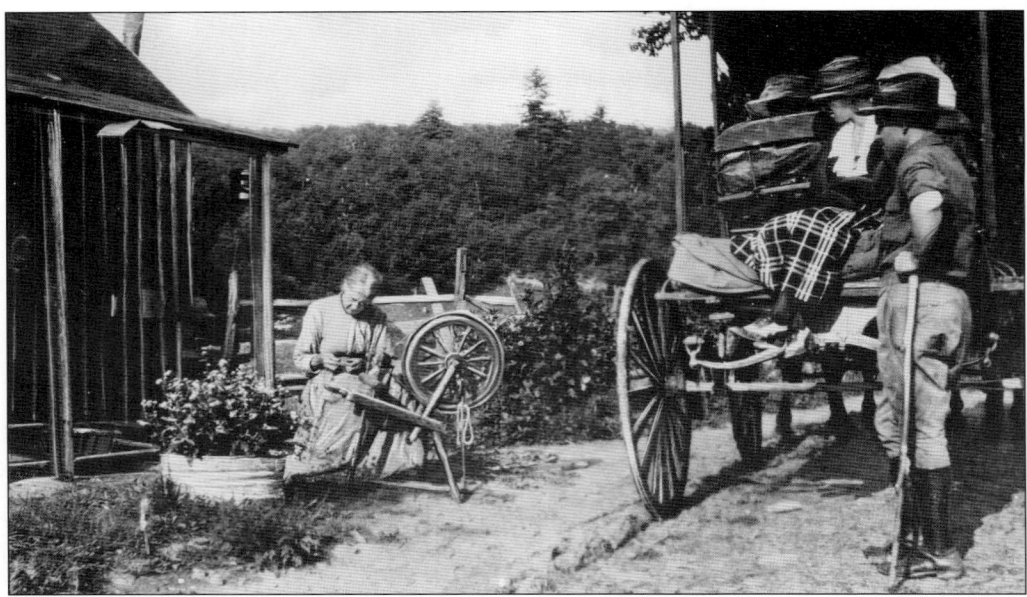

Spinning was an important part of family life to the hardy pioneer settlers, as they had to provide for their own subsistence. Using wool and flax, it provided much-needed materials for clothing. Visitors look on as an unidentified woman works her wheel in front of her home. (Courtesy of the North Carolina Collection, UNC–Chapel Hill.)

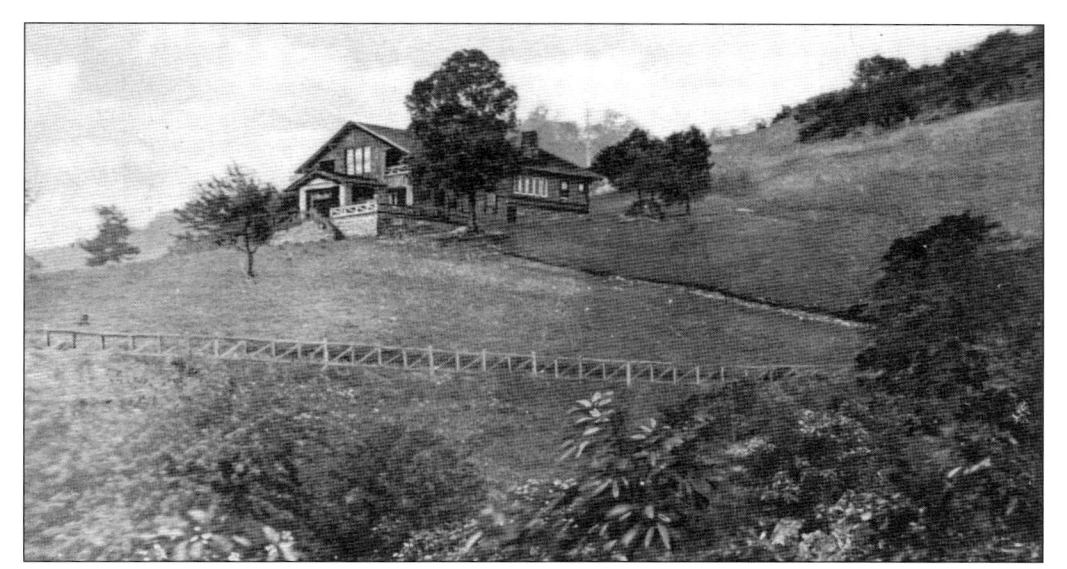

The most substantial cottage constructed in the community was the E. T. Cansler home on the side of Grassy Mountain. An imposing two-story structure, the Cansler home was one of the first built in the colony (being constructed in 1911). It was made of lumber from 300 chestnut trees. The view from the house of the southeast was most impressive, and it could be seen from miles away. It had a Delco electrical system, one of the first in the community. The house caught fire and burned to the ground in 1976 and was replaced by another cottage that enjoys the same majestic view. (Above courtesy of Davis and Jann Godwin; below courtesy of Carrie Washburn.)

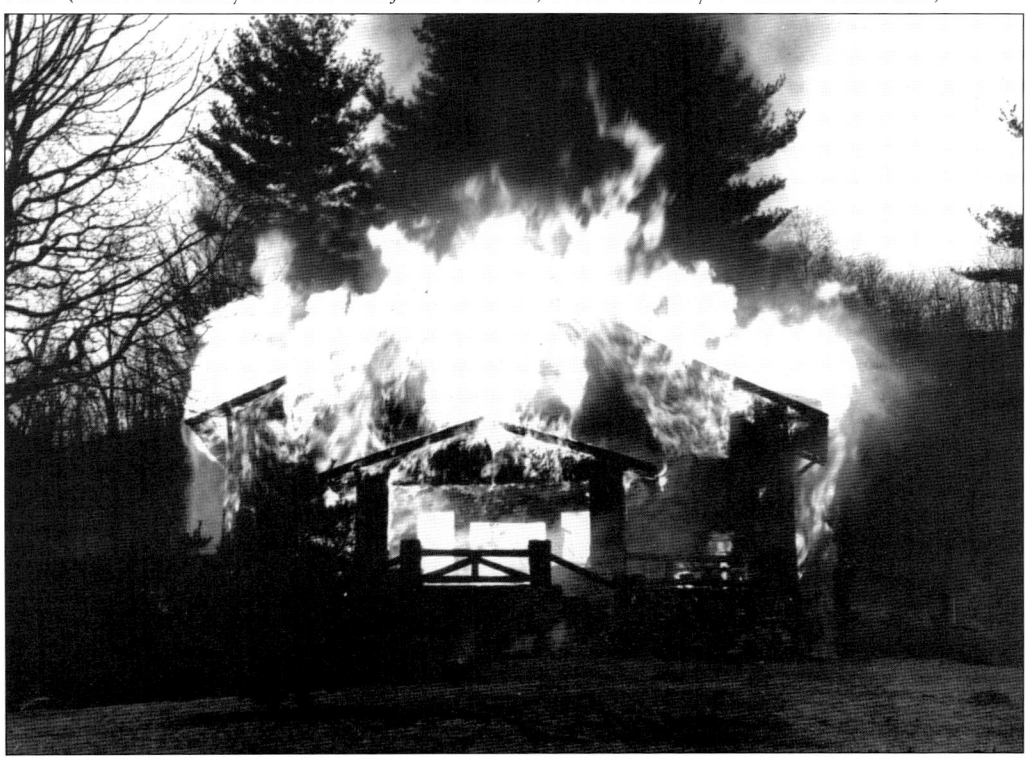

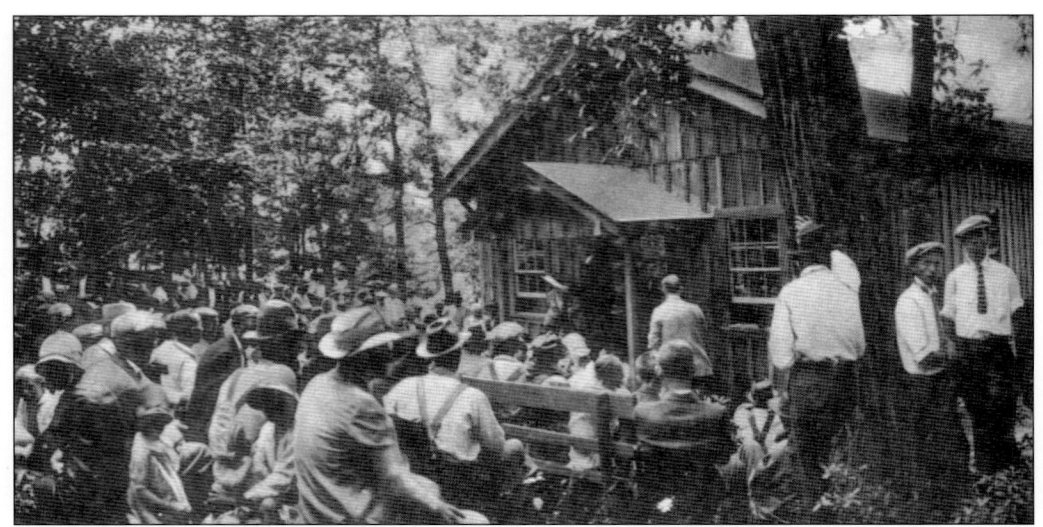

Geneva Hall opened August 1, 1928, with speeches by ex-governor Cameron Morrison on the League of Nations and R. O. Everett on the World Court. The Women's Guild of the Church of the Resurrection spearheaded the drive to build a community center that was named for Geneva, Switzerland. Originally located on land acquired for the Blue Ridge Parkway, it was moved uphill to a new tract and was replaced in 1959. (Courtesy of Mike Queen.)

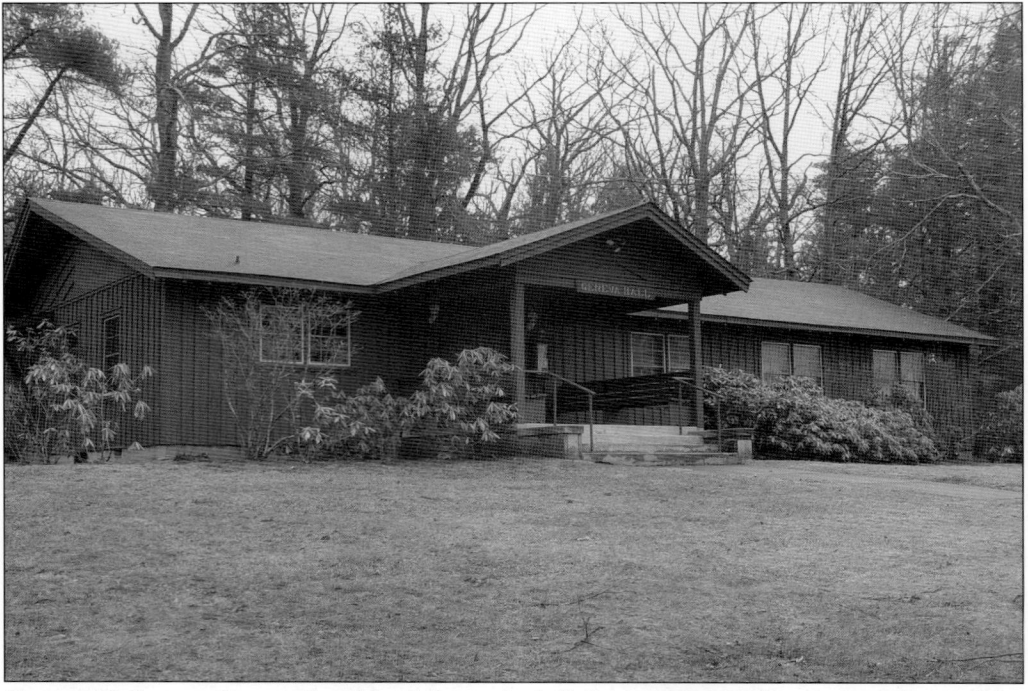

Geneva Hall started on a plot of land down the hill from its current location, in front of the present-day Little Switzerland Tunnel. It was relocated in the 1930s, and the original building was replaced with today's Geneva Hall in the early 1960s. Community events, family gatherings, wedding receptions, exhibitions, classes, and the famous square dance continue to make it an integral part of social life. (Courtesy of Marsha Biddix.)

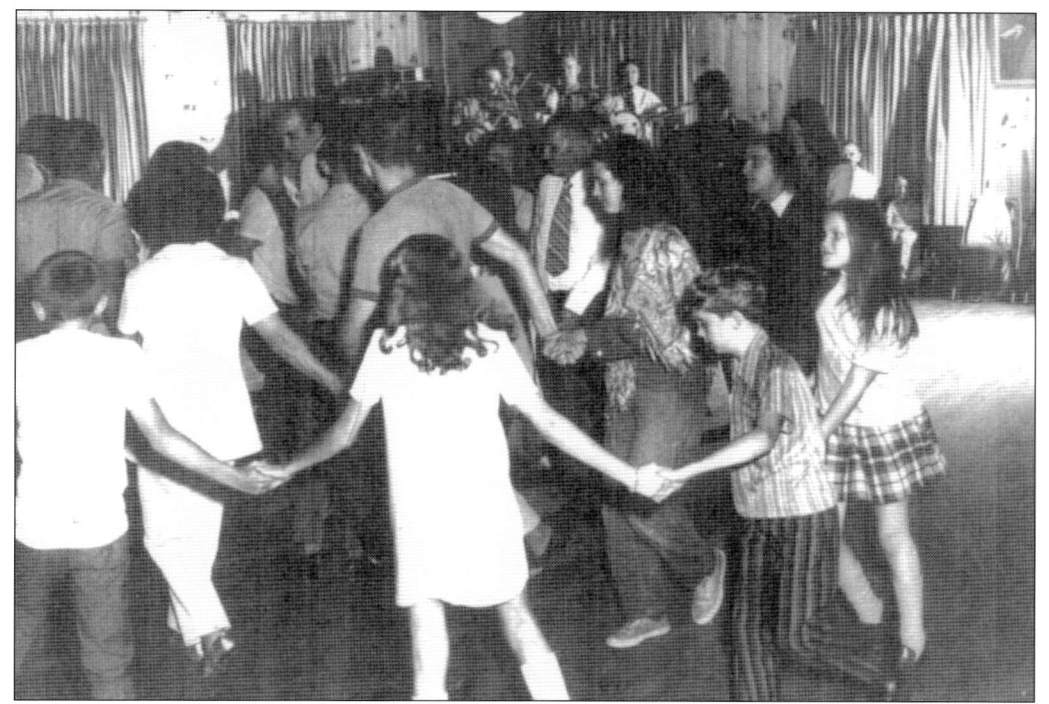

Geneva Hall has been the home of square dancing on Saturday nights for decades. North Carolina's oldest continuous square dance started modestly, with music being provided by phonographic record and piano, but starting in 1947, the Toe River Valley Boys (below, clockwise starting top left are E. C. Miller, Oscar "Red" Wilson, Clarence Greene, Gus Washburn, Cecil Burleson, and Charles Renfro) became a mainstay, providing the music through the 1970s. Today the dances are as popular as ever, and are held on Saturdays during the summer months. (Above courtesy of Bill and Judy Carson; below courtesy of Carrie Washburn.)

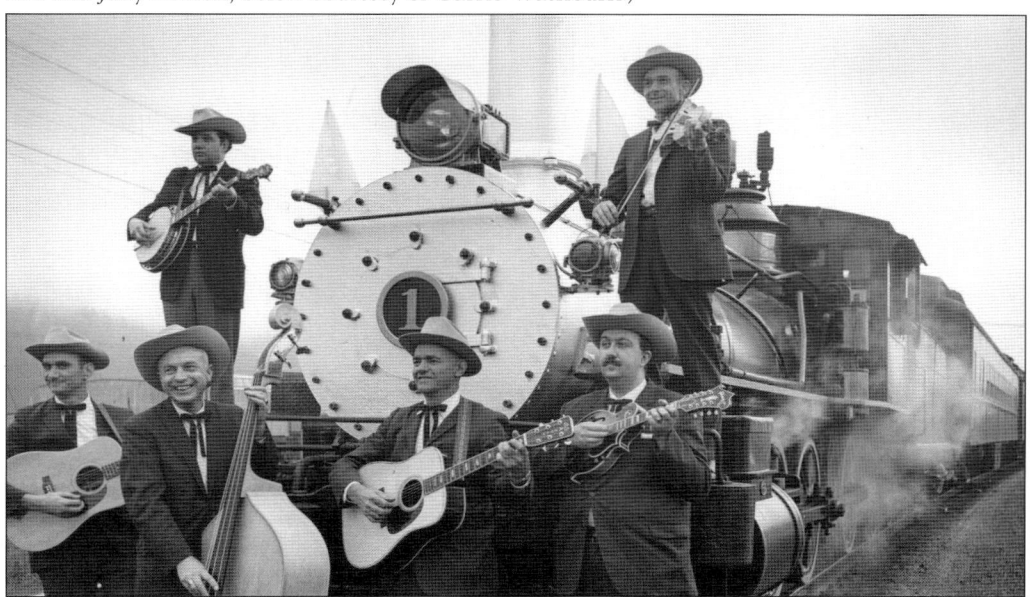

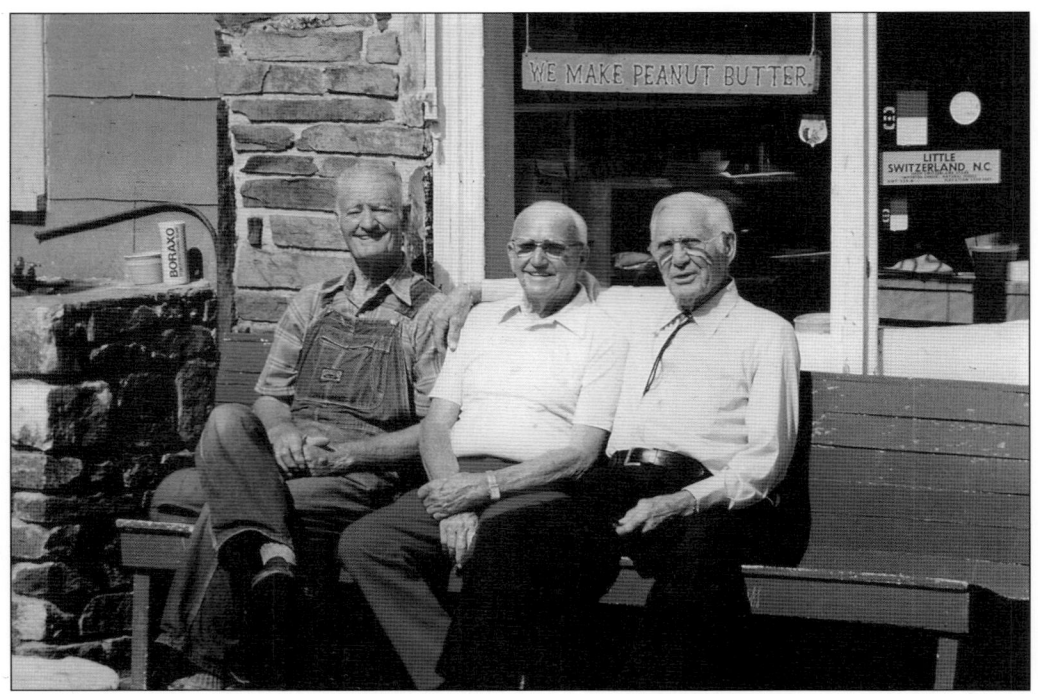

The Switzerland Store was the gathering place for community members to visit and socialize. Here, from left to right, Fred Self, Ralph Ramus, and Doc John Howell enjoy fellowship and the afternoon sun on the Liar's Bench in front of the store. (Courtesy of Eugene Self.)

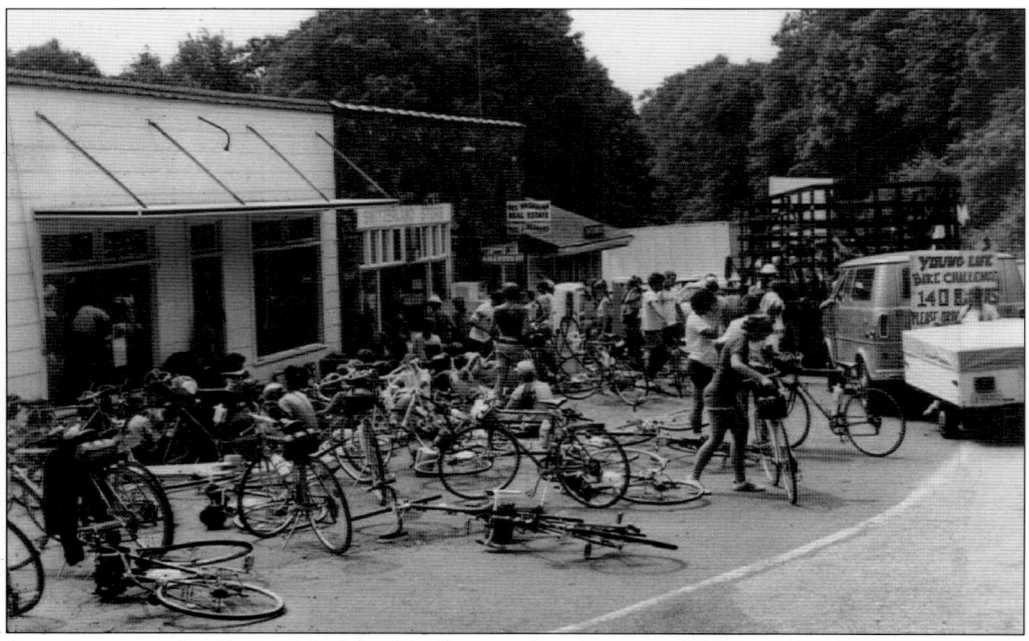

Participants in the Young Life Bike Challenge take a break at the Switzerland Store on July 16, 1974. The parkway is a popular route for cycling enthusiasts, and the Switzerland Store is a natural stopover for refreshments. (Courtesy of the National Park Service.)

Six

LIVING OFF THE LAND
MOTHER NATURE'S BOUNTY

From its earliest recorded history, Little Switzerland has been a source of beauty and riches. The origin of the Horse Stomp Mine below Rich Knob is lost in the mists of time, but ancient miners, long before the early settlers arrived, apparently found what they were looking for as they sunk a mine shaft some 700 feet in length but left no evidence of what they were mining. Some speculate that Hernando DeSoto or his men are responsible for the mine. Others feel that the Cherokees created it. As with the name of the mine, we may never know its true origin.

Mining, however, continued to be a major economic engine for the Little Switzerland area from the turn of the 20th century through the 1960s. The McKinney Mines, the Emerald Mine, and the Glenn Mine produced thousands of tons of feldspar that was hauled down Crabtree Creek on a "dinky line" railroad to the Carolina, Clinchfield, and Ohio main rail line at Wing in Mitchell County. When the quality of the ore diminished, the mines closed, leaving scars on the landscape to the present day. Some of the old mines are open to tourists for exploration and prospecting.

Tourism has always been a mainstay for Little Switzerland. From the 1910 opening of the original Switzerland Inn through today, visitors have made the community a destination for fun and relaxation year-round. Some have come here for a short visit, later deciding for more permanent ties with a place of their own. Real estate values have skyrocketed in recent years with a growing demand for summer and second homes on the mountain. Once again, the land is providing for residents, but in a new, unexpected way.

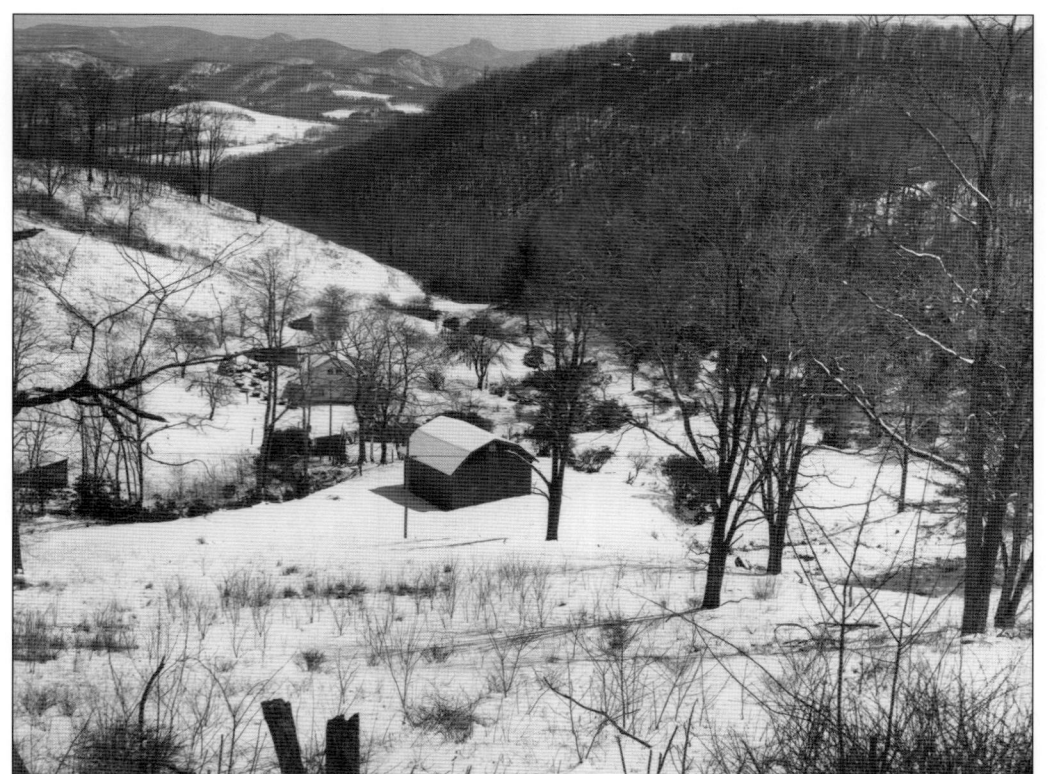

The Hollifield Farm appears snow-laden in this February 1972 photograph. Spoon Camp Road, one of the first paths into Little Switzerland, runs up the valley through the middle. Named for Peter Spoon of eastern North Carolina, who constructed a hunting lodge prior to the Civil War near the Switzerland Inn site, the road connected Grassy Creek and Chestnut Grove past Grassy Creek Falls. (Courtesy of the National Park Service.)

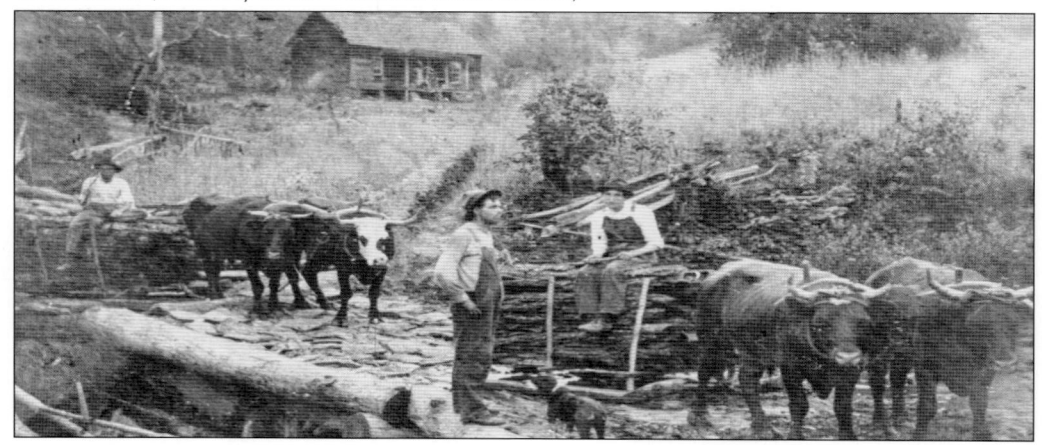

An occupation closely tied to logging was the tanbark industry. Bark from certain oak trees was combined with water to make tannin, which was used to dye leather. Other parts of the tree were used for building materials, particularly for the summer cottages. Here from left to right are Bob Burnette, Charlie Hollifield, and Jim Lowery hauling tanbark on the Marion Road in the Armstrong community. (Courtesy of John McKinney.)

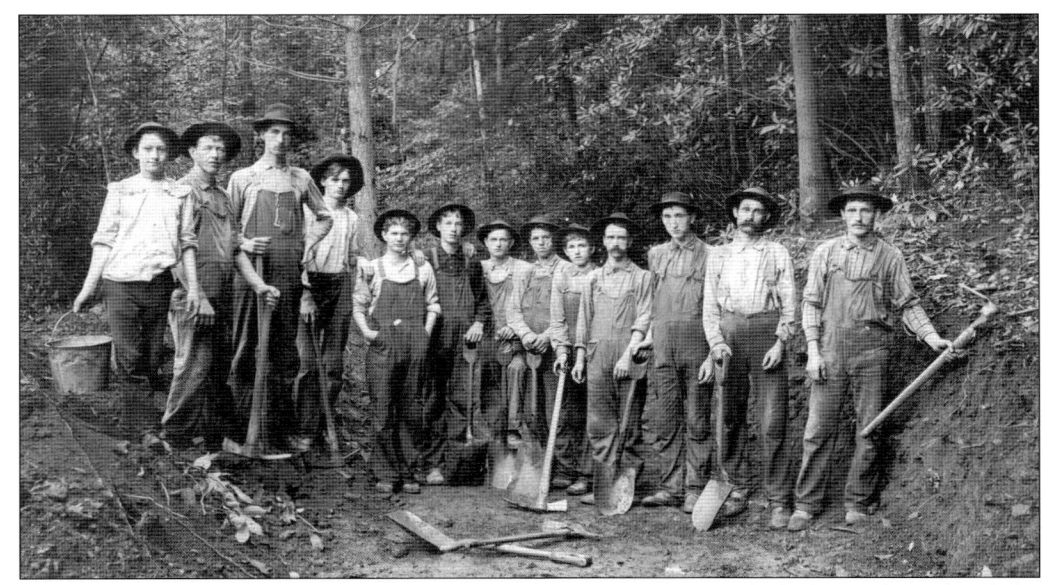

Wielding shovels and pickaxes, a crew working on the Armstrong dinky line takes a break for this picture, taken around 1910. From left to right, they are ? Eliotte, Elze Hollifield, Mansfield Lowery, Kelse Hoppes, Charlie King, Gudger Biddix, Ernest Bird, ? Eliotte, Oscar Elliotte, Asberry Biddix, Jim Lowery, Rom Hollifield, and unidentified. Narrow-gauge dinky railroads were run into the region to carry timber and mine ore. (Courtesy of John McKinney.)

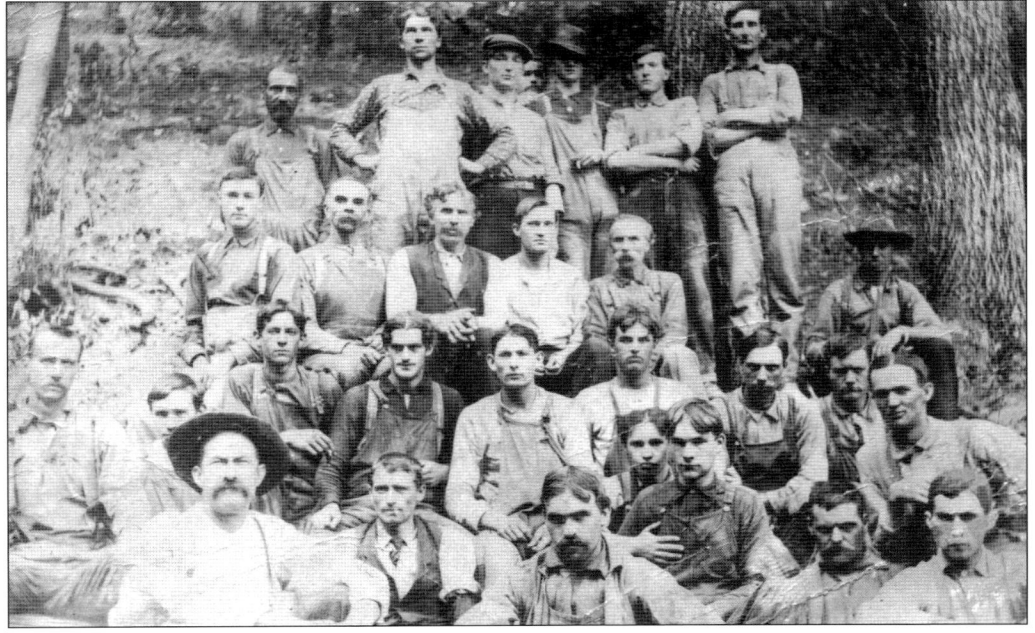

Logging was a profitable industry in the region in the early years. This camp of loggers in the Armstrong community around 1910 show the grit, determination, and hard work these men undertook to move the trees out of the then-virgin forest. Hillsides were extensively logged, with the trees being taken by dinky-line railways to sawmills, where they were processed. (Courtesy of John McKinney.)

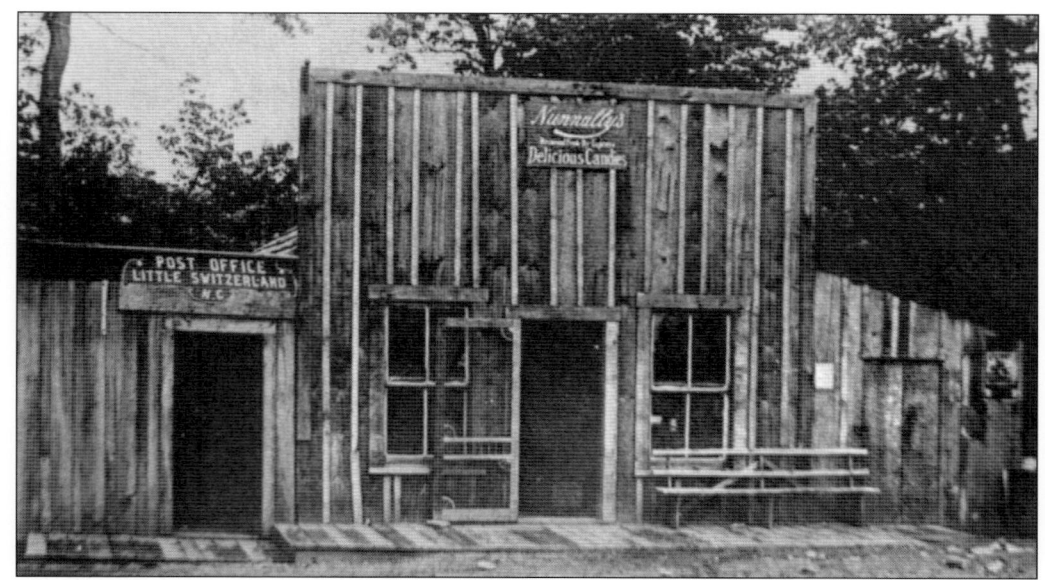

The original Switzerland Store and post office was located in this building on the site of the current Chalet Shops. It opened in 1913 and was the location of the first public telephone in Little Switzerland; Reid Queen later operated the store year-round for the community. He also ran the new store for a brief period in 1927. (Courtesy of Chris Hollifield.)

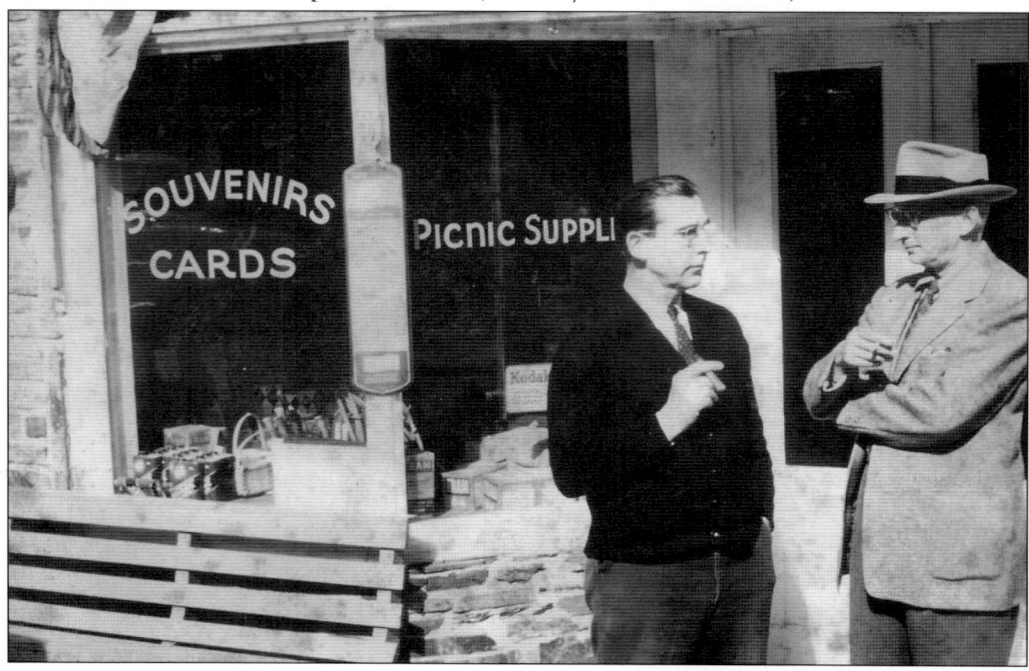

Pete Deal and Ken Norton enjoy conversation outside the Switzerland Store. Deal came to Little Switzerland in 1935, initially as a mining engineer, but was befriended by Judge Clarkson and later became proprietor of the Switzerland Store and postmaster for 33 years. He had a keen interest in the young people of the community. Norton was a frequent guest of the Switzerland Inn. (Courtesy of Ann Kernehan.)

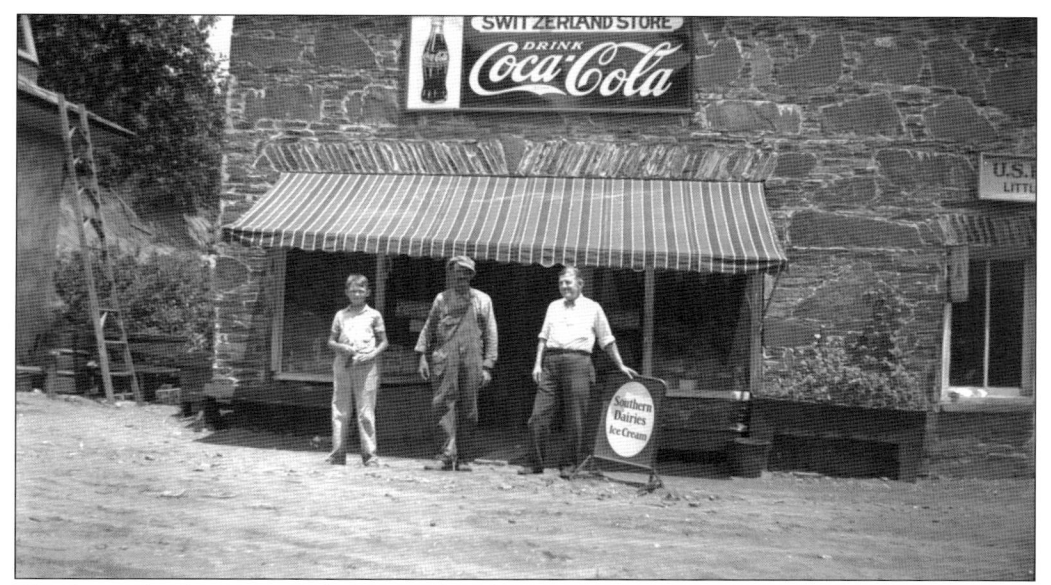

The Switzerland Store moved to a stone building on the Marion Road (currently North Carolina 226A) in 1927. Brevard Osborne, Judge Clarkson's brother-in-law, operated it until his death in a car accident in 1939. Pete Deal then operated it until the late 1970s. Pictured outside the store in 1933 are, from left to right, Reid Queen Jr., "Judge" John Jones, and Brevard Osborne. (Courtesy of Robert and Cama Merritt.)

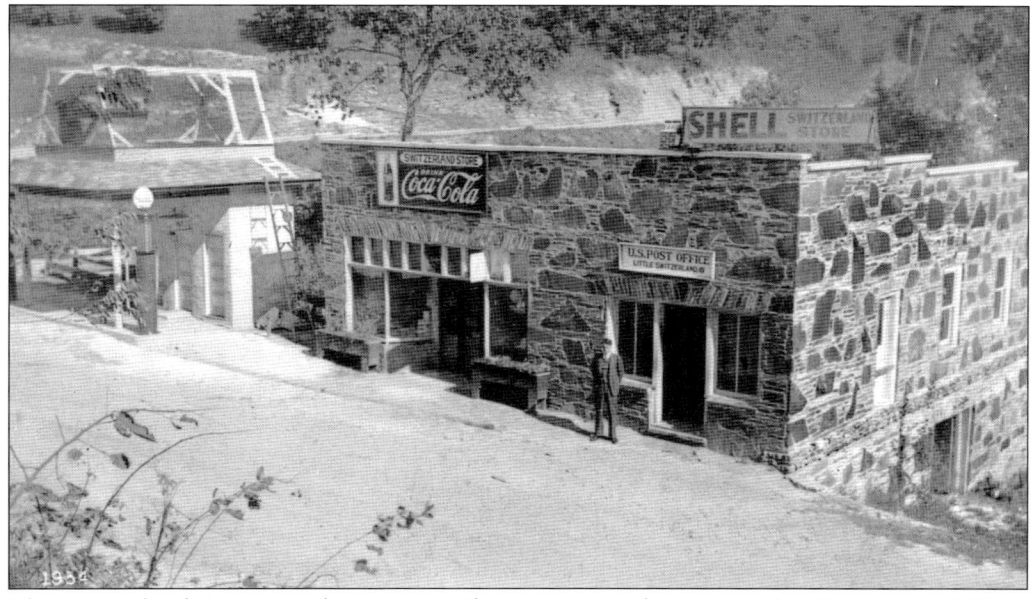

The Switzerland Store was the main retail operation in the community. Starting in 1913, it provided general merchandise and gasoline and served as the community hub. With the arrival of better roads and modern retail operations nearby, the store has increasingly catered to tourism and seasonal business, open only from May to November. (Courtesy of Robert and Cama Merritt.)

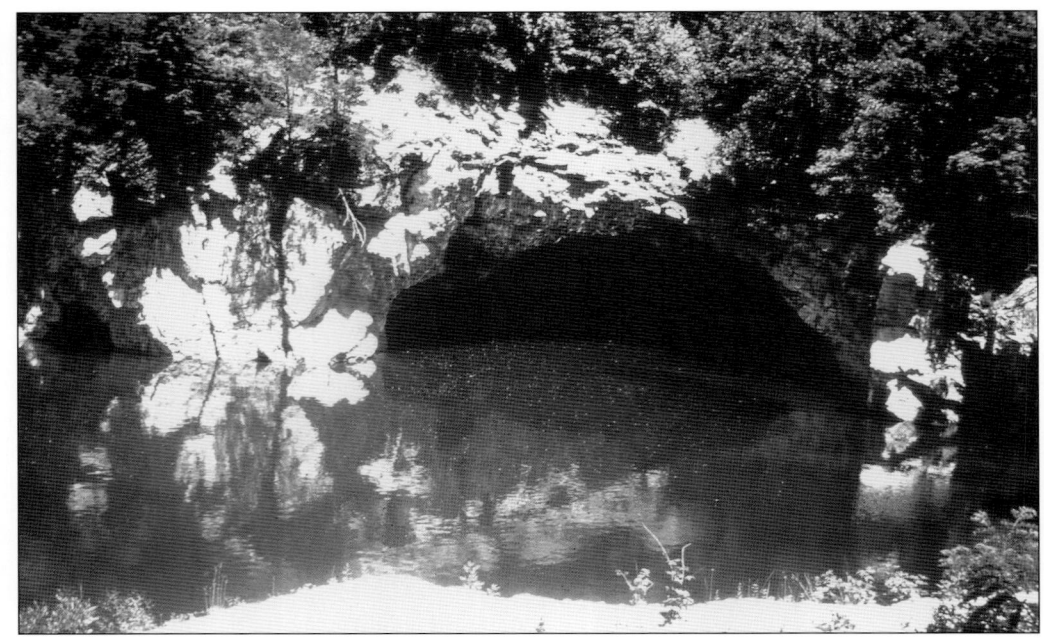

The Bon Ami Mine, located adjacent to the Big McKinney Mine, provided feldspar, which acts as the scouring agent in Bon Ami cleanser. Millions of pounds of spar were taken from these mines, helping homemakers with a variety of cleaning chores. The company abandoned mining in the 1950s, but small-scale operations continued into the mid-1960s. (Courtesy of Alan Schabilion.)

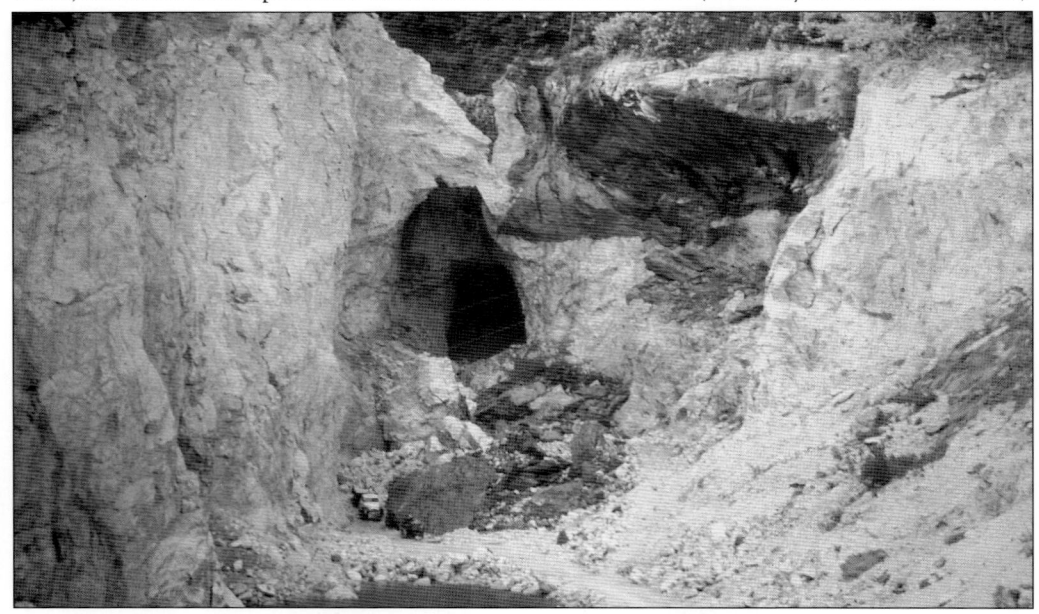

The Big McKinney Mine started operations in the 1920s, when the Carolina Mineral Company purchased mineral rights on the Dan McKinney property. A village, which included a commissary, church, school, and movie theater, sprang up in the valley below to house workers and their families. This was one of the largest feldspar mines and produced ore for over 30 years before it closed. (Courtesy of Alan Schabilion.)

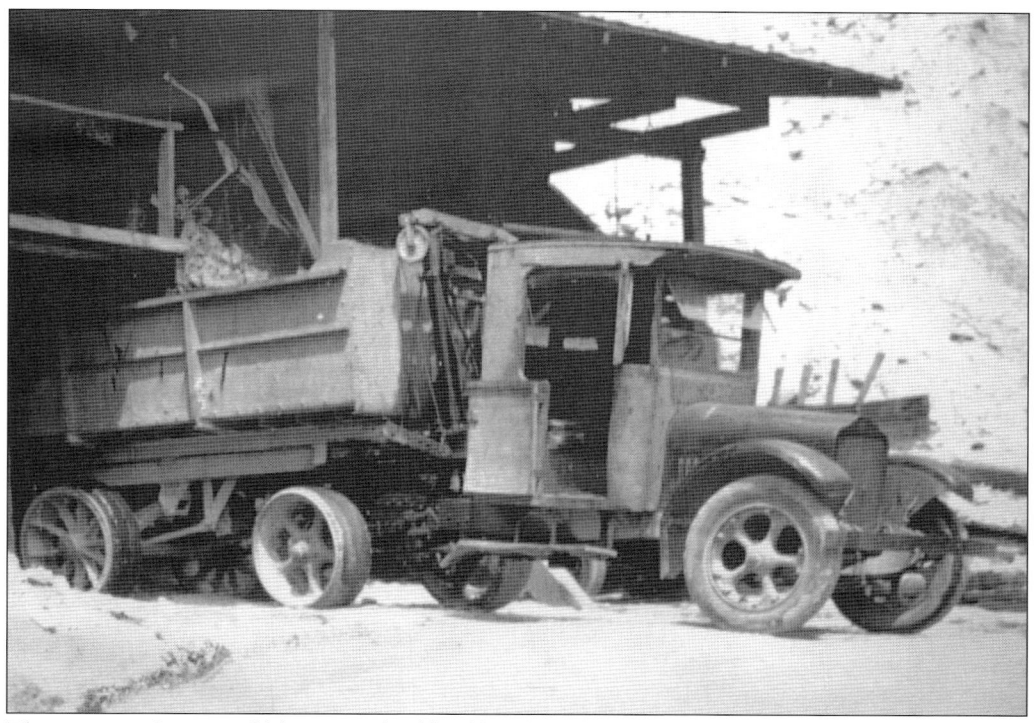

The process of mining feldspar involved backbreaking labor, and getting the ore to the processing plant presented major obstacles. A dinky line was constructed from the Clinchfield line at Boonford up Crabtree Creek to the falls. Miners would load dump cars, and later trucks like the one above, which would transport the ore to the dinky line, where it would be hauled to the Clinchfield. (Courtesy of Alan Schabilion.)

After the ore was blasted in the mine, it had to be sorted to eliminate unwanted materials, called "slate." This was accomplished by hand inside of a structure known as a picking house, pictured at right. From here, the ore was loaded to be transported to a processing location, where it was refined. McKinney Mine ore was processed at a plant in Erwin, Tennessee. (Courtesy of Alan Schabilion.)

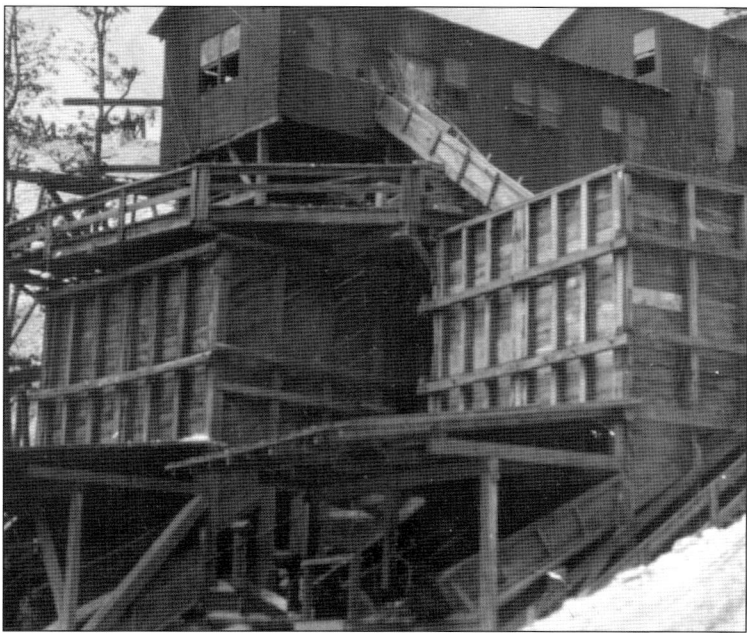

107

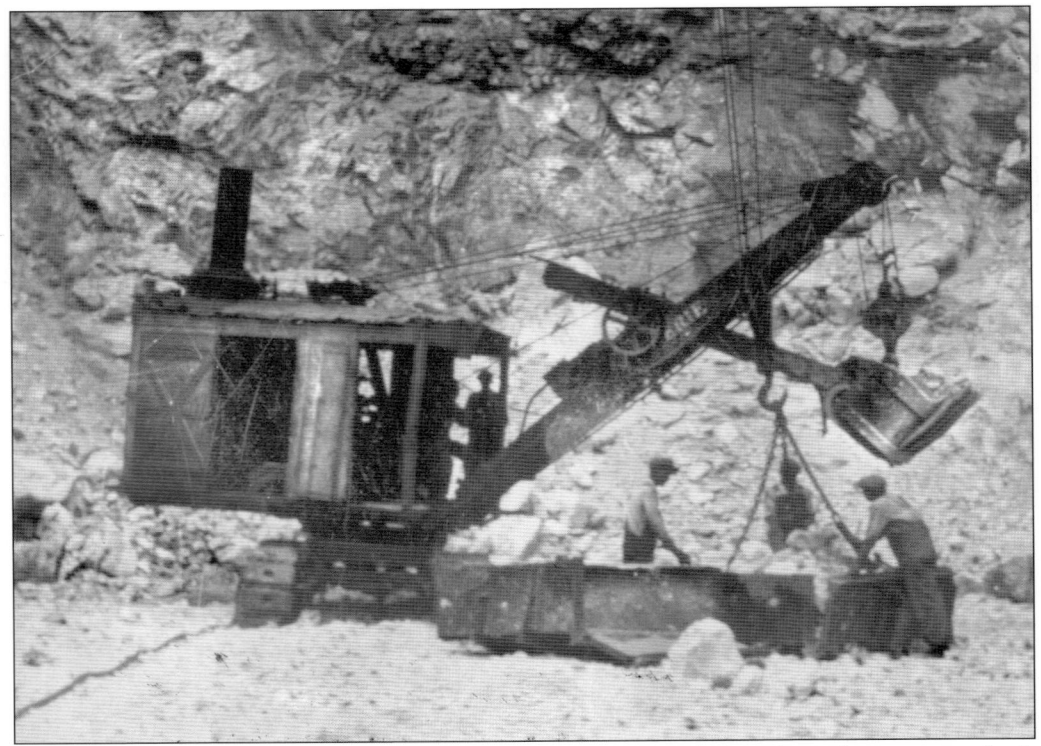

Early work in the mines was backbreaking, physical labor, done by hand. Mechanization, which was not introduced until the 1920s and 1930s, made the mines more productive. Steam shovels, like this one in the McKinney Mine, made the job of loading the ore cars easier and increased output from the mines. (Courtesy of Alan Schabilion.)

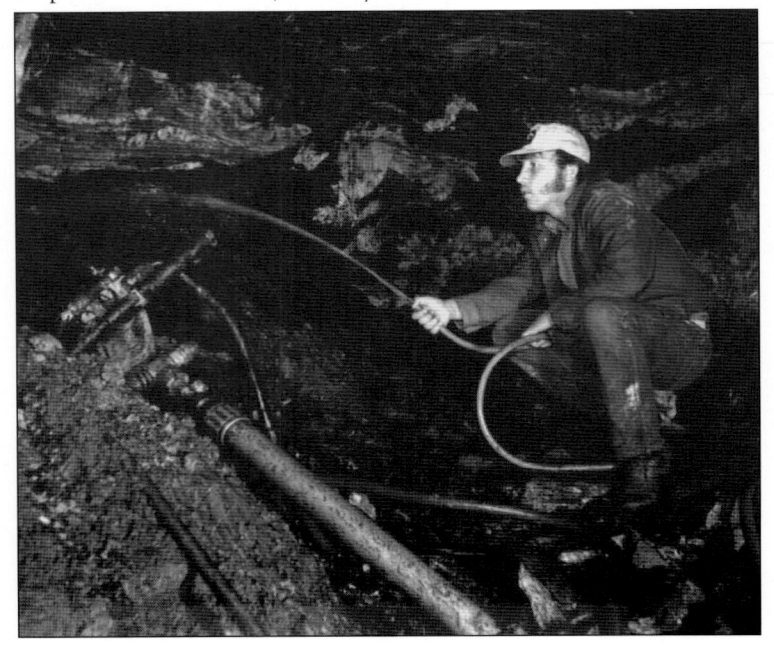

The Big Crabtree Emerald Mine, near Charlie Woody Mountain, was an early mining operation. Originally opened in 1894, the mine was operated for 13 years by Tiffany and Company, with other interests operating it from time to time through today. Several notable emeralds have been found at the mine, including one over 200 carats in size. (Courtesy of the National Park Service.)

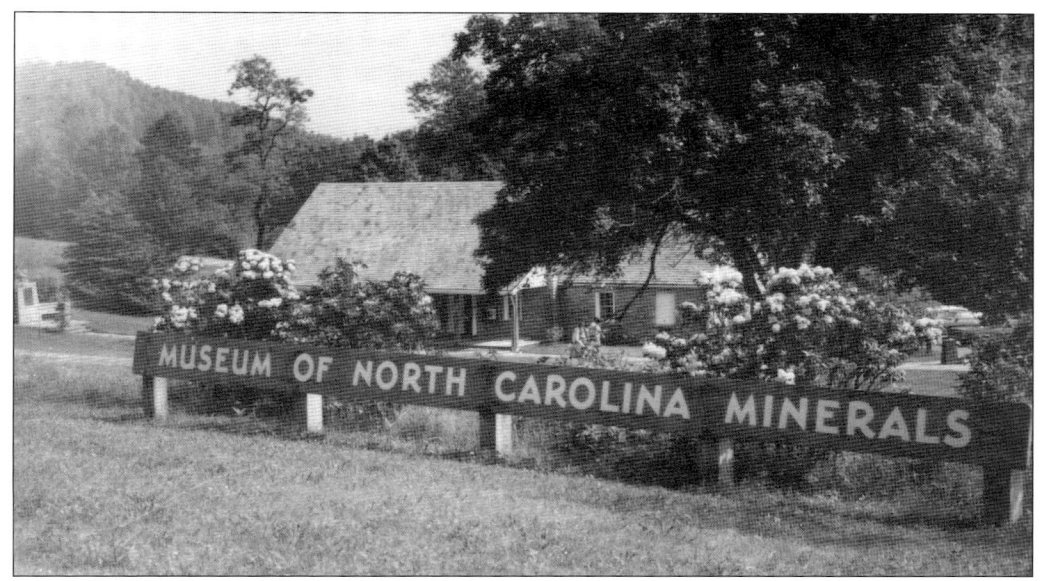

The Museum of North Carolina Minerals, located at milepost 331 on the Blue Ridge Parkway, tells the story of the Spruce Pine Mining District. The idea for a minerals museum goes back as far as 1939, but it was not constructed and dedicated until 1955. Visitors enjoy interactive exhibits that show how this region's wealth of minerals and gems developed and are used. (Courtesy of the National Park Service.)

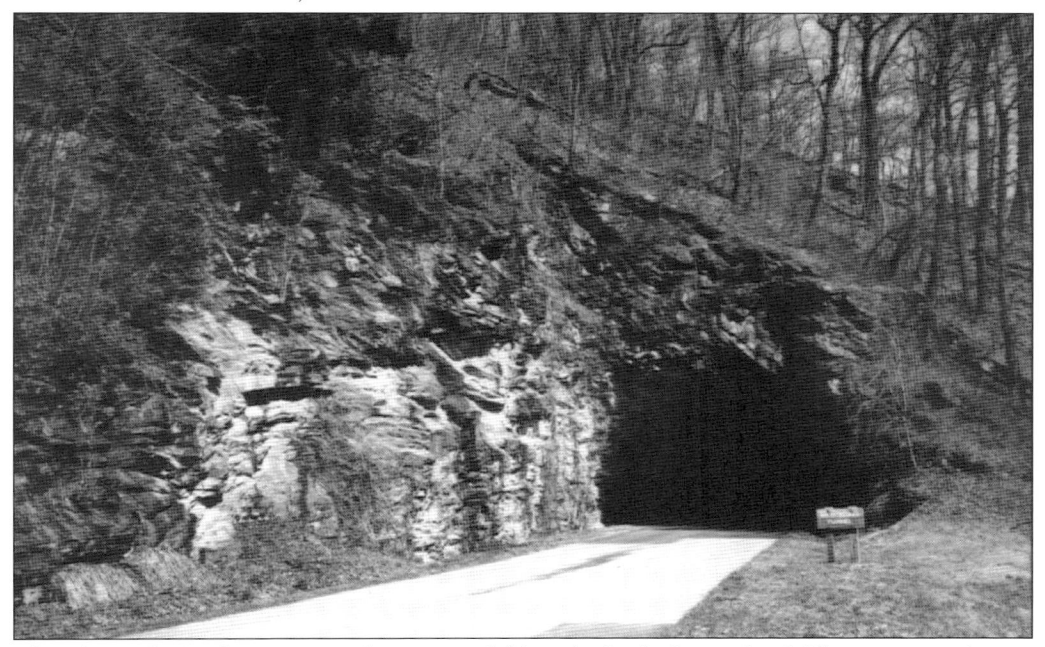

The Blue Ridge Parkway is a vital economic lifeline for Little Switzerland. The motorway brings thousands of visitors each season to the shops, attractions, the Switzerland Inn, Big Lynn Lodge, and Alpine Inn. Points of interest on the Blue Ridge Parkway abound in this area. Pictured is the Wildacres Tunnel, one of two located near Little Switzerland. (Courtesy of the National Park Service.)

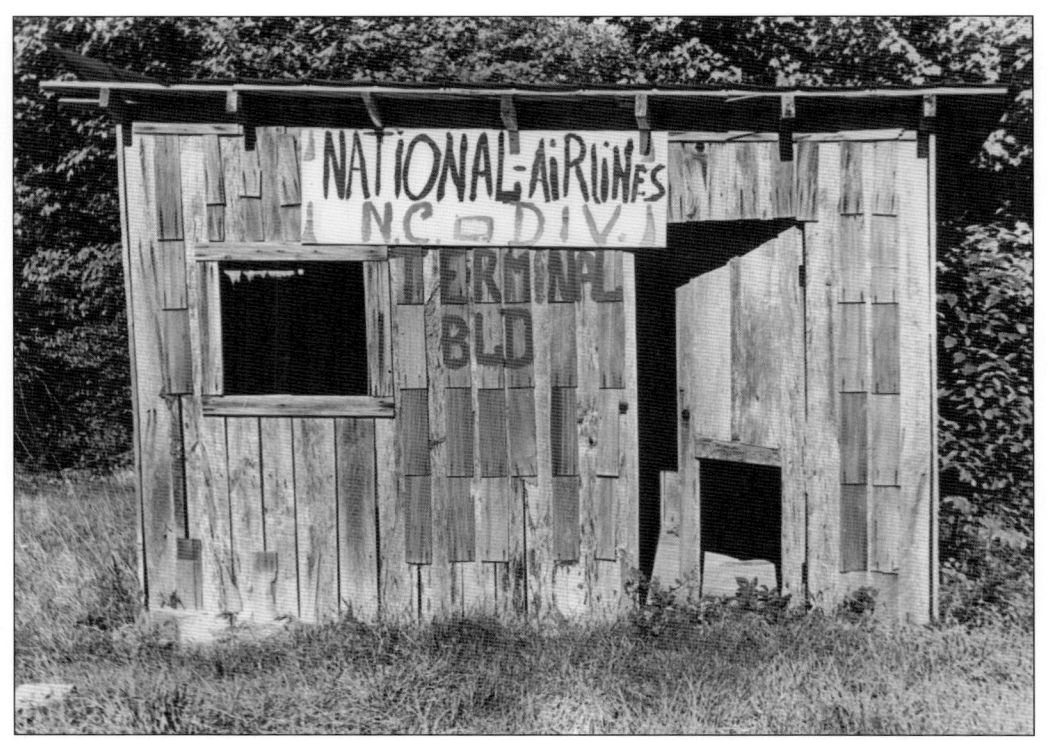

Strawberry Ridge was founded by Charlie Young and David Greene, who purchased land in the 1940s and began to sell lots from it in the 1950s. The development featured a grass airstrip, and some residents, including a couple of retired National Airlines pilots, christened a shed along it as the "terminal," shown above. (Courtesy of Bill and Judy Carson.)

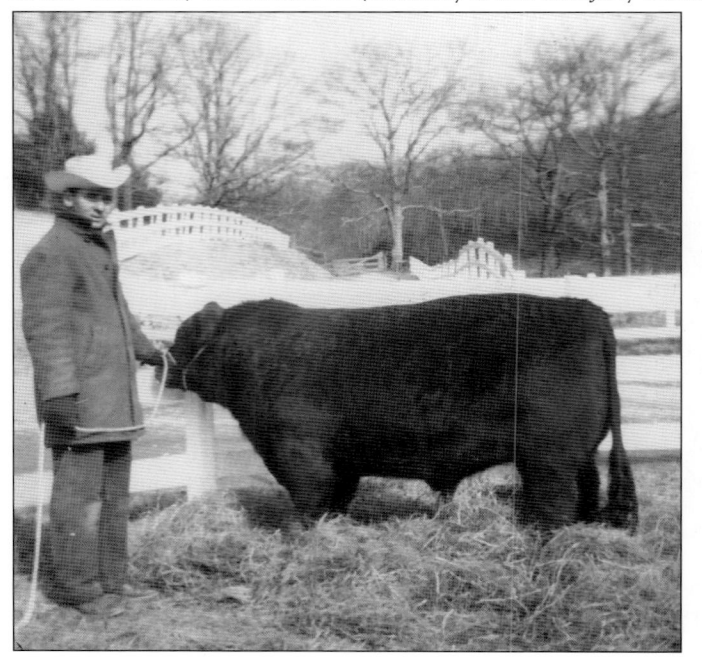

John McBee originally developed Rich Knob Farms in the early 1900s. The Hicks, Hand, and Howell families each owned it later. Joseph Walker ran horses and cattle on it in the 1960s and 1970s. Three couples from Florida then began a housing development in 1978. Pictured on the farm is Claude Burnette, longtime manager, with a registered Angus bull. (Courtesy of Greg S. Burnette.)

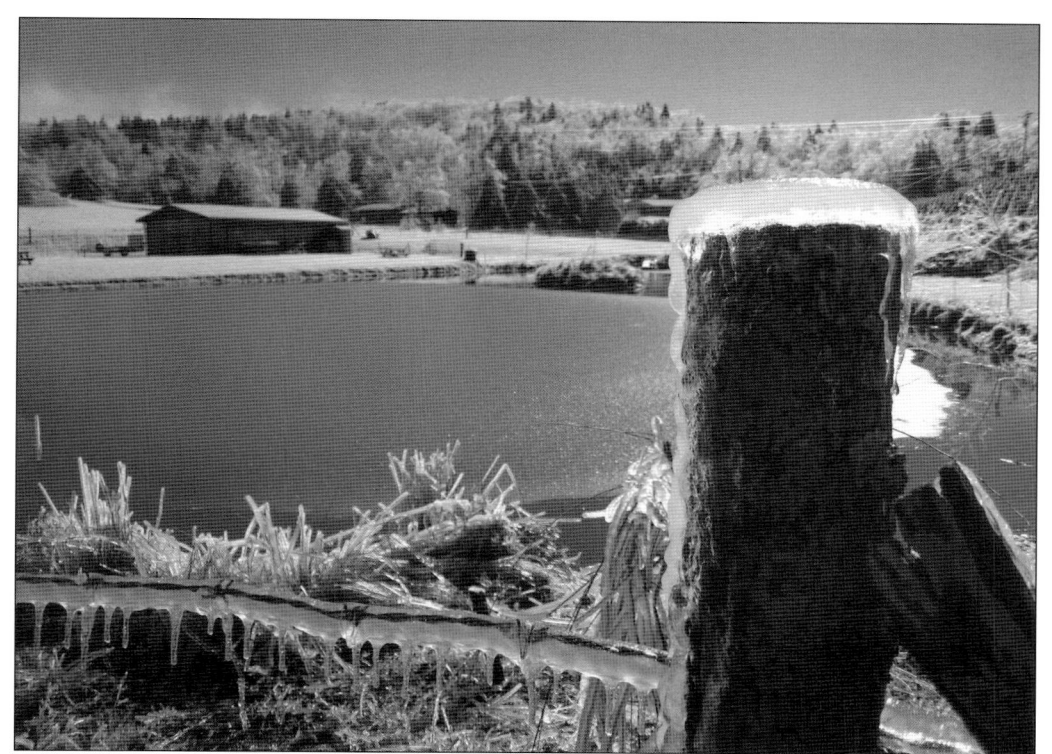

Alpine Village was a housing development started in the 1970s off McKinney Mine Road. The former Vera McKinney farm, it is one of the modern developments in Little Switzerland. Here the village is pictured glistening during an ice storm in 2008. (Courtesy of Kelly Gibson.)

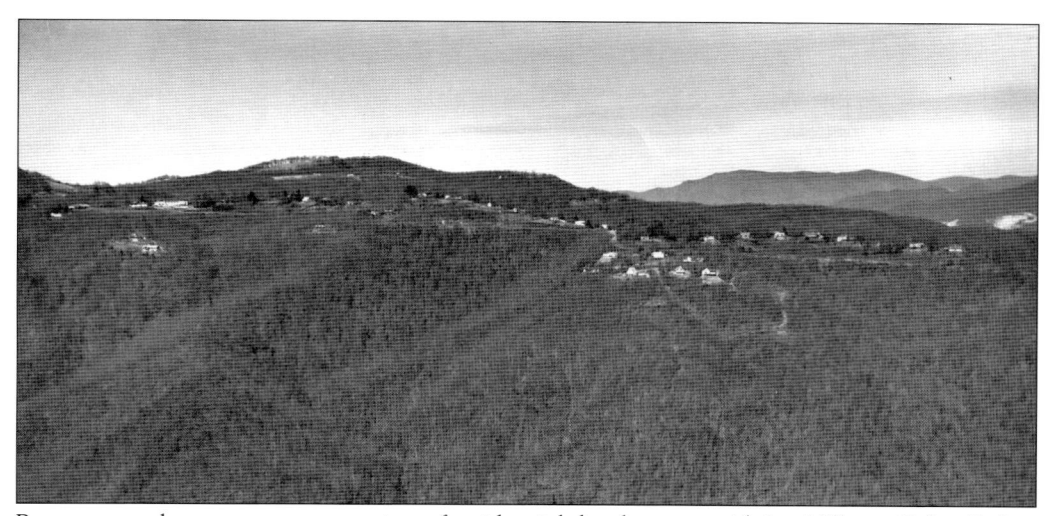

Recent years have seen an expansion of residential development. Alpine Village, Galax Ridge, Grassy Mountain, Lake Laurel, Osborne's Knob, Rich Knob, Strawberry Ridge, Sunset Acres, and Swiss Village appeared in addition to the original Switzerland Company offerings. Looking northwest, Sunset Acres appears in the foreground, with the Switzerland Inn at the upper left. Land values are increasing as more residents move in. (Courtesy of Carrie Washburn.)

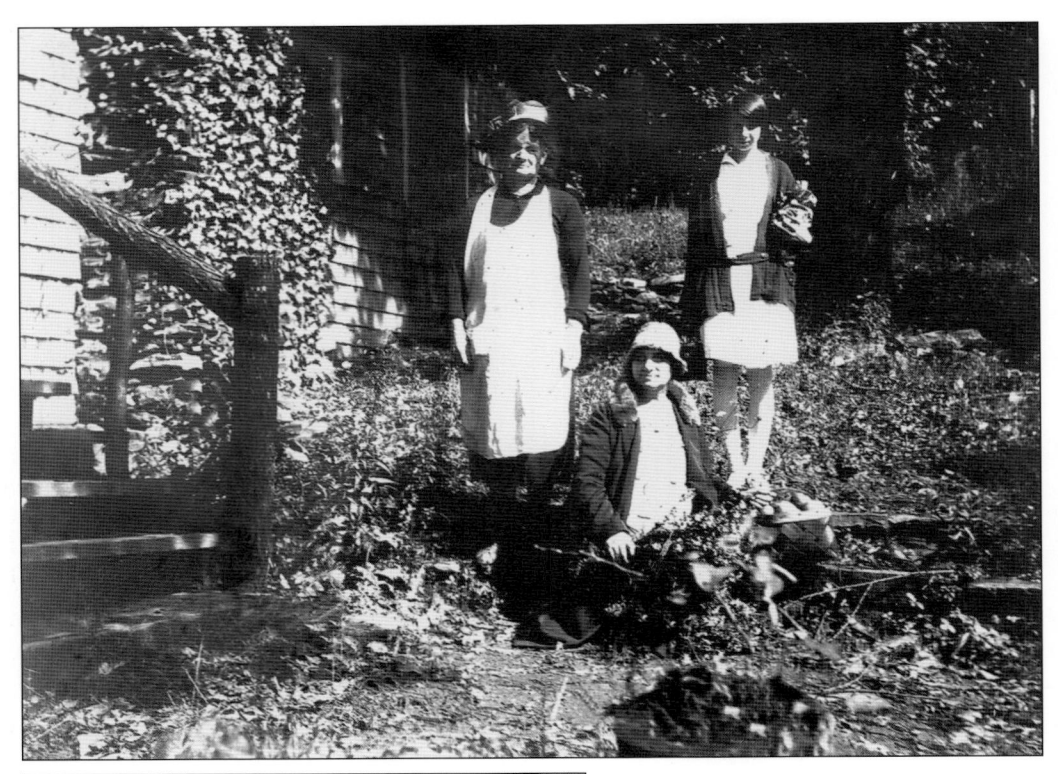

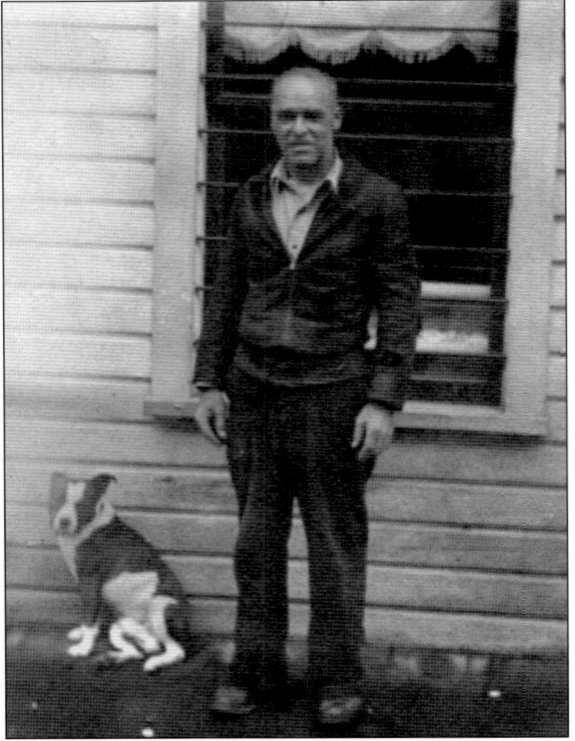

Local families often derived or supplemented their income by working for summer residents. Doing chores; selling fruits, vegetables, dairy products, and meat; and construction and maintenance were just a few of the tasks undertaken by the locals. Emily Burnette (left) and Intha Mae Ledford (also standing) are working for Minerva Avant (seated) at her home. (Courtesy of Greg S. Burnette.)

Barney Ballew was a local entrepreneur who operated several stores. An avid rock collector, he originally ran the Hard Bargain Store on Chestnut Mountain. He later opened a store in the Glenn community, along with one in Beaver Creek. He ran a wholesale grocery business with J. A. Heaton on Lower Street in Spruce Pine. (Courtesy of Tommy and Lillian Hollifield.)

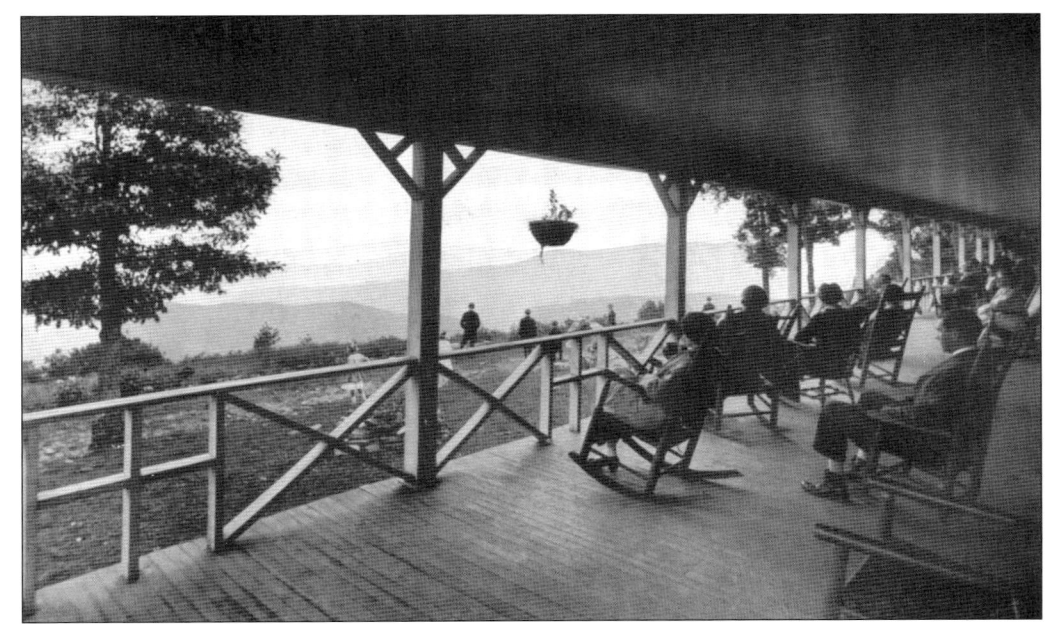

The front porch of the Switzerland Inn offered respite from the worries of life with a relaxing, scenic view, rocking chairs, and good conversation. Tourism has been a vital part of Little Switzerland's economy since its founding, and the Switzerland Company took great pains to promote its attractions. Guests enjoyed this unique spot for over 60 years before it was replaced with today's inn. (Courtesy of Sarah Clarkson.)

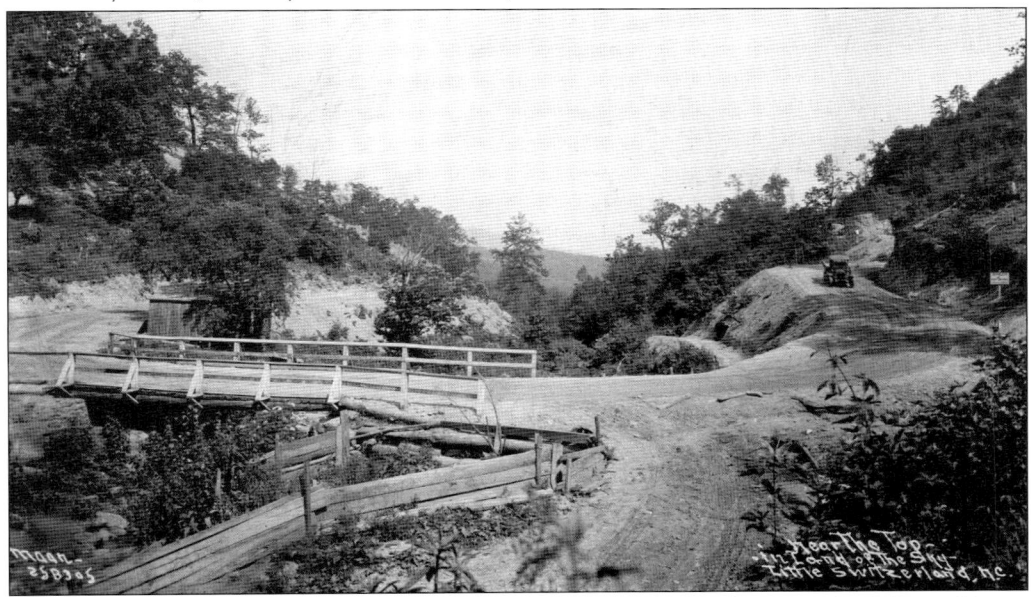

North Carolina 226A meanders up the Blue Ridge escarpment to Little Switzerland. Legend has it that a mule was taken to the bottom and set loose to wander home. The route the mule took was later made into a road. Judge Clarkson was a vociferous proponent of the route, fighting attempts to move it to Coxes' Creek, which is the home of the present-day North Carolina Highway 226. (Courtesy of the North Carolina Collection, UNC–Chapel Hill.)

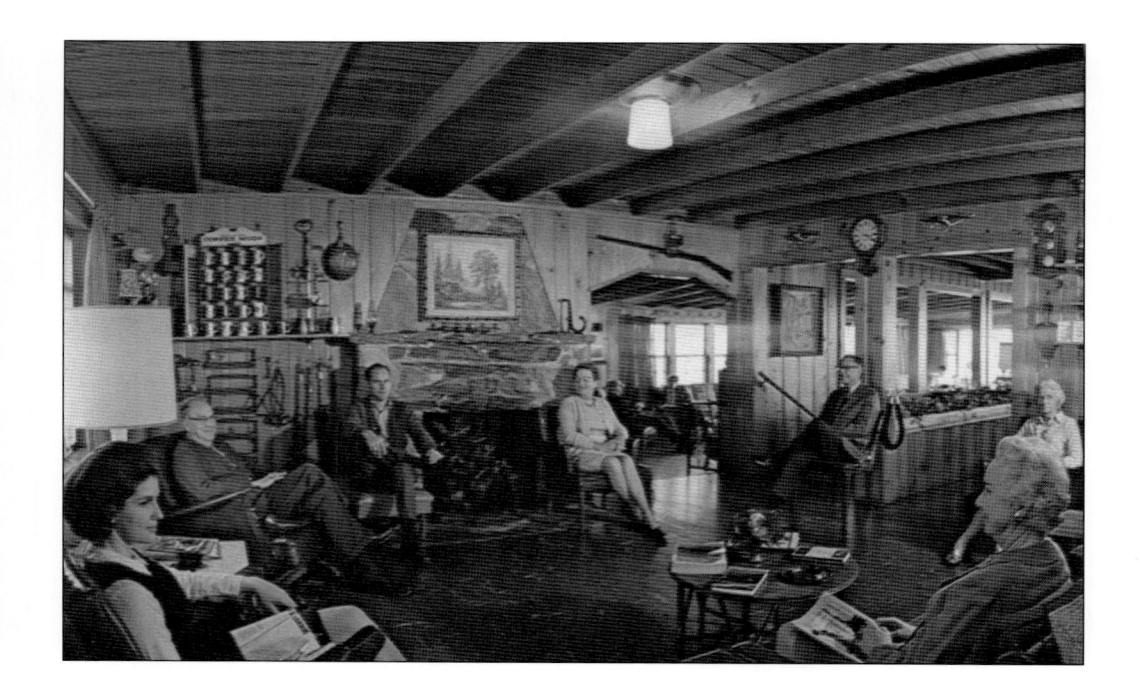

The Big Lynn Lodge began in 1938, when C. D. Bembow built cabins for his family. In 1945, John P. Johns bought the property and constructed the main lodge, along with some cottages. Located on North Carolina 226A at Lynn Gap, it was named by Cash Riddle for the famous tree that stood at its entrance. (Both courtesy of Davis and Jann Godwin.)

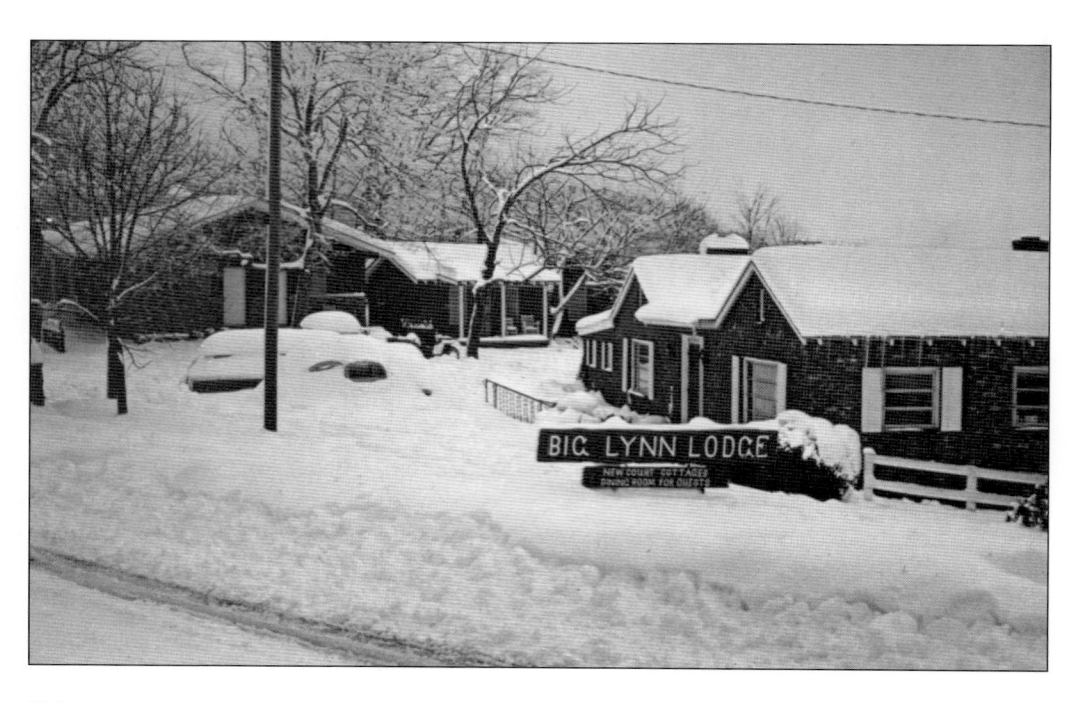

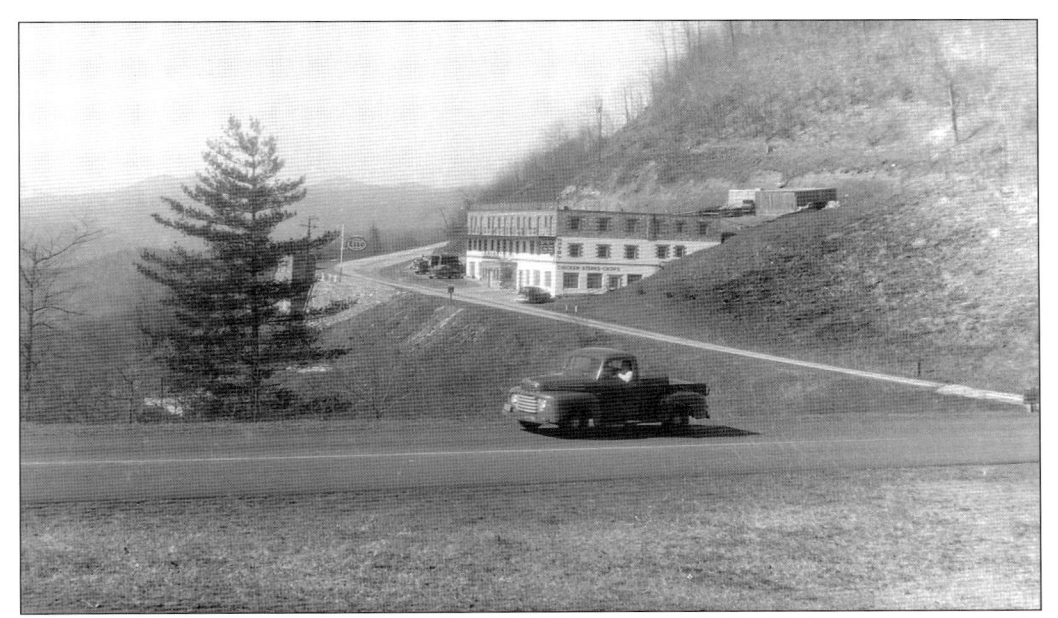

John Greer developed the Skyline Inn in 1948 after the Blue Ridge Parkway paving to Little Switzerland was complete. It and the Gillespie Gap Motor Court (later the Mountain View Motel) were the direct result of the road's completion. Little Switzerland also felt the Blue Ridge Parkway's effects, with its new connector road allowing visitors easy access to the Switzerland Inn and attractions. (Courtesy of Daniel Barron.)

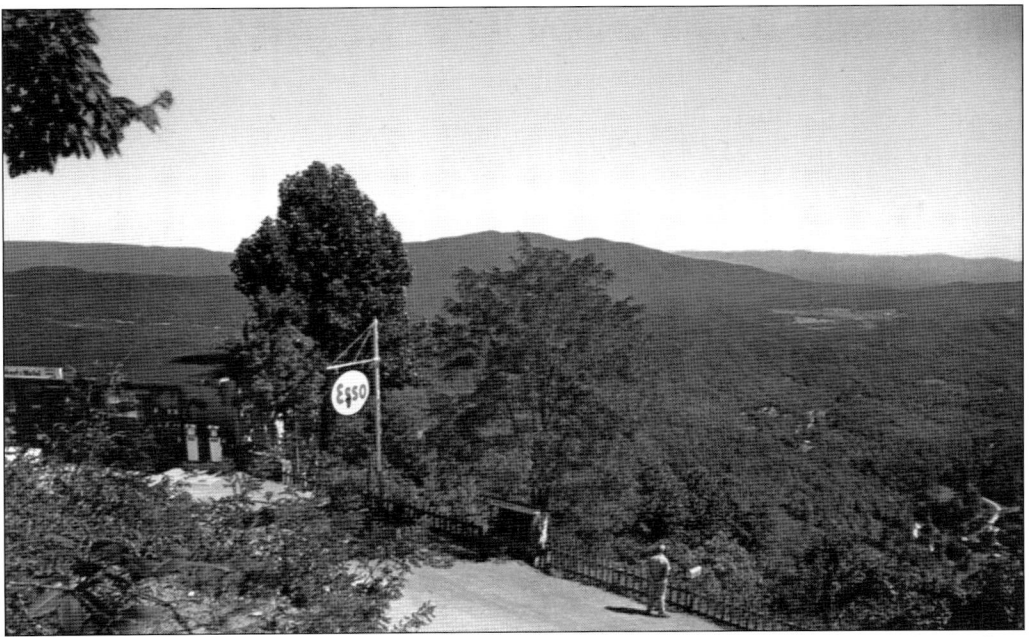

Dallas Hollifield established the Alpine Inn, located south of Little Switzerland on North Carolina 226A, in 1929. Originally known as the Alpine Lookout Motel, it featured a gift shop and restaurant along with accommodations. It continues to be popular with visitors for its scenic views and "the leaning lobby of Little Switzerland." (Courtesy of Davis and Jann Godwin.)

115

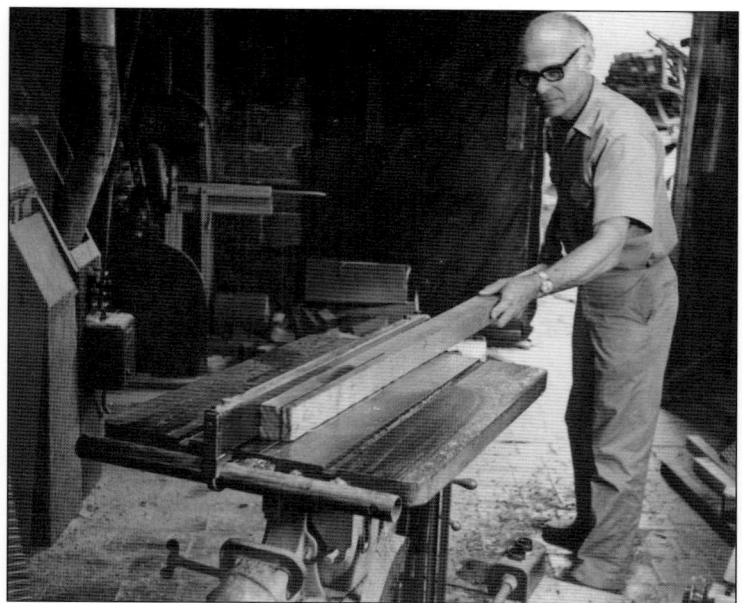

Woody's Chair Shop provided rockers for the porch of the original Switzerland Inn, along with several cottages. The Woodys have made chairs for over 100 years in the same location in nearby Grassy Creek. Their work is in the Smithsonian Institution, and they have provided chairs to notable politicians. At left, Arval Woody saws a board in the workshop in preparation to build a chair. (Courtesy of the National Park Service.)

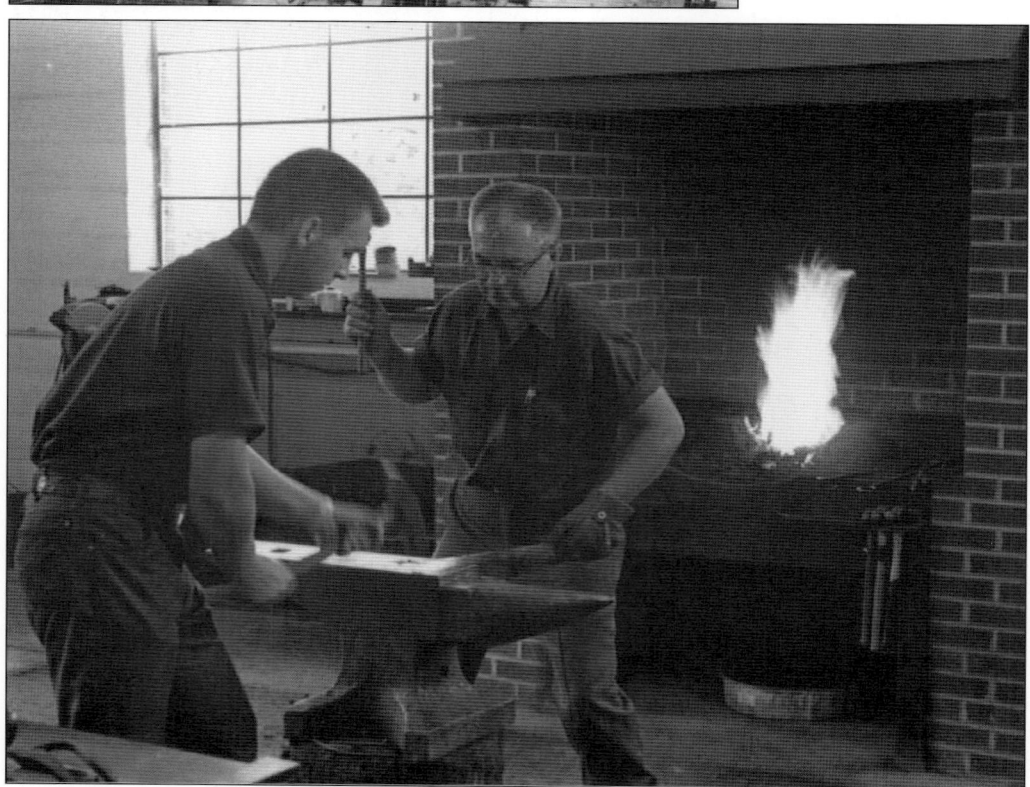

Bea Hensley studied blacksmithing under the tutelage of Daniel Boone VI and bought his workshop at Gillespie Gap. His work is known worldwide, and UNC Television adopted his Mountains to the Sea design as a logo. He gives regular demonstrations at his shop with son Mike, pictured at left above. (Courtesy of the National Park Service.)

Thayer Francis produced exquisite works of art using marquetry, a technique of applying veneers to a wood framework to make pictures. Honored as a North Carolina Living Treasure in 1988 (one of seven from Mitchell County), he was part of a folk art show at the Smithsonian Institution. He and his work were popular with Little Switzerland residents. (Courtesy of the National Park Service.)

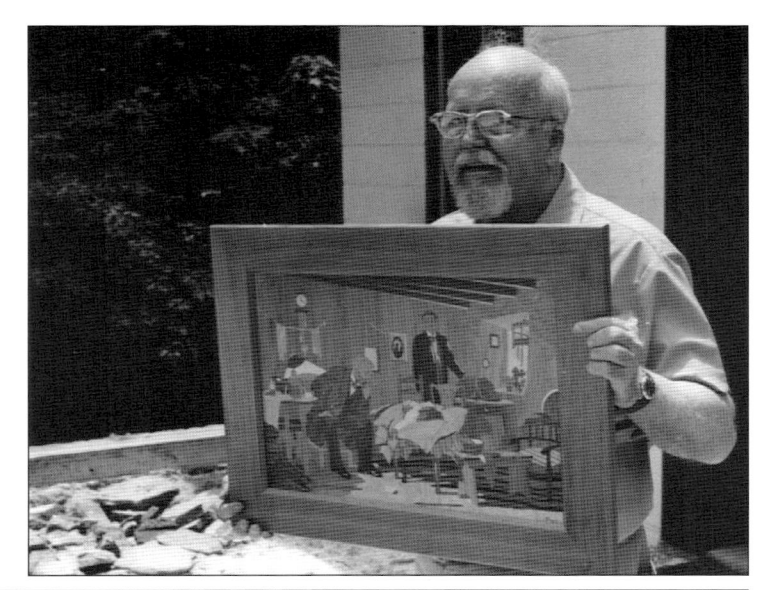

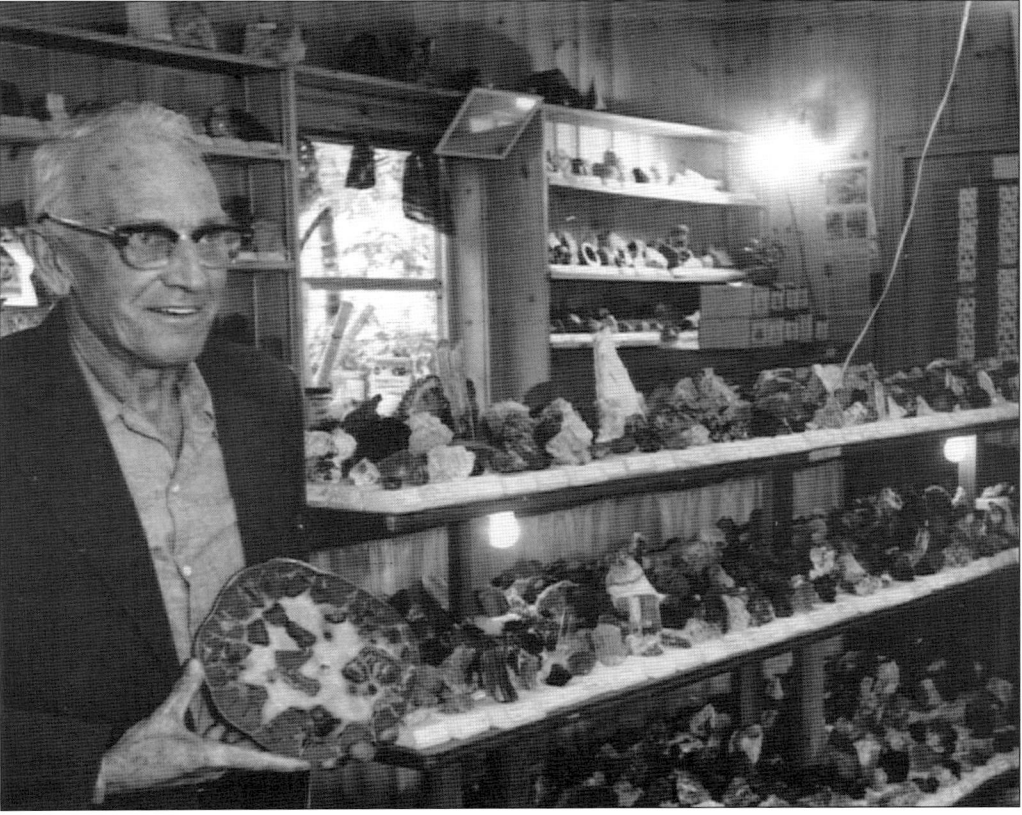

The popularity of gemstones mined in the region has increased exponentially in recent decades. Roby Buchanan was one of the first gem dealers in the region. He opened an establishment in the Chalet Shops to sell cut gems and minerals. He also taught lapidary and jewelry-making classes and was well known in the community. (Courtesy of the National Park Service.)

117

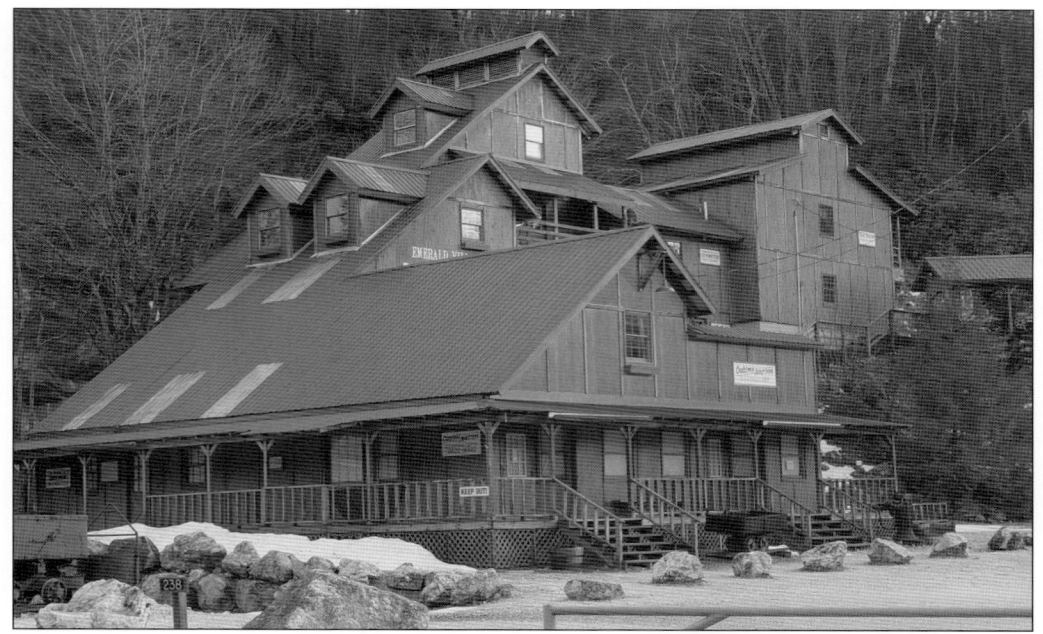

Emerald Village and the North Carolina Mining Museum opened in 1980 on the old McKinney Mine property. Robert Schabilion opened the attraction to honor and preserve the region's mining heritage. In addition to tours, visitors can pan for gemstones and see authentic antique machinery from the early days of mining in the Spruce Pine Mining District. (Courtesy of David Biddix.)

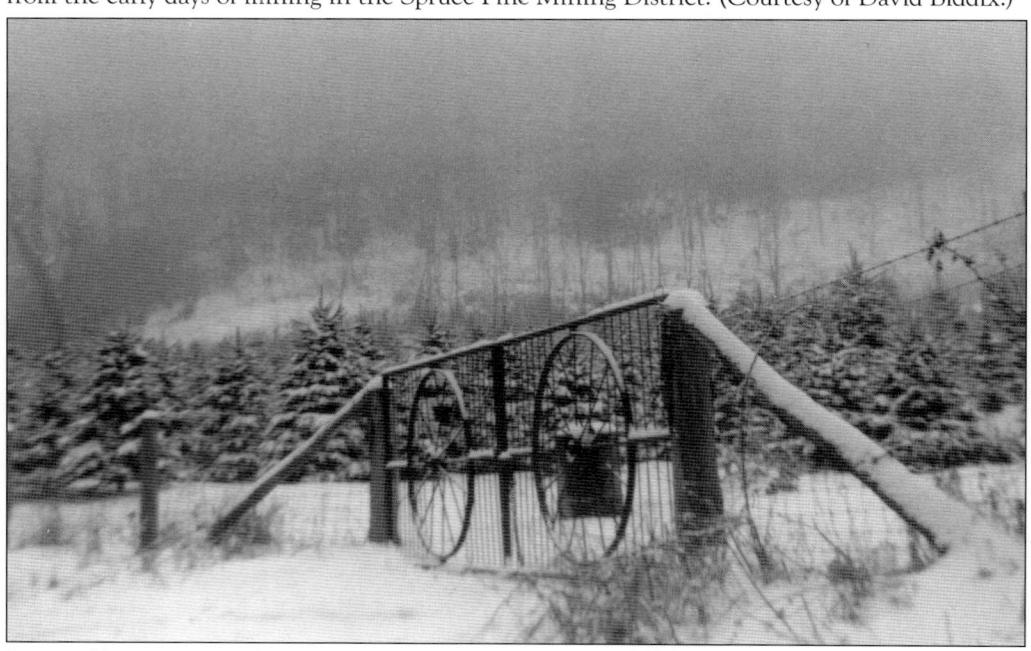

Pictured here in 1969, the Frank Hollifield Tree Farm on Chestnut Grove Church Road was one of the earliest Christmas tree farms in the region. Trees became a new way for farmers to grow a profitable crop. The tree industry continues to be a major economic force locally today. (Courtesy of Chris Hollifield.)

Seven

BEAUTY SPOT OF THE BLUE RIDGE
LITTLE SWITZERLAND TODAY

In many ways, modern Little Switzerland bears a marked resemblance to the community that Heriot Clarkson envisioned a century ago. A strong presence of summer residents swells the population of the community each year, returning for a season of rejuvenation on the mountain, while natives maintain their deep roots in the hills, some going back for centuries.

However, changes are beginning to occur. With the Blue Ridge Parkway's arrival and the opening of North Carolina 226 up Coxes' Creek, access to Little Switzerland has become much easier. This has led to increasing numbers of tourists, and many are returning to become part-time residents. Better access has also opened up economic opportunities for native residents, some of whom have begun leaving the community. This is leading to a more cosmopolitan population, one that is not as tight-knit as previous generations.

With growth, pressure on natural resources is also increasing. Demands for water and wastewater treatment, along with infrastructure needs, are forcing developers to make tough decisions on what can take place on the mountain.

Some feel that the community is as large as it needs to be, while others want to see continued growth. This dichotomy has opened a discussion on Little Switzerland's future. On the 100th anniversary of Clarkson's development, the community stands at a crossroads, celebrating the past while preparing for a future he would dared to have imagined.

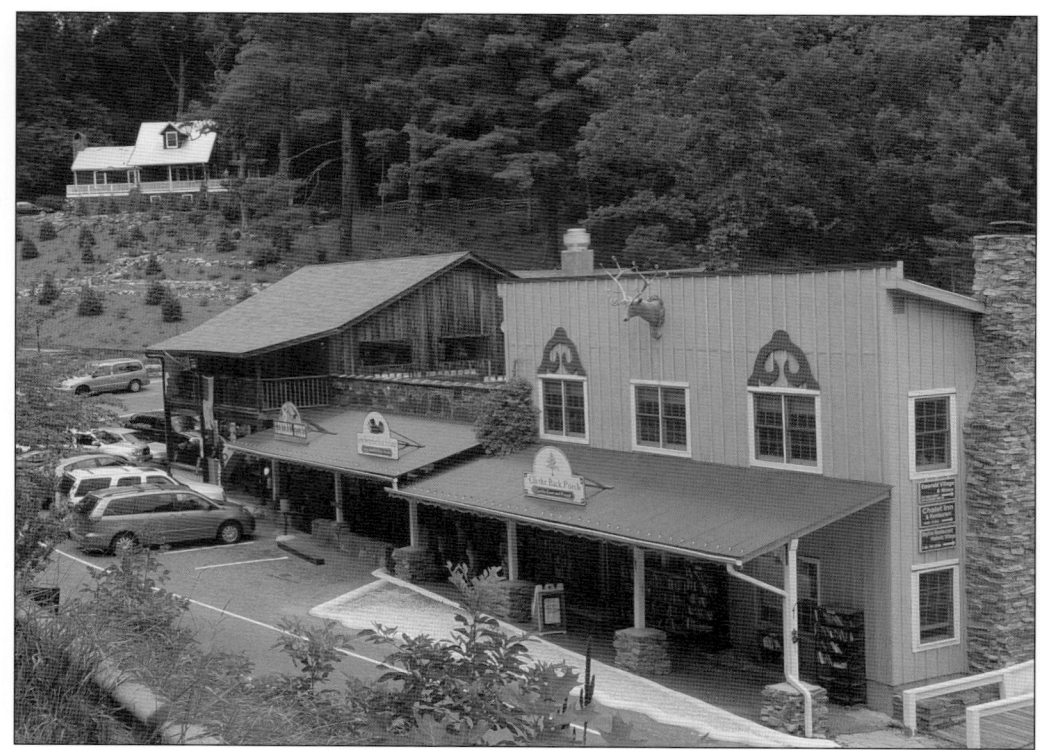

"Downtown" Little Switzerland today consists of the Switzerland Café (left), the Switzerland Store (middle), and Little Switzerland Book Exchange (right). They cater mainly to tourists and summer residents and are only open during the tourist season. (Courtesy of Chris Hollifield.)

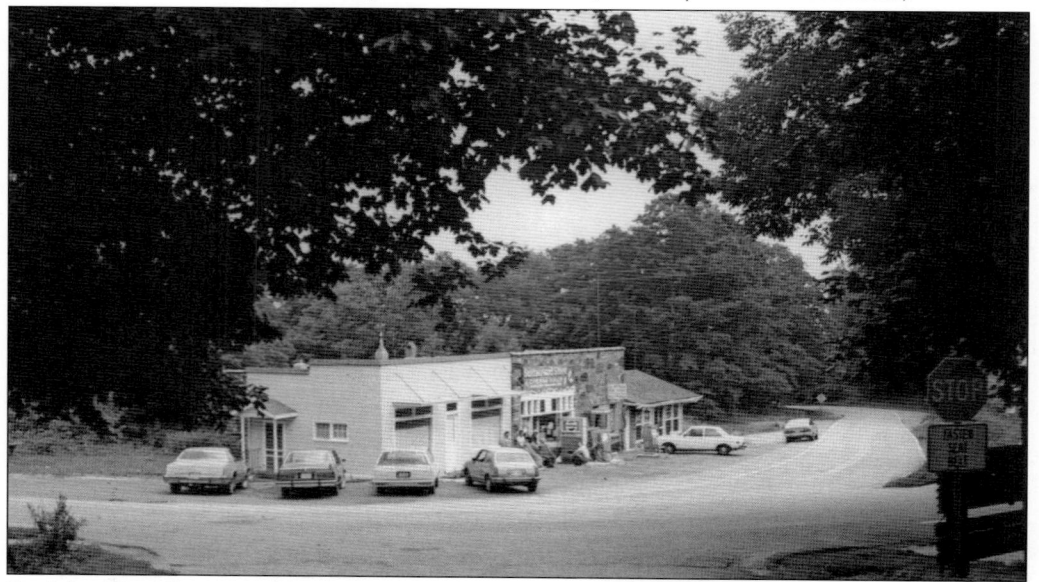

Dr. John Howell operated his dentistry practice in Little Switzerland in the 1970s in the old post office building (the white one in this picture). The post office was relocated across the road in a freestanding structure in 1976. (Courtesy of Davis and Jann Godwin.)

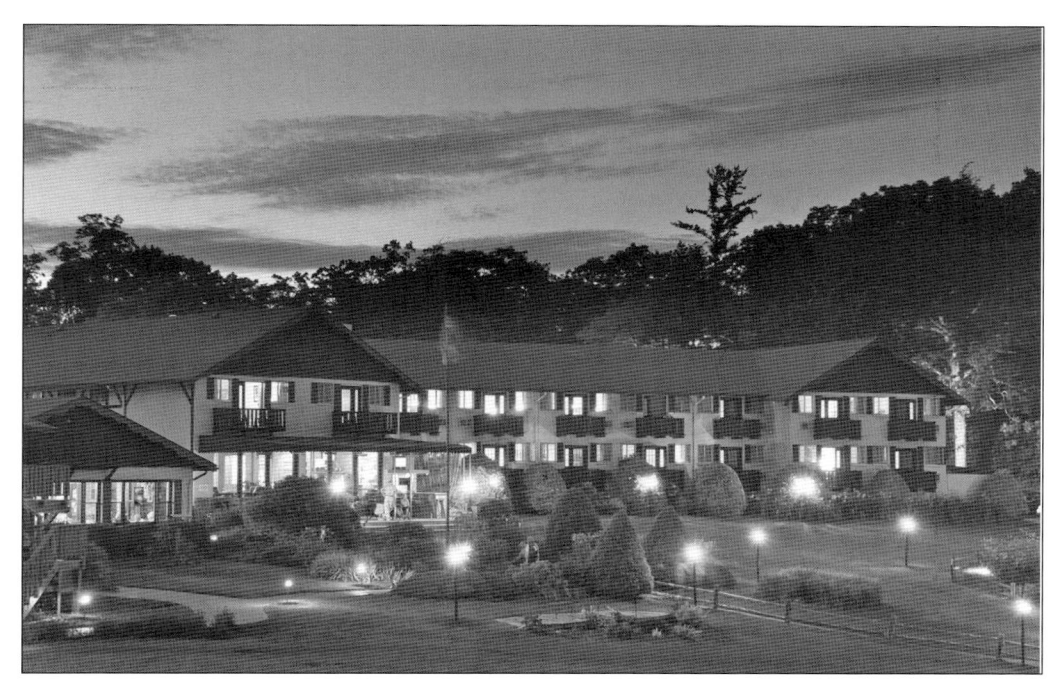

William and Wave Cessna purchased the original Clarkson home and Switzerland Inn, razed them, and in 1961 opened the Chalet Motor Lodge in their place. Robert Schwebke purchased the property in 1976. Gary Jensen Sr. purchased it in 1983 and renamed it the Switzerland Inn. He and his son, Gary Jr., have operated it since 2000. The shops behind the inn were opened in 1976 and cater to the tourist trade. (Both courtesy of Todd Bush, www.bushphoto.com.)

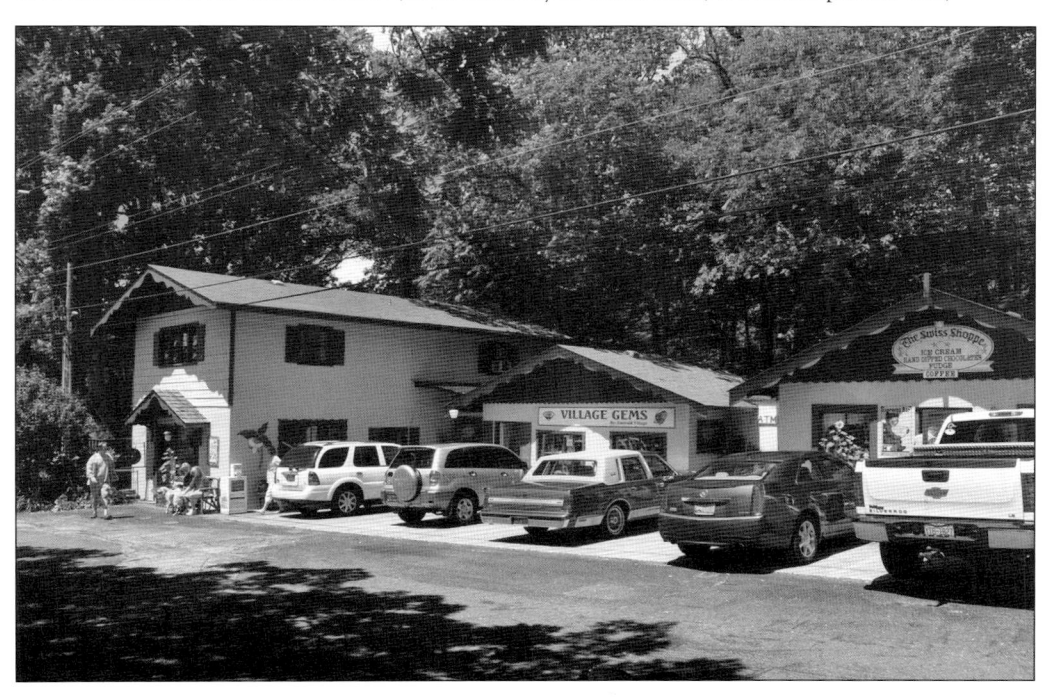

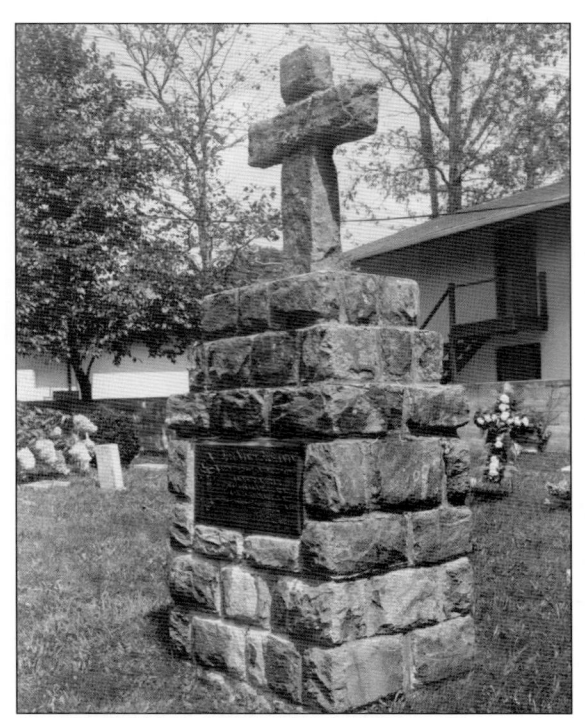

When Nancy Buchanan passed away in 1935, Judge Clarkson organized a committee of himself, Fons McKinney, and George Butler to erect a monument to the Mother of Little Switzerland. Interred in the Buchanan Cemetery behind the Switzerland Inn, the monument was dedicated in 1937. (Courtesy of Carrie Washburn.)

William and Nancy Buchanan's home sits abandoned on the Grassy Creek Falls Road. Constructed in the late 1890s, it still stands as a testament to the resilience of the mountain people. They overcame the challenges of climate, geography, and isolation to thrive and prosper in this mountain paradise. (Courtesy of Tommy and Lillian Hollifield.)

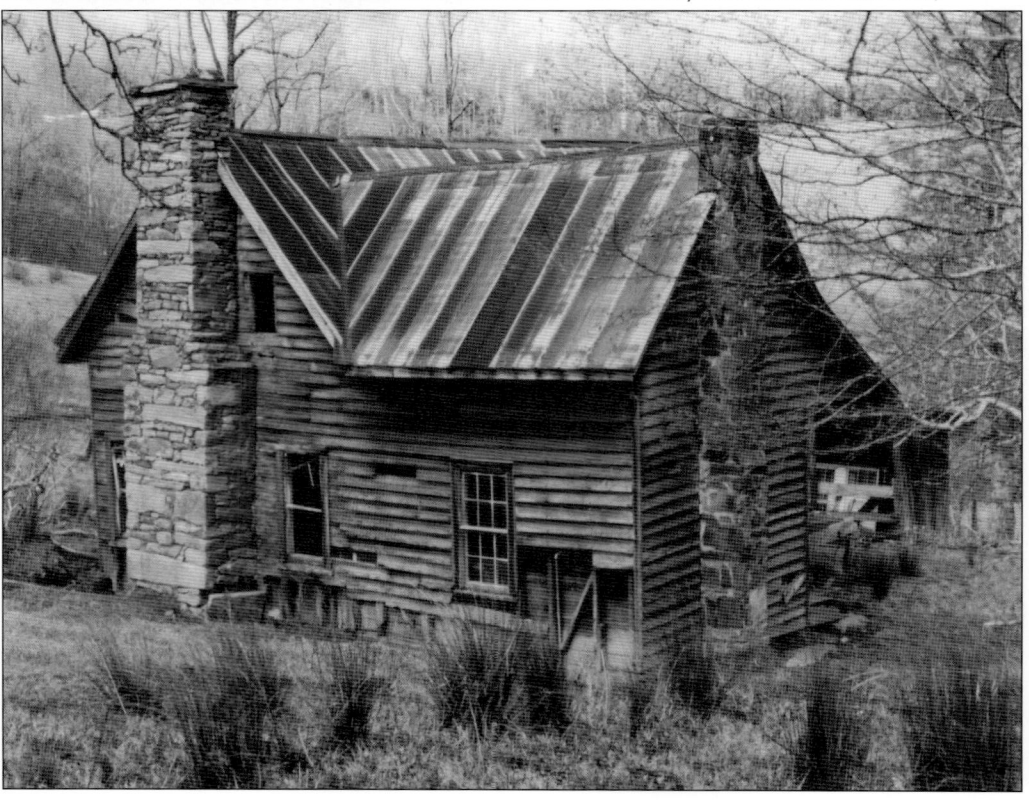

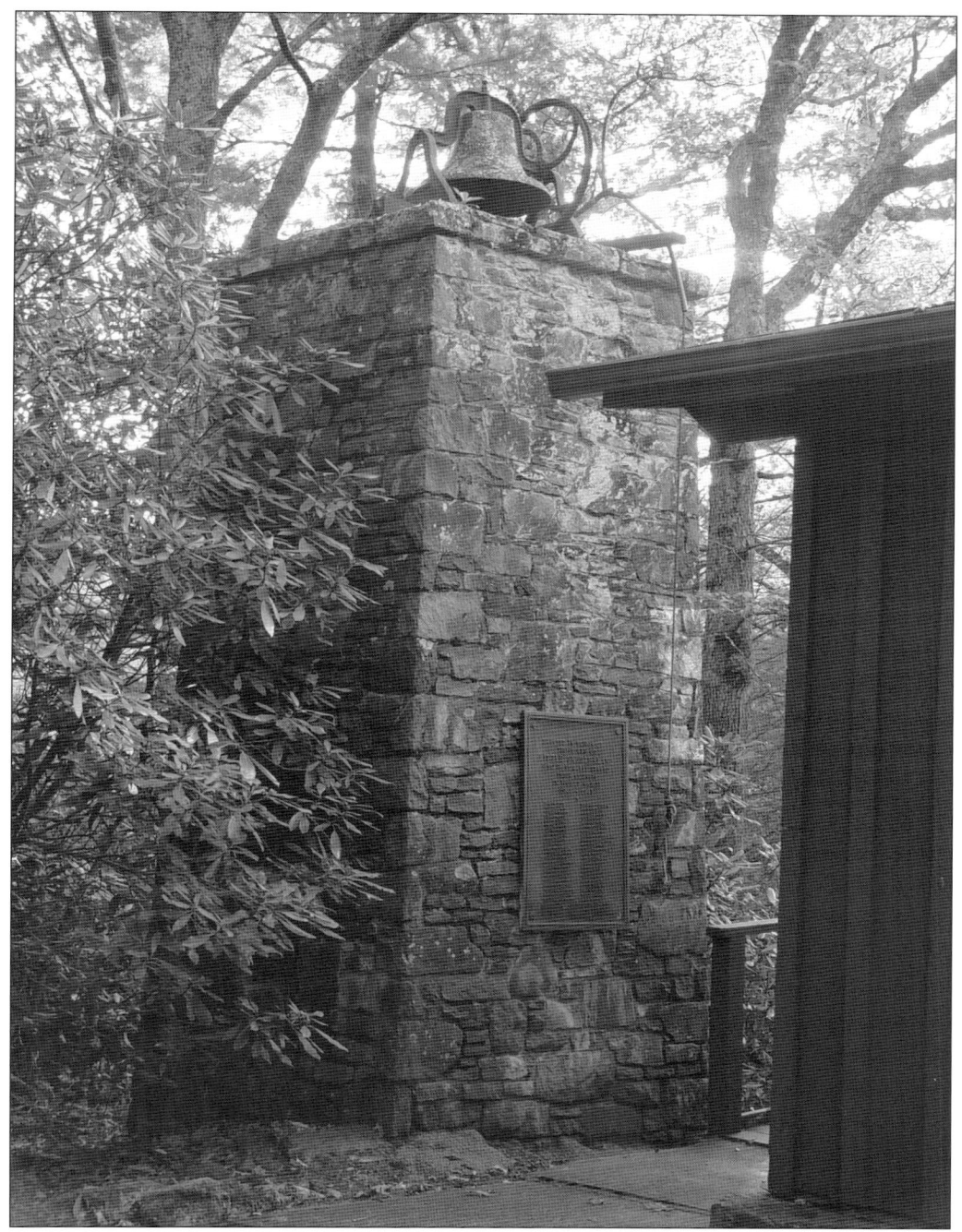

Plaques honoring the veterans of World War II from Little Switzerland and Judge Heriot Clarkson were removed from Kilmichael Tower after it was closed in the 1960s and relocated to a bell tower at the Church of the Resurrection. The memorial bell tower stands at the right rear of the church. (Courtesy of Marsha Biddix.)

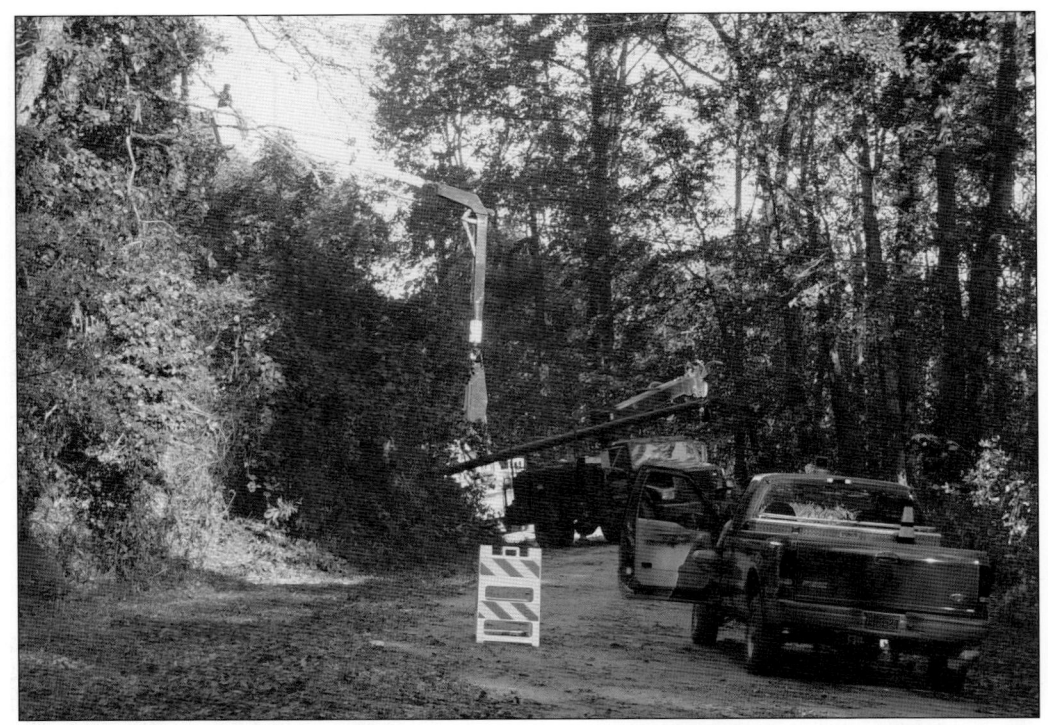

Hurricanes Frances and Ivan wreaked havoc on Little Switzerland in September 2004, downing trees and power lines, flooding creeks, and damaging roads. A section of the Blue Ridge Parkway nearby was closed for nearly two years following the storms to replace a section of the roadway. Weather plays a major role in the lives of residents, both summer and winter. (Courtesy of Marsha Biddix.)

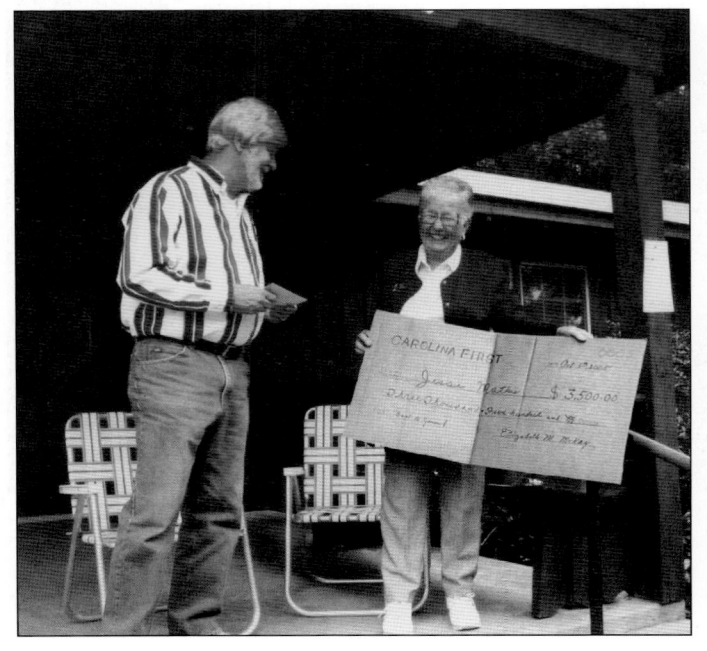

Longtime postmaster Jesse Mathis retired on October 5, 2005, and was honored at Geneva Hall by residents. He became postmaster in 1973 after Pete Deal retired and supervised its move to a new location in 1976. Jesse's smiling face behind the counter brightened many a resident's day. (Courtesy of Markine Ostling.)

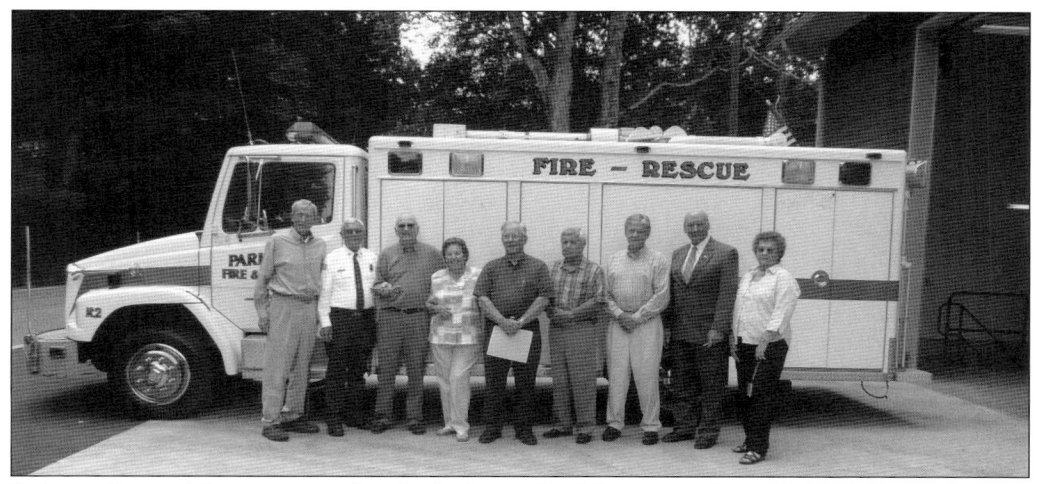

Parkway Fire and Rescue opened its Little Switzerland Station on June 29, 2008. Fire and rescue services for the community have been a challenge due to its location in both Mitchell and McDowell Counties. Pictured is the committee who worked to build the facility. From left to right, they are Fred Manning, Lloyd Glenn, Bill Carson, Mona Moody, Bill Hayes, Butch Renaldo, Dan McKinney, state representative Phillip Frye, and Joy Nash. (Courtesy of Bill and Judy Carson.)

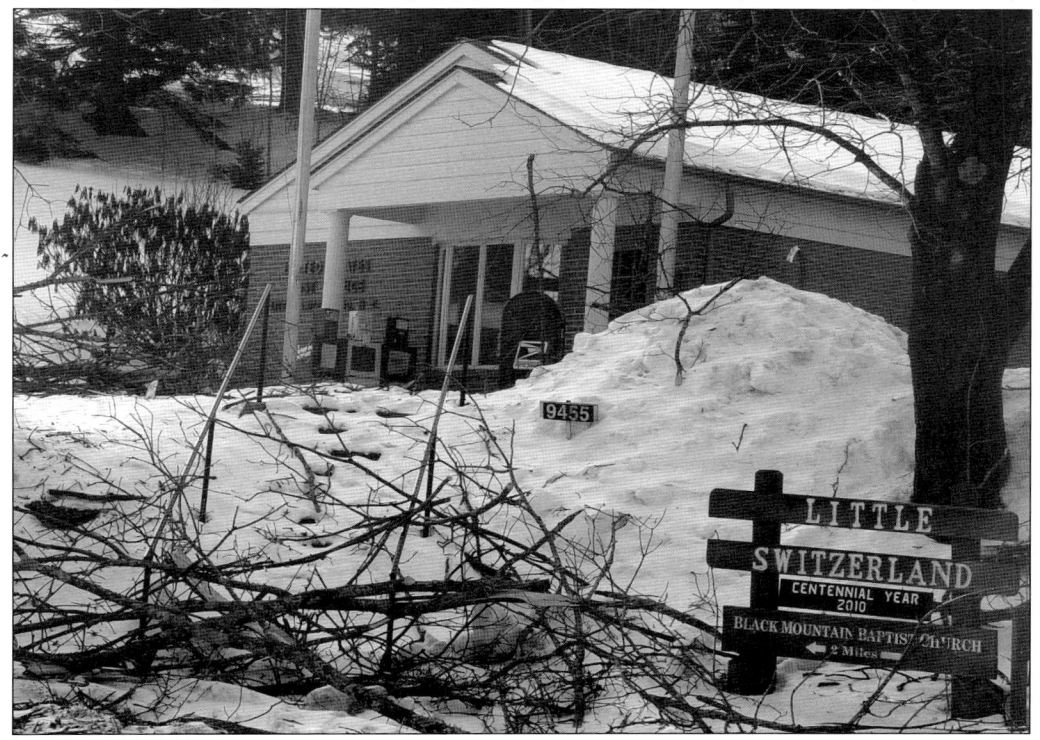

On December 18, 2009, a major winter storm brought 16 to 20 inches of snow to Little Switzerland, paralyzing holiday travel and delighting children. A week later, an ice storm brought devastation as trees collapsed, limbs broke, and power was disrupted. Some residents were without power for several days. Limbs are piled up outside the Little Switzerland post office, blocking the steps up from the road. (Courtesy of Marsha Biddix.)

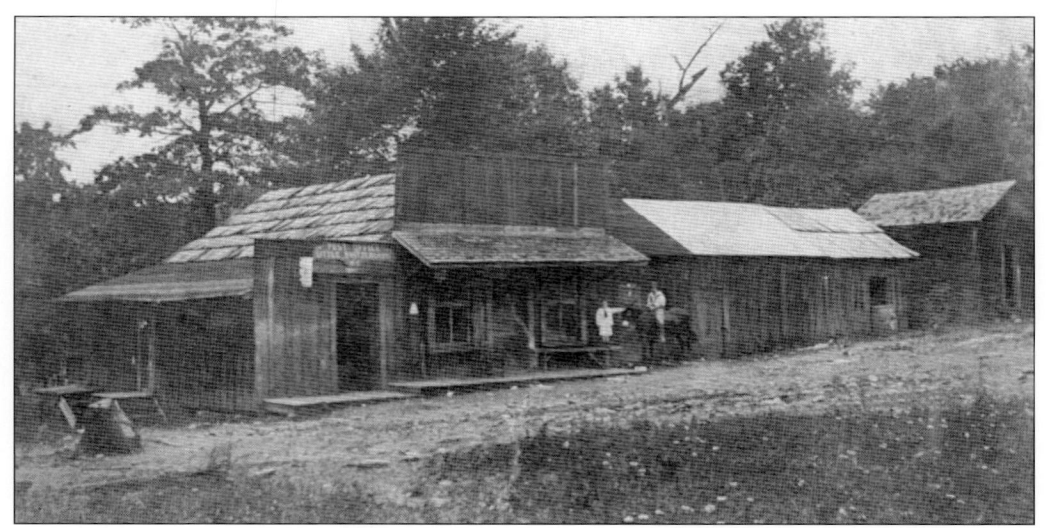

Originally known as the Commissary, the Switzerland Store was a vital lifeline for the community. This rare photograph shows the entire complex of buildings constructed by Heriot Clarkson, which included a post office and barbershop in addition to the store. It was Little Switzerland's "downtown" for the first 17 years of its existence. (Courtesy of Davis and Jann Godwin.)

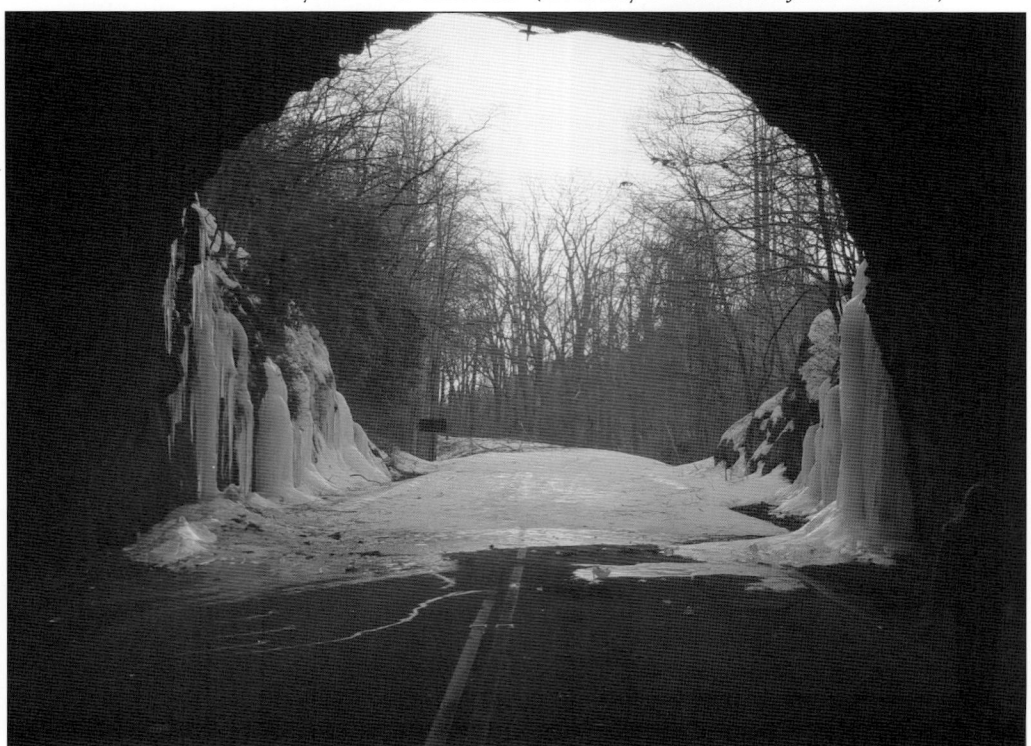

The opening of the tunnel presents a seldom-seen glimpse of winter, as the Blue Ridge Parkway is closed during bouts of inclement weather. Icicles grow from water seeping from the banks, and snow and ice paint the landscape. Little Switzerland is truly the beauty spot of the Blue Ridge year-round. (Courtesy of Marsha Biddix.)

Bibliography

Associated Press. "Award of $25,000 to Little Switzerland Company Upheld." *The Asheville Times*, November 8, 1939.
Bailey, Lloyd, ed. *Toe River Valley Heritage* (vol. 1–7). Durham, NC: L. R. Bailey, 1994–2008.
Chapman, Ashton. "Dreams of a Mountain Top." *State Magazine*, October 1974: 18–20.
———. "Little Switzerland Group Plays, Works Together." *The Charlotte Observer*, September 22, 1955.
———. "Mrs. Julia W. Wolfe Foresaw Resort At Little Switzerland." *The Asheville Citizen*, October 16, 1960.
———. "Tower Used Decade Before Dedication." *The Asheville Citizen*, August 24, 1952.
Duls, Louisa D. *The Story of Little Switzerland*. Richmond: Whittet and Shepperson, 1982, 1983, 1989.
Earley-Sheppard, Muriel. *Cabins in the Laurel*. Chapel Hill: UNC Press, 1935, 1991.
Hicklin, J. B. "Peace Shrine Nestles In Picturesque Hill Region." *The Asheville Citizen*, May 27, 1930.
Jolley, Harley E. *The Blue Ridge Parkway*. Knoxville: University of Tennessee Press, 1969.
———. *The Blue Ridge Parkway: The First 50 Years*. Boone, NC: Appalachian Consortium Press, 1985.
Joslin, Michael. *Appalachian Bounty: Nature's Gifts From the Mountains: A Collection of Essays*. Johnson City: The Overmountain Press, 2000.
Lord, William G. *Blue Ridge Parkway Guide, Milepost 291.9 to 469*. Birmingham: Menasha Ridge, 1981.
M'Afee, Hoyt. "Much Pride Shown in Little Switzerland." *The Asheville Citizen*, June 19, 1938.
McKinney, John. *A Common Thread: A Pictoral History of the Burnette, McKinney, Biddix, Hollifield, Brown and Mace Families*. Marion, NC: Self-Published, date unknown.
Mitchell, Pat. *Lifted to the Shoulders of a Mountain: A Story of the People Who Climbed a Mountain Before their Home Became Little Switzerland, NC. Their Strength and Courage Will Lift Them Up*. Bloomington, IN: iUniverse, 2007.
Schabilion, Robert. *Down The Crabtree*. Bloomington: IN: AuthorHouse, 2009.
Turner, Walter R. *Paving Tobacco Road: A Century of Progress by the North Carolina Department of Transportation*. Raleigh: NC Office of Archives and History, 2003.
Washburn, Carrie and Nellie Waycaster. "Histories of Chestnut Grove Baptist Church." Retrieved from www.chestnutgrovebaptistchurch.com.
Whisnant, Anne. *Super Scenic Motorway: A Blue Ridge Parkway History*. Chapel Hill: UNC Press, 2006.

Discover Thousands of Local History Books
Featuring Millions of Vintage Images

Arcadia Publishing, the leading local history publisher in the United States, is committed to making history accessible and meaningful through publishing books that celebrate and preserve the heritage of America's people and places.

Find more books like this at
www.arcadiapublishing.com

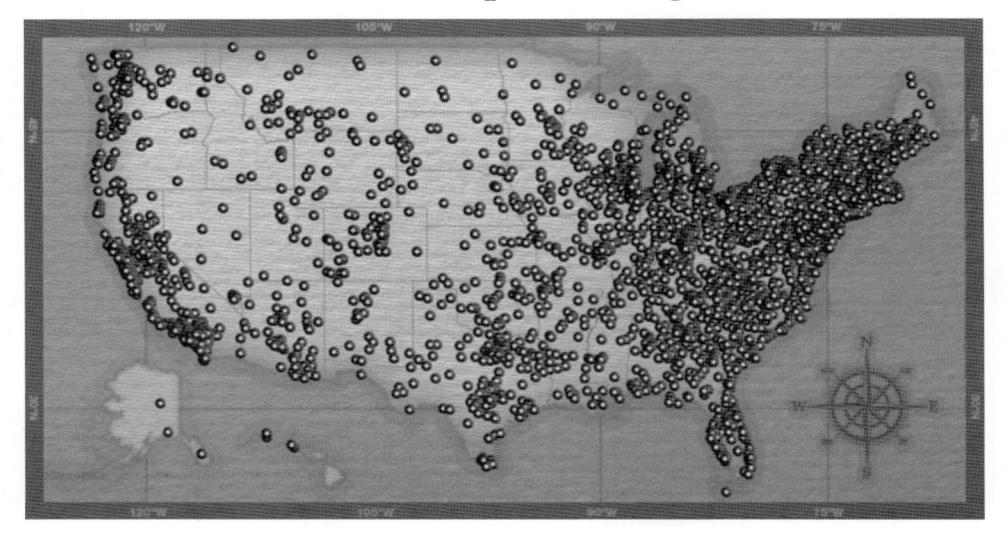

Search for your hometown history, your old stomping grounds, and even your favorite sports team.

Consistent with our mission to preserve history on a local level, this book was printed in South Carolina on American-made paper and manufactured entirely in the United States. Products carrying the accredited Forest Stewardship Council (FSC) label are printed on 100 percent FSC-certified paper.

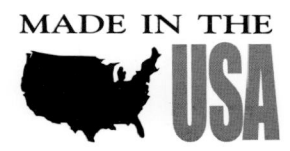

MADE IN THE USA